To Larry and Cleota Pugsley.

John A. Pugsley

COMMON SENSE ECONOMICS

YOUR MONEY

WHAT IT IS
AND
HOW TO KEEP IT!

The Common Sense Press, Costa Mesa, Calif.

PREFACE

The book you are about to read is true. The subject covered affects your life directly and more profoundly than any other social phenomenon. There are many opinions about the importance and correctness of economic actions; in the end there is only one truth, only one correct opinion. I firmly believe it is presented here.

I take no credit for the discovery and development of the basic economic ideas encompassed in the first chapter of this book. I can only recognize and extend my thanks to those writers and lecturers who, through their genius and skill, have caused me to understand economic and social reality and enabled me to penetrate the morass of fallacious argument that comprises current economic and investment thinking.

Who should get credit for the right thinking expressed in this book? On the ideas about economics and government interference in the marketplace, probably Ludwig von Mises deserves the greatest amount of credit. He was a world renowned Austrian economist who started writing early in this century. Although I haven't read all his works, nor can I say that all my conclusions are direct derivations of his ideas, his thoughts certainly were the seeds that influenced other writers who subsequently influenced me. I'm certain he would want to credit his teacher Eugen von Bohm-Bawerk, who in turn would credit Carl Menger, founder of the Austrian school of economics.

Both Murray Rothbard and Henry Hazlitt deserve star billing. Dr. Rothbard's book *America's Great Depression* was both shocking and exciting in its revelation of the causes of the economic debacle of the thirties. I have always been impressed by careful scholarship and adherence to scientific principles, and Dr. Rothbard's book was a fine example of both.

Henry Hazlitt's little tome *Economics In One Lesson* should be required reading for all economists, politicians, and businessmen around the world. In fact, it should be read by everyone. I probably never would have written this book but for his inspiration. Although I don't cite any of his other works, he's a prolific writer on the subject of economics and has devoted his life to purging the world of the black fog of Keynesianism.

One of the writers that Mr. Hazlitt gives credit to should also be mentioned, even though not specifically referenced in the text. That is Frederic Bastiat who wrote *The Law* way back in 1850. It is a masterpiece of timeless economic truth. Read it.

I warmly thank Thomas Paine for writing the original pamphlet *Common Sense* in 1776. Had all his thoughts and reasoning been followed, perhaps we would still be free today, and this book would not be necessary.

While giving credit, I shouldn't overlook those around me who offered the encouragement, advice, and physical aid to bring this book into being. Winston Griepp, LLB, good friend and counsel, gave the original inspiration and continuing confidence to start and finish the task. I would also like to thank Mr. John P. Dye, with whom I associated for several years, for introducing me to the basics of life insurance and mutual funds. Dr. Jack Hagadorn and Mr. John Thompson were the knowledgeable and considerate advisers who taught me the basics of investing in diamonds.

My staunchest supporter has been my wife, Gloria Terry. Her encouragement, as well as her help in editing the manuscript, was essential to the completion of the work.

Contents

INTRODUCTION

In the decade from 1966 to 1976, scores of public companies around the world have gained dubious notoriety: Natural Resources, Geotek, Carriage Company, Equity Funding, Groesbeck Company, Mont Beef Industries, Black Watch Farms, Urbanetics, Home Stake Production Company, Four Seasons Nursing Homes, Lockheed Aircraft, Herstatt Bank of Germany, Franklin Bank of New York, United California Bank of Switzerland, King Resources, and Penn Central Railroad are but a few. What do they have in common? Financial failure, and along with it the loss of billions of dollars of investors' money. Nor is it just single companies and their individual shareholders who have suffered. The stock market, even with inflation to buoy its value, is worth billions less than at the beginning of the period. Gold soared from $35 per ounce to almost $200, and then dropped again to about $100. Real estate values have risen, but with great pulses that have left tens of thousands of investors in the bankruptcy courts. Even those most conservative investors, the bond holders, have seen their wealth rise and fall in frightening waves as interest rates have reflected the chaos in the economy.

During much of the decade, this trembling in the financial markets has repeatedly spilled onto the front pages of our big metropolitan dailies as investors and speculators have rushed from asset to asset in a vain attempt to preserve purchasing power in the face of mounting inflation. Meanwhile, only with massive infusions of credit has the federal government been able to prevent a total flight of depositors from savings and loan associations, banks, and life insurance companies.

From every direction come cries of advice: buy gold, buy stocks, buy options, buy commodities, buy Swiss Francs, buy real estate. For every voice crying buy, another cries don't buy, stay away, do the opposite.

You, as an individual, live in this climate. Your goal is survival and the accumulation of enough wealth to provide for yourself when you no longer want or are no longer able to work. The reality is that few people have been successful money managers in the last decade, but fewer still are going to survive the financial and economic cataclysm that is yet to come. For the great masses of investors, the next ten years will mean the end of wealth. They are the ones who foolishly believe that the turmoil of the sixties and early seventies was nothing more than an aberration. To them, bonds are still the safest haven, the stock market is still going to go up in the long run, and prosperity is the name of the future. Without bothering to try to understand the root causes of the recent turbulent financial markets, they'll wander into the future handling their money carelessly (without even an understanding of what money really is) and taking their investment advice from salesmen, who are themselves ignorant of the underlying economic forces working in the marketplace. In the end they will fail financially, and that failure will sentence them to end up their lives dependent on the charity of the state.

Financial survivors will fall into two categories—those who become wealthy through sheer luck, just happening to own the right asset at the right time; and those of a more astute minority who will succeed because they have taken the time to understand the causes of the world's economic turmoil. Consciously or unconsciously, those who survive will be following the principles of natural economics outlined in this book. Those who read it carefully will find in the apparently simple economic analysis presented in the first chapter the roots of profound natural principles that govern all social interaction. It will become instantly clear that the economy of the world is operating on basic cause and effect, that the economic events of the past decade could have been (and were) accurately predicted, and that the calamities of the next ten years are virtually unavoidable.

No one can afford nor should he want to stop after reading *Common Sense Economics*. It is nothing more than an introduction, a mere guidepost to direct you along the road to financial independence. To achieve and maintain wealth you must study the subject thoroughly and deeply. You must ponder the thoughts, argue the premises, and analyze all the economic evidence around you to corroborate the theory. You must read the references, of course, and many more works that aren't cited. If this seems like too much bother, then you must have forgotten the lessons of your past. Perhaps you don't recall the tremendous difficulty of earning wealth to begin with, and the ease with which it has slipped from your grasp. How can anyone afford the luxury of remaining ignorant of the nature of money and the forces in society that so surely and silently control the exchange and value of wealth? Gaining a fundamental knowledge of economics and investments is the most important thing you can do for yourself in your lifetime. It is survival itself.

J.A.P.
Newport Beach, California
September, 1976

CHAPTER ONE

Money, Government, and You

WEALTH, THE ELUSIVE GOAL

Two friends each decided to build a house. The first, Jones, started by giving a lot of thought to the type of house that he wanted. He made rough sketches, lists of features, and penciled out his estimate of costs; then went to an architect, and together they sketched out room dimensions and floor plans. When he was confident the architect knew what was wanted, he commissioned him to go forward and design the house. Drawing on his knowledge of local conditions, etc., the architect decided on the general structural components of the building. With his knowledge of engineering and building materials, he carefully designed the house down to the very last light-switch plate. Then he had another meeting with Jones, the design was confirmed, and final adjustments to the drawings were made. From there, a contractor was hired, plans were filed, and materials were ordered. Inasmuch as the contractor and architect were honest, knowledgeable, and industrious, the house turned out exactly as Jones had wanted.

Smith, Jones' friend, took a more direct approach to his house. Rather than spend time fooling around with plans (he was very busy with his business at the time), he simply went down to the lumber company, ordered what appeared to be ample quantities of two-by-fours, plywood, cement, paint and plaster, and had them delivered to his lot. He arrived the following morning, along with his brother (a garage mechanic) and his wife's uncle (a dentist), and they set to work.

Unfortunately, his relatives soon tired of helping, and he found himself alone with the project. He hammered, sawed and did his best to design the house as he went along, occasionally cursing his lack of this or that material or wondering what in the world to do next. Fortunately, he could always call on his relatives for advice. (Although neither of them had ever built a house, they were more than willing to tell him how it should be done.) But, alas, the task was too great. In the end, he never finished. The project, as you can imagine, became an impossibility.

No one felt sorry for Smith, for everyone in the neighborhood recognized that he was a fool. You can't build a decent house without a lot of planning, and they pointed at Jones' house as proof. The whole thing was obvious.

Now, compare the problem of doing a simple thing such as building a house with the problem of becoming independently wealthy. Which would you say is easier? Almost everyone lives in a house of some sort, and someone had to build that house; so it might follow that home building is relatively easy. But it's only easy if it's done *right*.

And independent wealth? How many people who work for a living manage to accumulate enough wealth to become financially independent? According to U.S. Government statistics, only three people out of a hundred have enough wealth to provide themselves with an income of three thousand dollars a year at age 65. Why? Because they have all approached building a fortune the same way Mr. Smith approached building his house: without a design (goal), without knowledge of building materials (investment vehicles), and without knowledge of construction (how to integrate their investment program). Most don't even know how much money they want to accumulate, and they think nothing of getting their advice from in-laws. *As a matter of fact, most people don't even have a good idea of what money is.* Considering the difficulty of accumulating a fortune and the relative simplicity of building a house, doesn't it become obvious that failure to build a fortune is far more likely than success?

This book is going to approach the problem in its entirety. It will familiarize you with the environment in which you'll be building your wealth (the economy); it will tell you how to plan your goals; what money and wealth really are; and it will introduce you to some of the building materials (investments) that can get you where you want to go. When you finish, you'll be well on your way to becoming your own financial architect, and your chances of success at the single most difficult task in life will be increased a thousandfold.

IT STARTS WITH PRODUCTION

Survival, comfort, happiness; these are the fundamental conscious and subconscious goals of all individuals. To achieve them, each person labors to produce some usable product that can either be consumed or traded with others for products that can be consumed. The farmer grows apples, some to eat now and some to trade with the tailor for clothes. With good fortune, he'll have a few left over at the end of each year, and these he'll try to store for consumption at a time when he no longer wishes, or is able, to produce. It's this storing away of unused production year after year, usually in the form of money, that leads to independent wealth. Wealth is nothing more or less than an accumulation of production (or claims on production); when an individual has accumulated enough wealth to supply his total consumption needs for as long as he may live, he has then achieved financial independence.

There are two steps that must be climbed; first, producing enough so that you have surplus production (wealth) left over at the end of the year; and second, and by far the most difficult, preserving and hopefully increasing that wealth by using it to acquire more of the same. The challenge lies in doing this year after year in an economy in which almost all forces at hand are directed toward thwarting your efforts and robbing you of all you've gained.

Your formal education, assuming you're a professional, has taken fifteen to twenty years; and this does not count the years of practical experience necessary to achieve high earning levels. These years of sacrifice have been aimed at one objective: to enable you to *earn*. Consider how much time and energy you've devoted to learning how to utilize your surplus earnings. Probably very little. If you're typical, you don't have a clear idea of what money is, let alone an understanding of the complex problem of accumulating and preserving great amounts of it. If you don't take time to learn what wealth is all about, you may find that all the effort spent in developing a high earning ability has been wasted.

The objective of this book is to give you the expertise necessary to accumulate independent wealth using only your surplus production. To do this, you must understand enough about economics to be able to predict the future course of the economy by observing current events. In addition, you must recognize the relationships and relative values of all types of investment and savings vehicles, develop rational financial goals, and thereby design a strategy by which you can reach your goals in spite of external forces.

COMMON SENSE ECONOMICS

Of all the subjects taught in high schools and colleges, none is as dry, as dull, or as consummately boring as economics. Few people come away from their school years with anything but a distaste for this whole area of thought. It is obtuse, complicated, and it seems to have precious little bearing on the world in which they live. This view of economics is fundamentally false. Economics is, from the standpoint of both society and the individual, the one subject that most influences the human condition. From cradle to grave human beings must trade with others in order to survive, and economics is the science of trade. To the extent that natural economic laws are understood by the individual he will prosper; to the extent they are understood and followed by a society, that society will prosper. When civilizations rise it is invariably true that they are, even if unconsciously, following natural economic laws; and when they decline and fall it is because they pervert or ignore these laws.

In the world of science, we marvel at the beautiful simplicity that exists in nature; the endless interrelationships of matter that follow smoothly functioning natural laws. As scientists delve deeper and deeper into areas of the physical universe, the patterns and systems become more and more understandable. But in economics, the reverse seems true. The more books that are written, the more incomprehensible and complicated seem to be the patterns. It reminds one of the evolution of witch doctors' potions that start as natural remedies and after generations of mumbo-jumbo become wild, senseless gyrations that are both useless and dangerous.

In practice, it seems that most economists reject the scientific method as a valid approach to economics. They don't appear to have firm starting points (postulates) for their theories, and they fail to accept the fact that observation of past events is a useful tool. Consequently, history repeats itself endlessly, one society following another into economic oblivion, with the catastrophes of inflation, recession, depression, and monetary loss never ending.

The truth is that there *are* starting points in economics. There are laws of nature that apply to human beings and to the interaction between humans in trade, commerce, and all money matters. Understanding some of these laws will open your eyes to the true causes of the economic turmoil that surrounds us and enable you, as it enables the physicist, to predict the future.

In the last few years, the average American has had a myriad of economic terms thrust upon him. Inflation, recession, and devaluation have become household words and worries. Newspapers and magazines are filled with stories, articles, and editorials about the economy. Yet, believe it or not, *not one American in a thousand understands what is happening.* There are authors that for years have tried to bring an understanding of real economics to the individual. The maverick economists (if you use the word "maverick" to denote a critter that doesn't go along with the herd), including Ludwig von Mises, Murray Rothbard and Henry Hazlitt, have written scores of books that have proved and reproved that current solutions to economic problems are nothing but the wildest idiot's folly. The problem is not that no one understands; it's that the solutions to man's problems offered by these laissez-faire economists are not acceptable to the interests that wish to politically control the lives and wealth of the world. It seems inconceivable that anyone, even those prestigious leaders of economic policy such as professors Paul Samuelson or John Kenneth Galbraith could read Henry Hazlitt's book *Economics in One Lesson,*[1] and not understand the fallacies of their own positions.

You may have said that economics is too difficult for you to understand; you're more interested in your own situation and how to improve it. I take exception to that view. Economics is *not* hard to understand. It is, in reality, the simplest of all the sciences. When you get through with this chapter, you should have a sound knowledge about the way things *really* work and that knowledge is going to be your armor, your only armor, against the events that are going to financially devastate most individuals.

ECONOMICS IN ACTION—A MICROCOSM

It is one of the wonders of science that no matter how small or insignificant a piece of matter is, it still obeys all the laws of nature that govern the largest masses in the universe.

Thus, a piece of stone no bigger than a pea will act and react according to the same mathematical formulas that govern a galaxy. The beauty is that a scientist can study the pebble and project his observations into an understanding of a galaxy. When Galileo dropped a small and a large object from the leaning tower of Pisa and determined that they both hit the ground at the same time, the recognition of the significance of this observation changed the course of science for all time.

It's my contention that we, too, can use this technique to gain an understanding of economic events. Further, I contend that in economics, as well as in physics, the things that hold true on a small scale will be just as valid when applied to a large scale. We'll start by observing a small society, so small that it only consists of three families. The things you'll learn in this small society will enable you to understand equally well the forces at work within your worldwide society of three billion people. At least that's my contention. Judge for yourself.

In a small community, surrounded by mountains and completely isolated from the outside world, live three families: the Farmers, the Tailors, and the Carpenters. These three families toil all day long—six days a week, 52 weeks a year—and each produces a product. As you may have guessed, the Farmers produce food. They have an orchard, a field, and some animals; and they produce enough to supply themselves and to trade with the other families for their production. The Tailors produce clothes and fabrics; the Carpenters produce lumber and such useful items as tables, chairs, and fences. Each family is skilled only in the production of its own goods; each has specialized and learned to trade its production for the products of others. For the sake of this discussion, let's measure their production in "units." In an average year, each family produces three units of production, and to live comfortably, each family consumes three units of production. A diagram of the production of the community is shown in Figure 1.

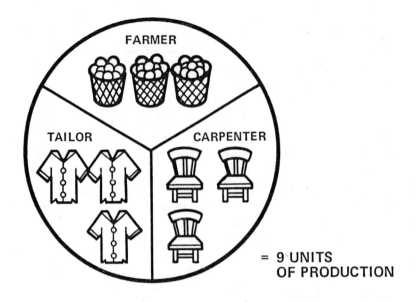

Figure 1

We can conclude that the total production of the community is nine units; its consumption is nine units; and therefore, its standard of living is nine units. Standard of living for our purposes will be defined as the total units of production that are consumed during a given time period by an entity, be it a whole society or an individual.

There are two possibilities for change in the standard of living of our community. First, the production of the community could rise. Second, the production of the community could decline. What could cause it to rise?

1. The inhabitants work harder.
2. They develop better production techniques.

What could cause it to decline?

1. They could work less.
2. They could forget how to produce efficiently.
3. They could lose production from natural causes.
4. They could lose production from vandalism or war.

Let's look at an increase in production first. If Farmer is successful in developing new planting techniques and produces twice as large a crop, our picture will look like Figure 2.

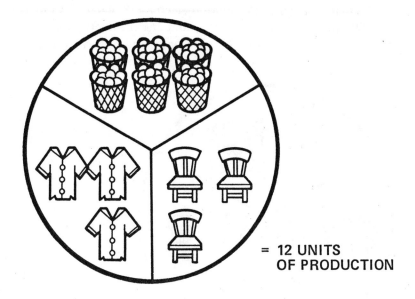

= 12 UNITS
OF PRODUCTION

Figure 2

Immediately, you recognize that the total production of the community has risen to 12 units. If they consume all the units, the standard of living of the community will have risen to 12. In other words, they are better off; they are more comfortable and better fed than they were before. If you also assume that a higher standard of living is something that is desirable, you would have to agree that things have improved.

Question: (Think carefully about this before you read further.) Assuming they consume the goods, *is there any way in which you could increase the production and not improve the standard of living of the community?* Since we've defined standard of living as the total goods consumed, it must be presumed that if the goods increase and the number of consumers does not, the standard of living must increase.

Now, examine a second and even more revealing situation. What happens when production decreases? What if vandals destroy part of Farmer's crop, and his production for the year is only one-half as large? He has now produced one and one half units, and our production diagram looks like Figure 3.

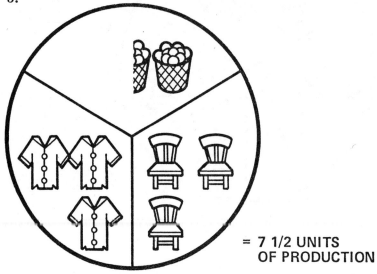

= 7 1/2 UNITS
OF PRODUCTION

Figure 3

The total production of the community has dropped to 7½ units, and the standard of living has decreased correspondingly. Each family now has a standard of living of 2½ units rather than three. They are worse off, right? Absolutely.

Now, here's question number two. Pay close attention. If you know the answer, which you probably will, you've taken a giant step toward being able to predict the future of the economy of the United States and the world. Inherent in this question and answer is the solution to every major economic problem facing the nation.

Question 2. If production *decreases,* can the standard of living increase? Can it remain the same? Or must it decrease? Remember, we are assuming a constant population that consumes all it produces. Look at Figure 3 and think. *You should be saying that obviously the standard of living must decrease if production decreases.* Obviously. If you are good at extrapolating and start with Question 2 and its solutions, you should now be able to answer the following question.

Which of the following programs are beneficial to a society, and which are destructive on an absolute basis?

1. Farm subsidy programs.
2. Wage controls.
3. Price controls.
4. Minimum wage laws.
5. Export tariffs.
6. Import tariffs.
7. Product boycotts (i.e., meat boycotts).
8. Anti-trust laws.
9. Grain acreage control programs.
10. Price control through destruction of livestock or other products.
11. Defense spending.
12. War.

If you can't apply these techniques to our small isolated society and thus arrive at an absolute answer, I'll help you out later on. Right now, I think you need some more background material on fundamental concepts. Let's talk about prices, money, banking, and inflation.

PRICES

What is meant by price? In our little community, we might say that price is a ratio at which one commodity can be exchanged for another. For example, one unit of food is *priced at* one unit of construction. One unit of construction can then be traded for one unit of clothing. It would look like Figure 4 as an equation:

PRICE

Figure 4

In the situation where Farmer only produces one-half a crop, some price ratios will change if he exchanges one-third of his production for one-third of Carpenter's production. Since he has produced only one and one-half units, he now exchanges one-half unit of his production for one whole unit from Carpenter. Thus, one-half unit of A equals one unit of B or C, and you might say that the price of farm goods has risen. Carpenter must pay the same amount for only one-half as much. Prices of farm goods have doubled in relation to other commodities. We have seen an *absolute* decline in the total production of the community. Goods are more scarce. There are only 7½ units where there were normally nine units.

But have we seen a *general* rise in prices? Farm goods have doubled, but what of other commodities? Hasn't the price of Carpenter's goods dropped? If price is a relationship, a ratio, we can certainly say that in relation to farm goods, Carpenter's products have dropped to half their former value. One-half a unit of Farmer's goods will now buy one whole unit of Carpenter's production. Thus, where one product has gone up in "price," the others have gone down.

You should be coming to a very interesting conclusion. In a barter society, there can be *no change in the general price level.* There can be no such thing as inflation! It can't be caused by scarcity, abundance, or even unions. One product can change in value in relation to the others; for example, if apples remained scarce, they would demand a higher price in terms of other goods. But those other goods would go down in relation to apples, and the general price level would not have changed. The other products, if their quantity remained constant, would not necessarily change in relation to each other. This isn't to say that the standard of living of the society won't change. Since it is based on absolute quantities of consumable products, when the amount of production goes up, the standard of living goes up; and when the amount of production goes down, the standard of living goes down. But prices? They are only relative ratios and remain constant.

Okay, then how do we have inflation? Simple. It is nothing more than an increase in quantity of the commodity used as the medium of exchange, while all the other commodities remain relatively constant. When the quantity of one commodity such as apples is increased, we know that they will become less valuable in relation to other commodities. It will take more and more of them to trade for the same number of some other product. If they grew as abundantly as leaves on every tree and anyone could have them for the picking, people certainly wouldn't be willing to trade their hard-worked-for products to obtain them. Any commodity that becomes abundant loses its value relative to the commodities that are useful but harder to produce. Thus, even gold, if it were as abundant as dirt, would be almost valueless as a commodity. It may have many uses, as does rock, but people would pay very little for it, because if it became too expensive they could dig their own.

Inflation, or as we normally use the word, a general rise in prices, is caused simply by an increase of the commodity known as "money." As "money" becomes abundant in relation to other commodities, the price of those commodities goes up relative to money. However, they may not go up in "price" relative to each other. One loaf of bread may still be exchangeable for one pound of apples, but both may jump from 10 cents to 50 cents as the amount of "money" in the society is increased.

MONEY

Before we go further, you're going to have to understand what I mean by money. If you've read Harry Browne's book *How to Profit from the Coming Devaluation*[2] (and I recommend it), you've already had a pretty good explanation of how money comes into being. It evolves from barter practices in almost every society. In our little three-family community, we could see it come into use. Assume that Carpenter wants to buy a shirt from Tailor. If Tailor needs no carpentry work done, or if the value of the shirt is too low in relation to the table that Tailor needs, Carpenter might use some other commodity he has on hand to trade—for example, some apples that he had left over from a trade with Farmer. In a barter society, any commodity that is desired by everyone in the community and can be divided into small trading units might easily become used as money.

The dictionary has several definitions for money, but most of them revolve around the idea that it is a commodity used as a medium of exchange. If Carpenter acquires apples from Farmer with the sole intention of using them as a medium of exchange, they most certainly have become money, and it should be easy to see that they could become a fairly standard form of money in the limited community I have described. Things could be priced in terms of apples, and for smaller purchases, each family could keep a few on hand just for trading.

In primitive societies, all manner of commodities have been used as a medium of exchange. Cattle, for example, are common as both a medium of exchange and a measure of wealth in agricultural societies. On some Pacific islands, stones have been used. North American Indians used beads or "wampum." Not all of these things are practical as money, of course. A medium of exchange that is to be most useful over a long period of time should have certain characteristics.

First, if I'm going to take a commodity in on trade with the hope of exchanging it with someone else for their products, I should be sure it's something they'll recognize and need. Then, I'll want to make sure it will last until I'm ready to trade. Milk, for example, might spoil if I kept it around too long and, therefore, would make a poor money. It should be divisible so that I can make small purchases with it, and there shouldn't be too much fluctuation in the quantity available, as we've already determined that the value of a product goes down as the quantity available goes up. Further, it would help if the commodity was relatively rare, so that a small amount was valuable. Then, a large purchase wouldn't be impractical, and the accumulation of wealth wouldn't present storage problems.

Money should take a certain amount of human energy to create. If apples are to be successful as money, they must represent the labor of the picker, grower, packer, etc. They must also represent the labor that went into the capital equipment necessary to aid the farmer in producing them, as well as the creative ideas that were needed to make their production easier. The value to you of any product depends on your willingness to give of your production in order to obtain it. That is, in a way, a measure of the amount of labor it would take you to reproduce the item for which you're trading. That value is made of human energy, ideas, and the capital mechanism necessary to produce it.

Real money, as I see it, is a kind of condensed form of human energy and ideas. The apple produced by Farmer is an example of this. So is a gold coin. It represents the ideas, labor, and equipment of the prospector, the miner, the smelter, and the mint—all condensed into one small coin. Of course, the effort by itself is not enough to make a good money. It must also be a commodity that has other attributes: it is wanted, useful (even if only for its beauty), durable, and divisible. Over the centuries and around the world, gold and silver have seemed to best fill the demand for a good money. They have all the attributes that make them nearly ideal—rarity, utility, divisibility, durability, and beauty—and because of these attributes, they are universally recognized and desired.

INFLATION

We started by asking where inflation comes from, and now perhaps we're ready to see how it could come about. Suppose we look at a society that used gold as a medium of exchange. The ruler of a country has taken on the task of creating coins out of the gold with his image stamped on them. Let's imagine that this society has produced one hundred gold coins, and they are used to trade for one hundred units of other production. Thus, they have a value of one unit of production, and the units of production of the society would be said to cost one gold coin.

The ruler himself is involved in trading with these coins. Finding that he is unable to live on the amount he's able to tax from the people, he thinks of a scheme. Every time one of the coins passes through his hands, he files off a little of the gold from the coin. Let's assume that he files off five percent. When he trades each coin again for a unit of production, the person receiving it doesn't realize that he's really receiving less gold than he expected for his product. He has come to believe that the coin represents a given weight of gold. Gradually, all the coins in the realm pass through the ruler's hands, and he now has enough gold filings accumulated to mint five new coins. He does this, and quickly spends them. Now there is no more gold in circulation than there was last year, but there are 105 coins in circulation and only 100 units of production.

1/100th of Total Gold Supply = One Unit of Production

1.05 Coins = One Unit of Production

Although it may not immediately become apparent, the increased supply of coins (money) will soon be used to bid for the available units of production (products), and the relative value of each coin will fall. Rather than one unit of production costing one coin, it will soon cost 1.05 coins. Inflation has set in. People will soon be talking about rising prices. Inflation would stop right there if the ruler stopped filing coins. But if each year he continued to file off five percent of the gold in all the coins of the realm, then inflation would continue at a rate of 5% a year. First, it would cost one gold coin to buy a product, then two, then three, etc. Donald J. Hoppe, in his book *How to Invest in Gold Coins*[3] tells about early Rome:

> "The earliest money of the practical Romans was neither gold nor silver but an ingot of copper—the as—weighing one pound. At first the as was passed by weight, but later it was stamped with the seal of the state, broken into smaller pieces and passed by sight. By the fourth century B.C., the as had evolved into a heavy round stamped copper slug, the as grave. With so large a coin passing by sight, the temptation surreptitiously to debase it by reducing its weight proved irresistible to authorities. By the middle of the third century B.C., the weight of the as had dropped to four ounces. By the end of the First Punic War,

around 240 B.C., it had shrunk to a mere two ounces,
and by 70 B.C., it weighed no more than half an
ounce."

In early times, filing, clipping or rubbing the metal of the
coins was not the only way rulers robbed the people. They
also alloyed cheaper metals with gold, and even created the
first "sandwich" coins of copper plated with silver. In Rome
in 15 B.C., Emperor Augustus established the "Aureus" at
126 grains of gold. In 60 A.D., Nero devalued it to 110
grains; Trajan again reduced it in 105 A.D.; by 200 A.D.,
under Severus of Caracallas' rule, it was down to 60 grains,
and by 268 A.D., under the rule of Gallienus, the coin no
longer contained any gold but was merely copper with silver
plating.

The history of currency debasement is intertwined with
the history of nearly every nation in the world. I'll have more
to say about modern techniques of debasement, but first I
should take the time to explain the evolution from hard
currency to paper money. It was this advance in "money
technology" that really opened the floodgates of economic
destruction.

BANKING

After the invention of paper and the printing press, the use
of receipts in trade became commonplace. You can imagine
how the evolution of banking might have taken place. A person
who had accumulated any significant amount of gold or silver
often found it safer to store his wealth with a reputable gold
dealer. That dealer would charge a storage fee but would
provide the safe vault necessary to protect against theft. The
depositor would receive a paper receipt for his gold which
would say something similar to "This is to certify that John
Doe has deposited 100 ounces of fine gold at my bank and
can withdraw it on demand," and it would be signed by the
owner of the depository. Gradually, these depositories
became known as banks and the receipts became known as

bank notes and were payable to the bearer.

The bankers soon discovered that a tidy profit could be made by loaning out the gold that had been deposited. By waiving the fee to the depositor and even offering him a rate of interest if he would agree not to withdraw his gold for a given period (a year, for example), they could then loan the gold and charge a higher rate of interest to the borrower, pocketing the difference. No one was cheated, and everyone received what was bargained for. The original depositor knew that there was some risk because the banker could fail to repay him, but a banker of good reputation found no lack of people ready to deposit gold and reap the profits of interest.

If the process stopped here, there would be no inflationary effect. The depositor has the unit of gold. He can trade it for a unit of production or hold it. No new unit of money is being introduced into the economy, and thus, there will be no resultant rise in prices. If the depositor chooses to remove the gold from circulation and not spend it (by depositing it in the bank), the economy will actually notice an apparent decrease in the money supply, and commodities would become cheaper in relation to gold. If the banker lends out the gold and the borrower spends it, it is no different than if the original owner had spent it. It is real wealth and is not inflating the money supply. Only now the borrower has the unit of production that the gold purchased, rather than the depositor. The depositor just has a receipt.

One thing could alter the apparent money supply, however. Suppose the depositor decides that before his gold is due to be repaid to him by the banker, he would like to make a purchase. He could take his receipt for the gold to a manufacturer and say "Sell me that wagon. I don't have gold right now, but this receipt can be exchanged for gold on the due date, and you can collect your money then."

At this point, if the manufacturer accepts the receipt in exchange for the wagon, we have seen our first inflation of the money supply, for now both the gold *and the receipt for the gold* have been used as purchasing media. Two units of production have been consumed, but only one unit of gold was used to pay for them. The supply of real money (the gold in circulation) has been increased by one paper receipt. If you followed the receipt back to its source, it would become apparent that it was the debt or note of the fellow who borrowed from the bank that was now being used as money. In other words, the individual that borrowed the gold from the bank had indirectly created a note which was now circulating in the community.

This process is known as "monetizing" debt. If the notemaker died and the note was never repaid, the community has lost a unit of its production which he consumed but never replaced with his own production. Anyone involved in the transaction might be the one to suffer the actual loss. It could be the banker if he makes good the gold receipt out of his own funds, even though the borrower never repaid him the gold. If the banker can't do this, the wagon maker, who now owns the gold receipt, would lose, for he now has nothing of value in exchange for his wagon. If he goes back to the original depositor and forces him to give back his wagon, or replace the worthless receipt with gold, it would then be the depositor who loses because he has lost the gold he deposited and has nothing to show for it.

The simple thing to remember in this analogy is that substitute money can be created in the form of an I.O.U., and if people in the community are willing to accept this I.O.U. in exchange for units of their production, the "money" supply in the community will be increased and prices will rise. Prices will rise because there is now apparently more money in circulation than there are products. If the debtor that originally creates the I.O.U. produces a product and redeems his note, the money supply will drop, and prices will fall back to their natural level. *But if the debtor repudiates his debt, someone in the community will have lost the production they originally traded for that note.* I hope that you are beginning to see that an increased money supply caused by monetized debt can be the cause of inflation. I also hope I have made it clear that a debt not repaid is a real loss to the community.

Let's take the next important step in analyzing the effect that this banker might have on the economy and on price levels. Suppose that the banker is approached by another person seeking a loan. He has no more gold in his vault, but he trusts the person applying for the loan, is sure he would be repaid on time and decides to take a chance. Since receipts that he has issued for gold on deposit have become accepted in the community in the past as money substitutes, he thinks to himself, "Why not just loan this person a receipt which will promise that the holder can redeem it for gold should they desire?" The banker's experience has told him that he usually has gold in the vault that people are storing, and most people would rather hold the receipt than the gold; therefore, it is unlikely that both receipts would be presented at once. What he has done is to double the supply of money substitutes in circulation in the community, and yet there is no product to back them up. If there were originally 100 pieces of gold and 100 units of production available to be purchased, there are now 100 pieces of gold *plus* two paper gold depository receipts that are being *used* as gold. There are now 102 units of purchasing power trying to be traded for 100 units of production, and the result is that the price of each unit of real production will now become 1.02 units of money.

If the banker continues and issues five or ten receipts for each unit of gold he has had deposited with him, he will place the economy of the village in increasing jeopardy. At some point, two or more of the holders of the receipts may decide to claim the gold that they believe they have on deposit, which will result in the banker becoming bank "rupt." In reality, the banker is taking I.O.U.'s from various people in the community, guaranteeing them, and then circulating them in the community as notes that are ostensibly as good as gold, since the banker has said that he will redeem them for gold on demand. If nothing goes wrong and his creditors repay him on time with real production (or gold), he can then redeem his "banknotes" with the gold. No one is the wiser, and he has profited handsomely from the interest he charged the creditors.

This has been the history of currency inflation the world over. Bankers increase their own lending power by creating banknotes and back those banknotes with the credit of the borrowers. Money substitutes are created out of paper and ink, then flow into the market place to bid up the price of goods. These notes don't represent existing production, but rather *future* production. They create a debt against the future and a very real distortion of the economy. Unfortunately the inflationary effects of monetizing debt in this manner cannot easily be traced back to the source.

THE GREAT FRAMEUP

There is a great deal of fuzzy thinking about where the responsibility for inflation lies (and here I mean the general rise in prices of commodities and services). Let's examine some of the more commonly blamed "culprits."

UNIONS

Many blame the unions, saying the increase in prices is due to excessive wage demands. In our simple barter-system community, when there were only nine units of production, what would the effect have been if one of the producers had demanded a higher price for his product? What if Farmer said, "rather than trading you for a unit of your production (a year's supply of clothes), I will raise my 'price' and demand two units of your production for one unit of mine." Now, since Tailor can only produce three units of production, he must either accept the food from Farmer at Farmer's price and have nothing left to wear himself, or he must refuse to trade and leave Farmer with all his food. Tailor may trade one year, out of necessity, but the next year he will either spend part of his time growing his own food supply, or someone else will come in to compete with Farmer, since he has become excessive in his demands.

Actually, when Farmer made increased and unreasonable demands for his product, the effect on the community's price level was the same as when part of Farmer's crop was destroyed; that is, the price of the farm products rose but the price of the goods they were being traded for decreased proportionately. There was no change in the *general* price level. The difference is that the standard of living of the community did not decrease in this instance because Farmer still had the balance of his crop and could consume it himself. His standard of living went up, while Tailor's went down. Other things being equal, free enterprise would tend to prevent this from happening as Farmer would immediately be driven out of business by competition if he tried to demand more than his product was worth in terms of human labor, capital, and ideas.

In this analogy, the unfair demands of labor are represented by the farmer, and in a community that did not have a paper money supply, unfair labor demands would simply wind up leaving the laborers out of work as either they would be fired, or the company for whom they worked would be forced out of business by competition. In any case, even if they received their raise and the company was not forced out of business by competition, *they would not have affected the general price level,* for when their products increased in price, the other products would fall in price proportionately. The laborers would be in a better position and the people they traded with in a poorer one, but only when the supply of money changed in relation to other commodities could there be inflation.

In conclusion, the unions aren't the culprits. Each union may have the power to raise the price of the product in which it is involved. If consumers are willing to pay the higher prices, then they must forego purchasing other items with those dollars.

Each union can only affect its own products, not prices in general. The blame has to be cast in another direction.

EXCESS PROFITS OF BIG BUSINESS

Many people would like to blame unfair profit demands of big business as the cause of rising prices. The same analogy used regarding unions still holds true. The price of one product in relation to other products cannot cause inflation whether the manufacturer raises the price or his laborers' wage demands cause the price increase. If the oil companies decide to increase gasoline prices in order to increase profits, they force a choice on you, the consumer. You must decide, when allocating your money, whether you value gasoline more than other items like food, clothes, and entertainment. If you do, you'll pay the higher prices for gas and forego the other things. The manufacturers of those other things will be forced to lower prices to continue marketing their products. Product prices are relative to one another; as one falls, the other rises. Like a teeter-totter. Only when all products are priced in terms of money can there be a general price rise and then only when the supply of money increases. It should be noted that if the money is real money (that is, a hard, usable commodity), the fact that its supply increases is not detrimental to the community.

If apples were the medium of exchange and there were suddenly an abundance of them, no one would be hurt because when an individual traded his production for a greater number of apples, he would be able to consume them. The real standard of living of the community would be increased. But when notes begin to be circulated in the community as substitutes for money and make a demand on the real production of the community, then real damage can be done. If the notes are never paid off, the persons holding them lose. While they are outstanding and circulating as money, prices are higher than they should be.

It should be realized at this point that prices could come down in two ways. The creditor can replace the note with real production, thus increasing the supply of products in the market-place and simultaneously reducing the supply of money substitutes, or the note can be repudiated, become recognized as worthless, and be destroyed. No new product has come into the community, but the supply of money substitutes has been reduced and thus prices of commodities other than the money commodity will fall.

No, big business is not the culprit either.

DECREASED SUPPLY OF PRODUCTS

It is held that increasing the supply of products will lower the rate of inflation. Since, as we have already discussed, the level of prices in any society is a ratio between the available products and the quantity of money bidding for those products, then it stands to reason that increasing the supply of products will lower the price level, providing the supply of money is not increased proportionately. There is no doubt the tremendous increase in production due to technological innovation that has occurred in the last fifty years in this country has camouflaged a great deal of the inflation, just as has the export of billions of dollars for foreign goods. But to attempt to cure inflation by saying we must produce more is to be exhorted by the hold-up man to work longer hours so you can replace what he is stealing. It does not diminish one whit the reality of the loss. Although you may not miss the standard of living you might have had without the past inflation, nevertheless, you have suffered.

A lower supply of products is not the cause of inflation; the cause is on the other side of the ledger.

THE SINGLE CAUSE

We have already demonstrated that the cause of inflation is an increased supply of money. The question now is, how does this come about in today's economy?

Purchasing media are created in our society through the mechanism of credit. A simple illustration of this can be seen when an individual deposits $100 in a bank. That deposit takes that amount of purchasing power temporarily out of the hands of the individual making the deposit. He is not bidding for products with that money and is, therefore, acting as a deflator of the price level. The price level in the community is lower than it would have been if he had used the $100 to buy a product.

The bank makes no profit if it merely holds the $100 of the depositor, for it must pay him interest, and therefore the bank is going to do one of two things with the $100. It is going to either buy some type of bond or it is going to loan that money to someone else. The law says that the bank cannot lend out the entire $100 but must keep a percentage of it as a reserve—this portion is known as the "reserve requirement" and the percentage is set by the Federal Reserve. Let's say that the bank is required to keep $15 and is permitted to loan out $85. The person who then borrows this $85 from the bank uses the $85 to purchase a product in the community; thus the price level in the community is now being raised due to the effect of this money bidding for available products.

When the seller of a product receives the $85, he normally takes it to his bank and deposits it. Thus, a second bank now receives a deposit of that $85, and now it attempts to loan it out. It also must keep a portion as reserve, and this time the loan to the next borrower is about $70. The next borrower uses the money to purchase a product, the seller again deposits the proceeds, and so the original deposit works its way through the banking system, being loaned over and over, and each time diminishing in size. Reserve requirements vary between city and country banks and between demand and time deposits, but the ultimate expansion of the original $100 could be to create loans of about $650.

In addition to being able to loan out money that is deposited by its customers, the bank also can borrow from the Federal Reserve, and from other banks, and relend those funds, again profiting from the interest differential. The Federal Reserve can thus influence the total amount of money in the community by encouraging banks to borrow federal funds and by lowering the reserve requirements.

FEDERAL SPENDING

The other major factor that determines the amount of money in the community, and thus the level of price, is federal spending. The money that the federal government spends comes either from tax receipts or from borrowing. Since taxes comprise money removed from the individual directly, spending of tax dollars does not inflate the money supply; if the government wasn't spending them, the individual would, and thus no new real demand is created.

When the government borrows to pay its bills, it issues treasury bills and bonds. Some of these are held by private investors here and abroad. Purchasing power is thus removed from the hands of the individual and given to the government. This is only inflationary to the extent that the individual was not going to spend that money, but rather to save it. Much of the government debt, however, winds up in the vaults of the Federal Reserve.

The actual process by which the government inflates the money supply is that it "attempts to sell securities to the public at a fixed price. If the public is not willing to purchase all of these *new* securities, the central bank intervenes in the securities market and purchases already outstanding govern-

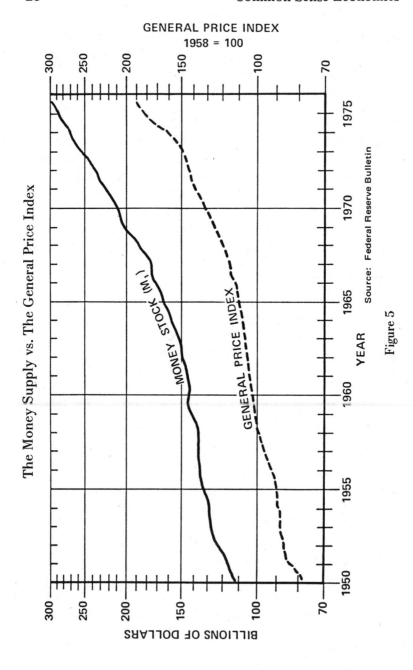

GENERAL PRICE INDEX
1958 = 100

The Money Supply vs. The General Price Index

MONEY STOCK (M₁)

GENERAL PRICE INDEX

BILLIONS OF DOLLARS

Source: Federal Reserve Bulletin

YEAR

Figure 5

ment securities from the public. In the process, the central bank gains an asset, the government securities, and creates a liability, the money paid to the private sector which finances the purchase of the newly issued government securities."[4] When these U.S. Government securities are purchased by the Fed, banks then have fresh money to spend or loan. This money starts its way through the banking system as a series of loans, just as did the money of the depositor we discussed previously. Whatever amount of the federal debt is monetized by being purchased by the Federal Reserve is injected into the banking system and is subject to the expansion, by way of loans, of that system.

For a more exact and detailed discussion of this system, read *Money & Markets; A Monetarist View* by Beryl Sprinkel.[5]

FOREIGN TRADE

Certain other phenomena can affect the money supply. First, foreign transactions can raise or lower it. If a product is purchased from a foreign manufacturer and paid for with American dollars, these dollars leave our banking system and the foreign product is brought in to replace them. The banks lose the deposit and thereby the ability to expand that deposit through the series of loans. The effect is deflationary. Thus, when the balance of payments is negative, the outflow of dollars causes prices to fall within the U.S. owing to the diminished supply of money.

Conversely, when the balance of payments is positive, that is when foreigners are buying more U.S. products than they are selling, those dollars are flowing into the bank accounts of American companies, and are thus available to balloon the deposits and loans of the banking system, and thus increase the money supply.

PRIVATE LOAN DEMAND

Another factor in the expansion and contraction of the

money supply is the level of borrowing by individuals and corporations from the banks. When loan demand is high and banks are fully loaned up, the money supply is greater than when they are not borrowing. Going back to our earlier example, it is easy to see that if the bank does not have a borrower for that $85 it has to loan, the subsequent deposits and loans are not possible either, and thus both the money supply and the price levels are held down.

A further factor is the amount of cash held by the public. If our original depositor decided to keep his $100 in cash in his wallet rather than deposit it in the bank, the bank would not have been in a position to make the $85 loan which led to the later loans. Certain times of the year the public holds more currency (such as at Christmas time) and at these times the money supply is suppressed.

There are of course other factors that act upon the supply of money such as the 'float' or funds in transit from bank to bank, and the amount of consumer credit outstanding between buyers and sellers that has not taken the form of monetary exchanges, but the effect of these small and temporary factors is not significant in the prediction of the overall money supply or inflation rate.

In summary, then, the following things are significant in determining the size of the money supply:

1. The level of borrowing of the Federal Government.
2. The demand for loans by the private sector.
3. The export-import balance.
4. The amount of cash held by the public.
5. Float and consumer credit.

Of these five items, only the first is of true long range significance. When the government borrows, it does so without any intention of repayment. Once that money is in the system, it stays and permanently bids up the prices of products. It should be noted that not all of the government borrowing winds up as a monetized increase in the money supply. To whatever extent private investors hold treasury debt—T-bills, etc.,—the money supply is not expanded. The supply is essentially the same as it would have been had the individual himself spent or deposited the money in a bank. Moreover, there is some difference as to whether the debt is held by foreigners or by Americans. When the Treasury issues a T-bill and an American buys it, the money is withdrawn from an American bank and deposited in the Treasury account, also at an American bank; but when a foreigner buys the T-bill, the money usually comes from a foreign bank, and thus enters our system afresh increasing the money supply by that amount. This has the same effect that a purchase of any American goods by the foreigner would have. For a clear illustration of the relationship between the money supply and consumer prices in the United States, refer to Figure 5. The money stock (M1) represents demand deposits of banks and currency in circulation.

In the final analysis, then, it is not the wage-demands of unions, nor the Arab cartels, nor the giant monopolies, nor the profiteering butcher who cause the inflation around you. All the wage and price controls, anti-trust laws, tariffs, and boycotts, will not only be futile, but they will in the end work against the society. Rather than cause lower prices, they will cause lower production. And with that lower production will come increasing efforts by politicians to "solve" the economic crisis through more government spending, and with that government spending will come the deficits that lead to more inflation. Modern inflation can be stopped only one way. By ending the inflation of the money supply. In our current system, that means putting an end to monetized debt.

> **An inflation free society would be one in which no debt would be allowed unless the lender loaned only claims to hard commodities. The elimination of monetized debt would eliminate inflation as we know it.**

THE ESTABLISHMENT SMOKESCREEN

"One difficulty about prescribing for inflation is that we don't entirely know how serious the disease is. . . . . . The argument made by those who demand very low rates has simply been inconclusive."

(Paul McCracken, former Chairman of the Council of Economic Advisors.)[6]

Let's scrutinize the above statement. The history of civilization is, in reality, the history of a series of societies, or nations, as you might call them. The people in each nation have come under the control of the leaders of a state or government by force or by vote. In either case, the leaders of the country (with the cooperation of the bankers) have always and in every case found it necessary to increase their funds beyond the amount they could collect through taxation. This is almost always done through some form of currency debasement. Whether the state borrowed from banks and monetized the debt, clipped coins, or simply ran printing presses to print new issues of notes, the results have always been the same: rising prices. As the state monetized debt and consumed the products and services purchased with those I.O.U.'s, the community as a whole was deprived of that production. The fact that the community felt it was receiving tangible wealth back in the form of "money" only served to confuse it. In the end, the confusion that resulted from this illusory wealth caused a fatal cycle of events that ultimately ended in the collapse of each of those states.

If you, as an individual, borrow money from someone and never repay that person, you have stolen from him. You are a thief. He is worse off; he has lost some of his wealth. When a state monetizes debt either by printing bank notes directly or by borrowing such notes from a bank without intention of repaying, it is just as much a thief of the society. The difference is that the victim becomes twice removed from his enemy. He can't tell by whom he has been victimized. The real loss falls on the population as a whole, and in such a camouflaged pattern that the results defy surface analysis. In other words, the theft is translated into rising prices, and the rising prices do the dirty work. When the victim feels the threat and tries to protect himself, he usually flails out at the symptom rather than the cause. The theft occurs when a person borrows money and does not repay it. The symptom is the rising price. As the individuals in society attempt to react to the symptom (rising prices), the trouble begins.

When the Congress votes to increase the national debt, as they have done periodically for years, how do you feel? Do you realize that what they're doing is borrowing money directly from *you* with no intention of ever paying it back? (Borrowing it from you, if you're a producer. Of course, if you're on welfare or unemployed, you have nothing to lend them.) Would you consider loaning someone money knowing that they had a long history of debt repudiation, and knowing that you may not agree with what they will do with the money once they've borrowed it? Of course, you wouldn't. But you're doing it anyway.

SYMPTOMS OF AN INFLATING MONEY SUPPLY

The most staggering revelation to come from a study of the economic history of past societies is that the sequence of economic events in the United States during the past fifty years has occurred repeatedly in dozens of other societies stretching as far back as early Macedonia:

1. Government needs more money than it is able to collect through taxation, so it issues paper money (or clips coins).
2. When the government spends this new money, business picks up.
3. As the increased supply of money percolates down through the society, prices begin to rise and business begins to slump.

4. To counteract the slump, the government issues more money.
5. Business picks up again, prices begin to rise, business slumps again.
6. People begin to distrust paper currency and begin to hoard gold and silver coins.
7. Government points finger of blame at gold hoarders and passes laws to stop hoarding (often confiscating gold, sometimes silver).
8. More inflation: prices begin to rise more steeply, people demand action and government passes price and wage control laws.
9. Shortages appear, rationing begins, black markets take over in place of regular markets.
10. Speculation begins to replace prudent investing as capital markets fluctuate up and down in concert with the business cycles.
11. Hard work falls into disrepute; people get rich (or poor) speculating; the thrifty lose all to inflation; more and more people go on relief as production falls and inflation forces prices out of the reach of the elderly and marginal producers.
12. As more people go on relief, government must tax the remaining producers more heavily until they decide to stop producing, and the situation begins to compound itself.
13. Stock markets oscillate wildly up and down, and finally drop; marginal businesses fail; prices fall to natural levels; currency is devalued to real levels; debts are repudiated; the country begins again.

The above scenario has been repeated in almost every society where the state has debased the currency. Everyone who is concerned about preserving his wealth should read *Fiat Money Inflation In France* by Andrew Dickson White.[7] It is a classic chronicle of the effect that fiat money had on the economy of France subsequent to the French revolution.

The parallels between France in 1789 and the U.S. in the 20th century are both obvious and frightening.

One has to wonder if President Roosevelt had ever studied the histories of countries that tried outlawing gold and inflating the money supply to solve their temporary economic problems. When he said, "it's all right; after all, we're borrowing from ourselves," had he heard of Macedonia, or the French economy of 1789? And what of President Nixon? When he instituted price controls, where were the scientists who said, "Let's observe the past before we act." If the saying is true that history repeats itself, could it be because no one consults history before they act? For Dr. McCracken to say that we don't really know the seriousness of the disease called inflation is totally absurd. The disease is *fatal.*

THE STATE SOLUTIONS TO INFLATION

Before every election the cries for programs to fight both unemployment and inflation rise from the political contenders. Although the causes of both these problems really did originate with the prior administrations, just as the political hopefuls contend, it is pure folly to believe that these would-be office holders, if elected, would be able to attack the root causes of either problem. If elected, they will do just what their predecessors did; they will make matters worse. They will spend vast quantities of money fighting the *symptoms* of both inflation and unemployment, and neither the expenditure of money nor the passage of laws will do anything but amplify both problems. Since inflation is really the source problem, let's look briefly at the rather standard remedies as suggested by Paul McCracken in his *Fortune* interview previously cited. His cure for inflation revolved around the following elements:

1. Fiscal responsibility.
2. Federal job-training programs.
3. Stronger anti-trust laws.

4. Control over unions.

5. Wage and price controls.

In light of our foregoing analysis of the causes of inflation, let's examine these "cures" one by one.

Fiscal responsibility by government is as attainable as a magic wand. Anyone who thinks the next administration will be elected to office on the promise that they will scrap the elaborate something-for-nothing welfare schemes of the previous administrations, doesn't understand the problem. Government costs are rising and will continue to rise.

What of number two? Federal job training programs are considered necessary because of the vast armies of unemployable, uneducated workers. Why are they unemployed? Because they have no skills. But to tell you the truth, no one is born with a skill. Every human being has had to learn one to become a producer. Assuming we've never had to rely on the government to tax us for the money to train these people before, why now? Because the system has made these people unemployable. The very minimum-wage laws that were effected to raise their standard of living have thrown them out of work. (See page 46 on Minimum Wage Laws.) They are not worth $2.30 (in 1975) an hour, and taxing the people to pay for training to make them worth $2.30 an hour is not the answer. The answer lies in letting the market be free to pay them what they are worth, and if individually they want more than that, they are free to educate themselves. But to insinuate that the unemployment of these people is in any way a cause of inflation is a rank absurdity.

Stronger anti-trust laws? In theory anti-trust laws were enacted to foster competition by preventing large companies from forcing smaller firms out of business. Granted, no company should be allowed to use *coersion* to damage another company, but analysed properly, it lowers everyone's standard of living to prevent businesses from properly utilizing their capital and know-how to produce their products in the cheapest possible ways. In effect anti-trust laws say that even if it's cheaper for two companies to sell their product if they join together versus operating as separate companies, no matter, they can't do it. The businesses that can't compete with the lower prices of the more efficient conglomerate scream that they should be subsidized, and that competition is unfair if it undersells them.

Nonsense. The consumer gets the best deal when the product is cheapest, and the product is cheapest when people can freely compete in the market place. The only monopolies that work to the advantage of the individual are those that are created and protected by the bureaucracy itself. As an example to prove the point, the U.S. Post Office would be out of business in six months if small businessmen were allowed to compete in the delivery of first-class mail.

Even if monopolies could fix prices at a level above what they should be, it wouldn't cause inflation. It would simply reallocate the resources of the individual consumer, as occurred in the example of excessive demands of big business and unions.

Control over unions? We have already discussed the fact that unions can have no lasting effect on prices if there is no government interference. They do not increase the money supply, and since an increase in the money supply is the *only* thing that can lower the value of money, unions are not guilty. They may cause the price of automobiles to rise. They may even cause a few companies to collapse. But their demands for higher wages do *not* contribute directly to the general rise in prices known as inflation.

Institute an effective program of wage-price controls? Suppose that Mr. Farmer is told that he cannot sell one unit of his apples for one unit of Carpenter's work. He must charge less. His price is now controlled and he must sell 2 units for 1. Immediately, his standard of living must go down, for he will trade off one unit of apples and only get one-half unit in return. He has two choices: he can trade, or he can refuse to trade. If he trades, he is less well off, and if this continues, he will probably go into another line of work where he can attain better rewards for his labor. If he doesn't trade, at least he still has his apples; but now a shortage of apples appears on the market, and the others must do without. Their standard of living drops or, at least, is distorted.

Since rising prices are nothing more than a symptom of an increasing supply of the money commodity, trying to hold them down will have about as much success as putting Band-Aids on measles. The fact is that not only will price controls be useless against inflation, they will have the effect of forcing producers to suspend production by making production unprofitable. This will lead to shortages. When the shortages appear, the government will say it must handle the allocation of the few supplies available, and we then have rationing. Rationing always leads to black markets. Remember World War II? If this is not readily apparent to you, read the headlines of every paper for most of 1973. Gas shortages, fuel shortages, meat shortages, grain shortages, paper shortages. And everywhere products available at twice the price on the black market. Did you think this was just coincidental? Or did you make the connections between the price controls and the shortages.

Argentina is a classic example of natural economic laws at work, as pointed out in *The Economist,* a London financial magazine.

> "Less than two years ago [in 1973] the government of Argentina was boasting a zero inflation rate, proclaiming an economic miracle. *Prices were tightly controlled,* and tourists could hardly believe their luck as they tucked into dollar steaks. Today a mile-long queue of taxis waits in vain for fares at the Buenos Aires airport. Coffee has disappeared from the market. Housewifes scour the streets in search of cooking oil, rice, and other staples, and queue up in front of stores to buy whatever is available before the price goes up. Shopkeepers are posting 'in mourning'

signs in order not to have to open up and sell goods at
half the price they expect to get in a hyper-in-
flationary while. Industrial workers are staging protest strikes up and down the country as they say a
45% wage increase is not enough . . . In the words of
one economist, Argentina has gone from concealed
crisis to open chaos. . ."[8]

The final and saddest of all the responses to this
money-supply inflation is that in the end, the propaganda
mechanism of the government points the finger at the very
businessmen who are being damaged the most by the system.
Without fail, the public, outraged and frustrated by its
inability to cope with inflation, assumes that it must be the
producer himself that is the cause. Now, you have the worst
injustice of all, the product boycott. Housewives marching
outside the butcher shop, picketing the merchant, and in the
end driving him out of business. With him, go the meat-
packers and with them go the cattle farmers. As we already
know, when you destroy production, down goes the society's
standard of living.

The great Austrian economist, Ludwig von Mises, summed
up the establishment's response to the failures of these wage
and price control programs:

"History is a long record of price ceilings and
anti-usury laws. Again and again emporers, kings, and
revolutionary dictators have tried to meddle with the
market phenomena. Severe punishment was inflicted
on refractory dealers and farmers. Many people fell
victim to persecutions which met with the enthu-
siastic approval of the masses. Nonetheless, all these
endeavors failed. The explanation which the writings
of the lawyers, theologians and philosophers provided
for failure was in full agreement with the ideas held
by the rulers and the masses; man, they said, is
intrinsically selfish and sinful, and the authorities
were unfortunately too lax in enforcing the law. What
was needed was more firmness on the part of those in
power."[9]

Those words, written more than 25 years ago, described the past, but they also hold true today and will so tomorrow. The great majority of economists and writers around the world flatly state that controls have failed for lack of teeth, and the political solutions to the inflation-recession cycle continue to be the same symptom-fighting folly as in the past.

Inflation is not caused by rising prices. Rising prices are a result of inflation. All the price controls, whether through jawboning or at the point of a gun, are exercises in futility.

To assume that any political party would, or could, have any long term answers to the country's economic problems is folly. To plan your own financial future based on the belief that this administration or the next, or the next, will provide us with the leadership and programs that will finally cure inflation will most certainly lead to your financial demise.

THE FEDERAL DEFICIT

The Federal government plays an ever-increasing role in your life; certainly far more so than could have been conceived by the founders of America two centuries ago. The most direct contacts are known and felt by everyone: federal jobs, government contracts, income taxes, government regulatory agencies, etc. But perhaps the most significant and in the long run the most tragic connection each of us has with government is through the federal deficit.

In the first 100 years of the country, the concept of federal spending was pretty well understood. The government levied taxes to the extent necessary to finance its operations. Deficits, other than in times of war, were rare if not nonexistent. By 1929, after 153 years of independence, the U.S. had run deficits totalling only $16.9 billion. By 1939 these had grown to $39.9 billion, thanks to the government's massive attempts to buy our way out of the inflation-induced depression of the 30's. The advent of World War II changed the picture dramatically, however, and we emerged in 1946 with a government debt of a staggering $250.7 billion. By 1959, thanks mostly to the defense expenditures for the Korean War the debt had grown to $287.8 billion.

The 1960's saw the avent of the Great Society measures of the Kennedy and Johnson administrations and a social philosophy that said increased wealth for all could be achieved by redistribution of the existing wealth. Massive social welfare programs coupled with the Vietnam War brought federal deficits to $61 billion for the decade.

But the end was nowhere in sight. Whatever administration was in power, the deficit spending went on. The first five years of this decade, July, 1970 to June 1975, federal deficits totalled $108 billion, almost twice those of the previous ten years. Almost half of that came in one year, 1975. This 1976 fiscal year the deficit will reach more than $70 billion, or almost twice the deficit of the previous year, and *close to the total for the entire first half of the decade.*

How about the administration's estimate for next year? Well, President Ford's projected 1977 budget seeks to hold spending to $394.2 billion, and if this happens, we would run a deficit of $43.6 billion. But we have learned to take budget estimates with a grain of salt. As the London *Economist* pointed out in their January 24th issue,

> "When the budget for [1975] was presented two years ago, its figures were presumably taken seriously by economists, politicians and the general public. Yet the deficit turned out to be $43.6 billion instead of the $9.4 billion estimated originally. The thing is becoming a joke.
>
> "The fact that the totals in the President's budget—outlays, receipts and deficit—are no longer to be taken seriously is now increasingly recognized by economic analysts and is noted in this budget. . . For example, he proposes some $20 billion of expenditure reductions, most of these requiring action by Congress to change existing law. . . about as likely as the appearance of palm trees in Alaska. . ."

Moreover, the current budget forecast assumes further recovery from the recession, which would bring in more taxes and lower unemployment costs; it assumes an inflation rate of only 5.9% this year; and it assumes that Congress will forego further tax cuts. If we are realistic, we will assume the opposite. Congress will spend more money, try for more tax cuts, inflation will probably heat up, and unemployment will not improve substantially. The result under these conditions will be a budget deficit not of the $43.6 billion estimated by Ford, but a more realistic $75 to $85 billion. *Thus in just two years we will have equalled the total deficits of the previous fifteen years!*

Recognizing the calamitous social costs of inflation in economic turmoil and social upheaval, it would behoove us to peer a little further into the future.

In September, 1975, Arthur Andersen & Co., a leading national accounting firm, published a study titled *Sound Financial Reporting in the Public Sector.* It dealt with the misleading nature of the government system of accounting, pointing out that the U.S. Government does its accounting on a cash basis, while most businesses use the accrual basis.

The basic difference between cash accounting and accrual accounting is that in cash accounting the only items included are those actually paid, or those for which payment has been received, while in accrual accounting any item which has been purchased and delivered, whether paid for or not, is included. For example, the amount of income taxes owed to the government, but not collected, would not show up in a cash-basis statement of income and expenses, but would be listed in an accrual-basis statement. Likewise, in accrual accounting if the government collects social security taxes from an individual, the amount of future benefit that is then owed to that individual becomes an expense on the day the liability is incurred rather than at the time the benefit is paid out.

It should be apparent that if you were trying to evaluate

the financial position of an individual, merely knowing what income he had received for the past year, and what checks he had written, would not give you a clear picture. You would need to know also what debts he had incurred that would need to be paid in the future, as well as what monies were owed to him that had not yet been paid, in order to understand his real financial status.

Arthur Andersen & Co.'s study points out that the government budgets are misleading for this very reason. They show only the income actually received during the year and the checks actually written. They completely overlook the fact that many bills are incurred, but remain unpaid. The greatest of these is the future retirement benefit due government employees and social security beneficiaries.

The study covered the fiscal years ending June 30, 1973 and June 30, 1974. According to the government's cash-basis accounting the deficit for 1973 was $14.3 billion and for 1974 only $3.5 billion. But according to Arthur Andersen & Co., if accrual system is used instead, the budget deficits for those years are far different. Under the accrual method, the 1973 deficit comes to a staggering $86.6 billion, *six times as great as the reported deficit!* In 1974, things are even worse. Instead of the $3.5 billion of the cash basis, the accrual basis shows *a deficit of $95.1 billion, or a deficit 27 times greater than shown.*

The problem is simple: the Congress and Administration have found that they can buy goods and services today, receive these things and disperse them to the public, while not paying for them until much later. Furthermore, they don't even need to reveal these future debts on their balance sheet. These debts will fall on the shoulders of the future generations.

Clearly, the federal budget is out of control. Political promises have been made to past generations that are now being paid by us; promises are now being made to us that will be borne by our children. The extraordinary deficit of the

1976 fiscal year will be at least $70 billion by the cash accounting method. By the accrual method it will be a more realistic *$200 billion.* Today we pay the piper for yesterdays fun, yet we haven't learned and the dance goes on.

The great questions today are: Will inflation continue? For how long? At what rate? The answers hinge on only one factor: the size of the federal deficit. A quick review of the above figures should answer the question. The next decade promises to be the most disturbed period in American history. There is no administration that could survive attempts to repudiate the promises made to the tens of millions of veterans, government employees and social security beneficiaries. Consequently, the wealth now held in the form of monetary assets by all of us must become worthless in the face of the massive currency inflation that lies ahead.

THE MYTH OF
GOVERNMENT ECONOMIC PROGRAMS

Before leaving the subject of government "solutions" to our economic woes, I think I should take time to cover some other political fiascoes.

Earlier in the book, I said that when you apply any set of conditions to a simple three-family society, you should be able to arrive at the same results as though you applied the conditions to a society of three billion. Also, I mentioned that there was a simple way to tell if a government program was beneficial or detrimental in the long run. If you remember, I asked the question: "Is there any way you can decrease production in a society and simultaneously increase the standard of living?" For example, could a lone hermit spend half as much time gathering food as he has in the past and be better off? It seems fairly obvious that the answer is *no*. Here's the magic question that you should ask yourself when someone suggests a "program" for improving the country. In the long run, *does the application of the program tend to increase or decrease production?*

AGRICULTURAL CONTROLS

Let's take some of the government programs, one at a time. In the thirties and late forties, farmers lobbied to maintain price levels in the face of falling farm prices, claiming they were being forced out of business due to the low prices. In response, Congress passed a number of agricultural acts extending back into the thirties. The purpose of these acts was to protect the farmer; the result was land taken out of production by paying the farmer not to grow crops, meat production reduced by having livestock slaughtered and buried, and foodstuffs made scarce by the purchase and destruction of enormous quantities of other farm products. The incredible stupidity of the process was told in a story in *Life* magazine in the March 20, 1950 issue. They tell of how the government spent $500 million on potatoes to support the price, but then couldn't figure out what to do with them:

> "The Agriculture Department then sprayed blue dye on its sacks of potatoes, to keep them from being sold for human consumption, and dumped them back to farmers for use as animal feed and fertilizer. But the dye colored only the top potatoes in the sack, and there grew a strong suspicion that many farmers simply threw away the colored ones and sold the others right back to the government, thus cashing in a second time. Finally, the government offered to sell its surplus to needy foreign countries at 1 cent per 100-pound sack, one of the greatest bargains ever recorded. Unfortunately, potatoes are so difficult and expensive to ship that even at this remarkable price there was trouble finding takers; the best customer was a man from Spain who said he could use 50,000 tons, chiefly because the sacks in which they were packed would be worth around 30 cents each in his country. There things stood until last month, when the government's stocks had mounted to 50 million tons and everybody was getting desperate. Then the Agriculture Department found a new method to dye the potatoes with a colored salt that is supposed to

> seep down into the sack and touch every single one.
> It now appears that the potatoes will all be used for
> hog feed or dumped into fields to rot into fertilizer.
> Potatoes aren't really much good as fertilizer, but
> even so this is probably the best possible solution
> because the potatoes were bound to rot anyway, and
> an outlying field is the ideal place."[10]

Potatoes weren't the only problem commodity, the article
goes on to say:

> "In addition to the 76 million pounds of dried eggs
> which will never be eaten and the potatoes which will
> rot, the government has accumulated a vast amount
> of other stuff. Most of it, fortunately, is more edible
> or useful than the dried eggs and less prone to
> spoilage than the potato; in fact it is perfectly good
> farm produce and would be very useful to have if
> only someone could figure out what to do with it. To
> put the size of the surpluses into everyday terms, the
> government has enough:

WHEAT to bake 12 loaves of bread for every man, woman
and child in the world.

CORN to make all the cornstarch, corn sugar, corn syrup
and corn oil that the U.S. will use in the next five years.

BUTTER to bake a birthday cake for every child under 15
in the U.S. for the next 10 years.

COTTON to produce 54 house dresses for every U.S.
woman.

PRUNES to give every member of Congress a dish for
breakfast until approximately September of the year
3239."

In light of the foregoing discussion and assuming that you
agree that you can't enjoy a higher standard of living if you
have less to eat, were these agricultural acts beneficial or
detrimental to the country?

MINIMUM WAGE LAWS

In 1938, the government passed the Fair Labor Standards
Act, which included the first minimum wage law. They said
no one, with the exception of agricultural workers, domestic

help, and retail trades workers, could be paid less than 25 cents per hour. The minimum wage was then raised to 49 cents in 1939, 75 cents in 1950 and so on until it reached $2.30 in 1975. Was this good or bad? If it is good for the country if production increases and bad if it decreases, let's apply the situation to our small community and see the direct effect.

Suppose the state says our farmer cannot pay his apple pickers less than one bushel of apples a week. If these workers don't pick enough to justify that wage, the farmer might begin to lose money at his business. He would soon lay off those workers and stop producing apples. Losing this production would be detrimental to the standard of living of the community, and the workers would be affected most because they would be unemployed. Granted that if they were efficient workers and there was ample profit in the employer's product, he might be able to raise their wages and still produce. In fact, he might be able to raise the price of apples to compensate for the increased labor costs. But it would still be taking production away from the carpenter or tailor and lowering their standard of living if he raised his price.

In reality, a minimum-wage law has the absolute effect of driving the marginally-profitable producer out of business and leaving all the unskilled laborers unemployed. The very law that is designed to aid the poorest workers only succeeds in throwing them out of work and cutting the supply of products available to the community. Everyone loses. No wonder Dr. McCracken calls for federal job training programs for the unemployed. It seems only fitting that the bureaucracy that causes a worker to lose his job should retrain him for another. Pity that you and I and the apple farmer have to pay for that retraining through taxes.

EXPORT CONTROLS

On a number of occasions in the past, Congress has passed laws controlling exports. In 1973, bills were introduced to limit the export of cotton, wheat, and various other commodities. The reason suggested was that we couldn't afford to lose these products, which were in such short supply. Does this tend to increase or decrease production?

It must be assumed that a producer will try to sell his produce to the highest bidder and also that a larger demand for a product will result in more of that product being produced. Generally, a greater demand, although initially causing a higher price, eventually results in lower cost, as production facilities are improved to supply the increased demand.

Establishing export controls decreases the size of a producer's market. Moreover, it prevents him from obtaining the maximum price for his production, because the only reason a person would ship his products out of the country rather than sell them locally is that the foreigners are willing to pay more. If other producers can export and he cannot, those exportable products will be more profitable. It will tend to limit the production of one item in favor of another. To say that the production is lost to the community when it is exported is nonsense; if the farmer trades with the carpenter, it doesn't matter whether the carpenter is in his valley or in another state or another country. He still has the benefit of the carpenter's work when he makes the trade. If the U.S. ships wheat to Japan and in return Japan ships automobiles to the U.S., the rise in wheat prices due to lower wheat supplies here is offset by the decrease in auto prices due to increased auto supplies.

TARIFFS

Since modern nations look at jobs and full employment as a measure of prosperity, anything that threatens employment becomes a target for the wrath and action of parent-like governments. After all, what higher function can government perform than to insure the right to meaningful and productive labor for its citizens?

One of the requirements for a healthy industry is a stable market in which it can sell its products. Advocates of protectionism contend that when foreigners step into the marketplace and offer competitive products at a lower price, local industries suffer. When unable to compete, an industry can be bankrupted, with consequent loss of jobs to the workers involved. It's pointed out that cheap foreign products destroy the business, throw the workers out on the street, cause local merchants to lose business, and even affect the suppliers to those merchants. Furthermore, the government loses the tax revenue from all these citizens, and thus the economic damage spreads in ever-widening circles.

Faced with the responsibility for preventing this type of economic hardship, governments can employ a number of tools. First, they can impose import duties (tariffs) on incoming goods. This brings the effective price of the foreign product up to or above the price of its domestic counterpart. Second, they can offer subsidies, directly or through tax breaks, to the domestic manufacturers and their employees who are hurt by foreign competition. This allows the local manufacturer to sell his product at a lower price and still realize an adequate profit. Third, governments can restrict imports by setting maximum quotas for incoming goods.

Examples of efforts to protect domestic workers and industries are replete in the pages of the press:

The Wall Street Journal, August 28, 1975:

> "A 'buy British' fever is mounting in the United Kingdom, strengthening the hand of protectionists who want to slap controls on imports. Import controls are 'a tolerable possibility' if the government decides to spur employment by stimulating the economy this fall, as appears necessary, says F. D.

Black, Deputy Director of the National Institute of
Economic and Social Research, a prestigious independent study group. Some leftwingers in the Labor
Party government, union officials, and academics
been advocating import controls for some time to
preserve jobs in Britain."

The Wall Street Journal, August 27, 1975:

"The Amalgamated Clothing Workers Union peti-
tioned the Labor Department to supply benefits to
20,000 members of the union said to have lost work
due to rising imports of men's wear. The Trade Act of
1974 provides weekly cash benefits and other aid to
workers whose jobs have been 'importantly' affected
by imports."

The Economist, London, August 9, 1975:

"The 150,000 wine growers of the French Midi,
are out on the road again, disrupting the holiday
traffic at its height, stopping cars, painting out road
signs, and handing out leaflets in French, German,
English, and Italian. . . Their complaint is simple:
they are not getting enough money for their wine. . .
The trouble is that French wine traders can get Italian
wine for blending more cheaply than domestic
products. . ."

The Wall Street Journal, August 4, 1975:

"As the excess of U.S. exports over imports begins
to dwindle, there is the danger that protectionist
sentiment will revive. Such sentiment is by no means
dead now. The Treasury this year has been looking
into such varied imports as canned pork shoulders,
leather handbags, and processed asparagus to determine whether they were being 'subsidized' by the
exporting countries. . ."

The Wall Street Journal, August 4, 1975:

"The Labor Department's decision making 18,000
Chrysler Corp. workers eligible for special trade-re-

lated jobless benefits seems certain to trigger further applications from the United Auto Workers' Union. The Department ruled that the workers were either unemployed already or in danger of losing their jobs later as a result of increased imports of automobiles and parts from Chrysler plants in Canada."

The Wall Street Journal, August 11, 1975:

"The Treasury tossed to the U.S. International Trade Commission the thorny issue of whether foreign autos are being 'dumped' in the U.S.

"As expected, the Treasury formerly announced that it will investigate allegations that foreign autos are being sold in the U.S. prices below those in eight home markets, in violation of the U.S. Anti-Dumping Act. If the Treasury ultimately finds that dumping is occurring, it would refer the case to the Trade Commission for a full scale investigation. If the Trade Commission finds injury, special dumping duties would be assessed. The Common Market has warned the U.S. it is prepared to take a retaliatory measure against U.S. goods should the government rule that dumping is occurring. The market countries believe that the Treasury investigation represents a protectionist policy. . ."

Protectionist sentiment is strong in almost all nations, just as it has been for centuries. Rare is the government that doesn't try to pamper its industries with a shield of protective measures. In fact, so constant is the voice of protectionism, that we rarely hear an argument to the contrary.

Protectionism vs Economic Reality

Way back in 1844 Frederic Bastiat, a French economist, in a publication titled *Social Fallacies* used Robinson Crusoe to illustrate the realities behind protectionism. W. M. Curtiss repeated Bastiat's parable in his fine little book, *The Tariff Idea*[11] back in 1953, and it bears repeating again.

"You remember how Robinson Crusoe managed to make a plank when he had no saw."

"Yes; he felled a tree, and then, cutting the trunk right and left with his hatchet, he reduced it to the thickness of a board."

"And that cost him much labour?"

"Fifteen whole days' work."

"And what did he live on during that time?"

"He had provisions."

"What happened to the hatchet?"

"It was blunted by the work."

"Yes; but you perhaps do not know this: that at the moment when Robinson was beginning the work he perceived a plank thrown by the tide upon the seashore."

"Happy accident! He of course ran to appropriate it?"

"That was his first impulse; but he stopped short, and began to reason thus with himself:

" 'If I get this plank, it will cost me only the trouble of carrying it, and the time needed to descend and remount the cliff. But if I form a plank with my hatchet, first of all it will procure me fifteen days' employment; then my hatchet will get blunt, which will furnish me with the additional employment of sharpening it; then I shall consume my stock of provisions, which will be a third source of employment in replacing them. Now, labour is wealth. It is clear that I should ruin myself by getting the plank. I must protect my personal labour; and, now that I think of it, I can even increase that labour by throwing back the plank into the sea.' "

"But this reasoning was absurd."

"No doubt. It is nevertheless the reasoning of every nation which protects itself by prohibition. It throws back the plank which is offered in exchange for a small amount of labour. Even in the labour of the Customhouse officials it discovers a gain. That gain is represented by the pains which Robinson takes to render back to the waves the gift which they had offered him. Consider the nation as a collective being, and you will not find between its reasoning and that of Robinson an atom of difference."

Bastiat went on at delightful length with his allegory extending it to the situation wherein a stranger came to trade with the castaways and was met with the same strangled logic. Yet in just this brief example a perceptive person will have to agree with the narrator and realize that any form of protective measure that attempts to halt the import of lower cost goods is, in some degree, as destructive of the well being of the nation's inhabitants as the casting back of the plank was to Robinson.

The perversion lies in the concept that the good of the nation comes from the labor performed by the inhabitants. Full employment becomes the goal, rather than the more thoughtful concept of obtaining the most consumable products for the least amount of labor. Bastiat pointed out that the confusion stems from observing that which is seen, and ignoring that which is not seen. What was seen by Robinson was that he would lose his job (that of shaping a plank) if he accepted the gift from the waves. What was not seen was that the same amount of effort that was going to be expended in shaping the plank, could be put to some other use. By doing some other task he would wind up with both the product of the new labor and the use of the plank as well.

What is seen in a nation's economy when low cost imports are allowed to compete with high cost domestic products is that jobs are lost, just as Robinson would have lost his. The jobless workers and idle plants are highly visible evidence of the damage. What is not seen is that those same laborers and that same idle factory could be put to work manufacturing some other product that was needed, and then the society would have a second product to add to the imports, and thus a higher standard of living for everyone. But the new products are not yet in existence, and the only thing that can be immediately seen is the unemployed worker. Since unemployed workers are not the ones directly benefited by the imports, as was Robinson, they loudly shout their disapproval. Those who benefit from the use of the low-cost

imports are not so visible or so vociferous. Thus the
politicians who make their living by attending to the
demands of the vocal minority are ready and willing to
"protect" the interests of the nation and the affected
workers.

Who Does "Dumping" Hurt?

Whenever a person or a nation is offered a product at a
price below what they would otherwise have to pay, that is
their good fortune. If Japan decides to subsidize its automobile industry in order to allow it to "dump" automobiles
into the United States at an artificially low price, that is not a
loss to the U.S. It is a gain. The loss accrues to Japan. They
have expended labor and received less in return than they
should have. It doesn't matter whether they give the autos
away, or charge any price below that of the American
manufacturers, the difference is only one of degree.

Nor does it matter what the product is. If the sky opened
up and suddenly started raining wheat, how could anyone
claim that to be a calamity? Would not the whole world be
better off? Yet the protectionists would have to say, no, it
would an economic disaster in as much as all the wheat
farmers would go out of business. This in turn would
precipitate a depression of the highest magnitude. They
would cast the free wheat into the sea, just as Robinson cast
back the plank. Whether it's wheat, automobiles, or leather
handbags, the consequences of protective measures are
equally harmful to the nation that employs them.

Why Not Subsidies?

Well, if we don't prevent the products from coming into
the country, certainly a subsidy to the injured industries
would be appropriate. Or would it? If you take money from
the consumer in the form of taxes, and give it to the
inefficient workers, how has the consumer benefited from
the low-cost import? It is as logical as Robinson's keeping the

plank he found on the beach, while making another one and tossing it into the waves. The benefit to the country will come when the workers displaced by the more efficient foreign competition find a new occupation in which they can be efficient. They won't do this as long as the taxpayer is forced to reward them for their inefficiency.

In the short run, low-cost imports do cause unemployment. But in the intermediate and long run, they do not. If I have $20 to spend and a domestic manufacturer offers me a leather handbag for $20, when I make the purchase I then have nothing left. If a foreign purse maker sells me the same bag for $15, then I'll have the bag and $5 left over to spend on something else, say a belt. I now have two items, and the belt industry is benefited by the purchase that I wouldn't have made otherwise. In addition, the $15 I spent on the handbag will go to the foreign manufacturer, and eventually will find its way back into this country to purchase an American product. When it does, some other American manufacturer will be benefited by that $15 purchase. For every worker injured by the low cost foreign handbag, another is benefited. Since this competition tends to cause people to be employed where they produce the most efficiently, the whole world is better off.

There is one sure way to determine whether any economic policy is sound, and that is to ask if it ultimately causes a higher or lower standard of living for the nation. Any time you read that your government is erecting tariff barriers, supporting threatened industries with subsidies, or interfering in any way with free trade between individuals or nations, you must realize that your standard of living is being lowered as a result. It's just a matter of common sense.

ANTI-TRUST

In most areas of governmental intervention in the economy, there are two opposing factions: those who believe government control is necessary, and those who believe in the sanctity of the free market. There is one area, however, where there seems to be almost no disagreement. Most laissez-faire advocates and interventionists alike agree that the public welfare is damaged by monopoly power, and they seem to stand together in believing that a thoughtful application of anti-trust law is necessary to save the public from the ruthless and economically devastating actions of modern industrial corporations.

Even Adam Smith in his *Wealth of Nations* denounced private monopoly. He observed, "People of the same trade seldom meet together, even for merriment and diversion, but the conversation ends in a conspiracy against the public, or in some contrivance to raise prices." Today, if there is an argument over anti-trust laws, it is not an argument over the basic concept, but rather over their application and enforcement to achieve the maximum public good.

The concept of monopoly power is rather simple. A seller who is effectively able to eliminate competition can set his price higher than he would be able to if competition existed, and thereby the price he charges may be unfair to the public and his profits unreasonable. The objective of anti-trust legislation is to maintain competition.

Federal laws to combat monopoly power started with enactment of the Sherman Anti-Trust Act of 1890. This Act provides that every contract, combination in the form of trust, or conspiracy in restraint of trade is illegal, and any person who monopolizes any part of trade is guilty of a misdemeanor. This act was followed by the Clayton Act of 1914, which states that price discrimination favoring one buyer over another (except when this can be justified by real cost savings) is illegal. In addition, a seller cannot, as a part of the contract, preclude a buyer from doing business with the seller's competitors, nor can a company acquire ownership of another company if this tends to create a monopoly.

The history of court action against monopoly power began shortly after the enactment of the Sherman Act with two cases: the E. C. Knight case involving the sugar refiners, and the Northern Securities case involving the railroads. The first major battle, however, was with the Standard Oil Company.

John D. Rockefeller started in the oil business in the mid 1860's, practically at the very beginning of its history (the discovery in 1848 that kerosene could be distilled from oil started the industry). By 1880 his share of the now booming market had climbed to about 80 percent and he was undisputed king of the industry. His refining company, Standard Oil of Ohio, had significant interests in oil fields, pipelines, tank cars, and storage facilities, and massive bargaining strength with railroads. As new firms entered the refinery business and failed during the decade of the 70's, Standard had bought them up. The giant's cost efficiency could not be matched. In addition, volume allowed it to demand and get significant rebates from railroads in the shipment of oil.

By 1880 Standard of Ohio owned 14 firms completely, and had large stock interest in 25 others. In 1882, to get around a tax provision of Pennsylvania law, the Standard Oil Trust was formed. This trust was ruled illegal by the state of Ohio in 1892, and seven years later the stockholders formed Standard Oil of New Jersey as a legal holding company. Public sentiment turned against the company in the early 1900's with publication of Ida Tarbell's *The History of the Standard Oil Company,* and in 1906 the Sherman Act was invoked against Standard. Standard was convicted of being a monopoly, that conviction was upheld by the Supreme Court in 1911, and the company was ordered dissolved back into its original companies.

This was a landmark case. The biggest trust had been attacked and defeated. From there on down to the present day, company after company has fallen to the power of the anti-trust legislation. Tobacco, steel, aluminum, shoes, electrical equipment, salt, newspapers, railroads, and foods; all have been attacked, split up, fined, and in many cases the executives have suffered imprisonment as they were proved guilty of abusing monopoly power to the detriment of the American public.

Today, our courts and newspapers are replete with anti-trust actions. The most noteworthy in recent years was the civil suit brought against IBM by Telex in 1973 in which IBM was accused of monopolizing the peripheral computer equipment market. Telex was initially awarded $259.5 million, but this judgment was overturned on appeal. (In any case, the suit opened Pandora's Box for IBM, as numerous smaller firms, heartened by Telex's victory, filed their own civil anti-trust actions against the giant.) The major drug companies were recently convicted of monopolizing the market for certain brand name prescription drugs, and were forced to rebate millions to drug customers. Another rebate order was levied on the potato chip industry in 1975 in a similar price fixing case.

As inflation gets more severe, anti-trust action will probably accelerate. Critics of business point at monopoly (or "market") power as a major cause of inflation, and cite aggressive anti-trust action as an absolute necessity in the fight against higher prices.

There seems to be no doubt that with the almost universal acceptance of the theory of monopoly power and its "antidote," anti-trust legislation, cases will multiply in the coming years. In fact, even many supporters of anti-trust are becoming alarmed at the profusion of suits and the tangle of precedent-setting decisions that are effectively hamstringing the business world in pricing and merger decisions. Where will it all lead? And what effect does it all have on you and me as individuals or businessmen? To understand this, it is necessary to examine basic concepts.

Morality and Pragmatism

As in most economic problems, there are two vantage points from which to make judgments: the moral and the pragmatic. The greatest good for the greatest number of people, which is the pragmatic view, really becomes the basis of a definition of morality. However, when morality is defined in this way, it becomes totally relative to the opinion of the person making the judgment. Even Charles Manson, in his warped way, believed that through mass murder he was setting up a better society.

If, on the other hand, you tie a concept of morality in with the right of an individual to own and control his own affairs—his property, his money, his life—then any interference with that individual's right to make voluntary exchanges with others would be seen to be an immoral act. Certainly in this case, anti-trust legislation would have to be deemed immoral, for it is a direct interference. Suppose I have the only potato chip factory in existence, and I decide to sell my chips at $50 per bag. If someone buys a bag it is a voluntary exchange between us, and no interference takes place. By setting a value on my property (the chips) I use no force or fraud in making the customer part with his money—we have made a moral transaction. If, however, a third party steps in, claims I'm charging an unfair price, and forces me, through the power of the law, to sell my chips *involuntarily* at a lower price, then that act has to be deemed to be immoral.

Of course, by selling chips at $50 a bag I would severely limit my market, and if I achieved any success at all, competition would soon pop up. Unless I took affirmative action to compete with the lower prices my new competitiors would charge, or figured out a way to eliminate them from the market, I would soon lose the customers I had, and would go out of business. This natural magnetism in the market that attracts competitors wherever high prices are maintained is the very force that keeps prices down. It is this competition then that the anti-monopoly laws seek to insure.

The anti-trust laws, rather than enhancing competition, tend to eradicate the very mechanisms by which it produces its beneficial effects. After all, it isn't the competition that we want, it's the effects of competition. The laws penalize the strongest and subsidize the weakest; they destroy the incentive for innovation; they discourage efficiency.

The case of Standard Oil is a good example of this. Standard undercut their rivals' prices. Why? Because they were so efficient that no one could produce oil as cheaply as they could. They received rebates from the regular rates railroads charged. Why? Because they were the railroads' largest customer, and in addition financed and built their own loading and unloading facilities. They bought out numerous competitors. Why? Because they were able to operate profitably at low prices, and their competitors were not. Were the buyers of oil products hurt by Standard's practices? At the point of Standard's dissolution, prices of petroleum products were *the lowest in history,* and the quality and variety was the largest. It was to Standard's advantage to continue to develop new products, reduce the price of existing products, and expand their market. All these things meant higher profits; certainly it did not work to the disadvantage of the buying public.

Standard was not hurting the petroleum market by its actions, nor was it acting immorally in its battle with competition. In lowering its petroleum prices it was only exercising control over its own property. Its contracts with its suppliers were voluntarily executed by both parties. Its purchases of interests in ancillary products like storage facilities, pipelines, and tank cars in no way interfered with the property of its competitors. The problem was not that Standard was trying to interfere with the property of its competitiors. The problem is just the reverse. Smaller businesses, unable to compete with a more efficient, able firm, turned to the coercive power of the state to interfere with the property of their more successful rival. In fact, almost every anti-trust action has been instigated by one business against another. Businessmen have found the anti-trust sword a convenient, taxpayer-subsidized weapon to use against competition when they are unable to compete on the basis of their own talents.

If morality, by our definition, is opposed to the concept of anti-trust law, how about the bigger issue of pragmatism? If an atmosphere of competition enforced by law could truly provide for greater good for all involved, then perhaps the moral question should be overlooked, or morality should be redefined as being that condition wherein the greatest number achieve the greatest good. Some of the greatest moral teachers, many of whom have been gifted advocates of limited government and laissez-faire, have stated that private monopoly is detrimental to the public welfare.

The lower the price on a product, the larger the market; therefore, any producer has an ongoing incentive to expand his sales through price reductions and quality improvements regardless of the competition. This is illustrated by the case of Polaroid Corporation, with its patented Land camera. With no other competitor in the instant photography field up until 1976, Polaroid still saw fit to constantly improve the quality and bring out new innovations, as well as steadily reduce the price of its cameras. The potential profits of an expanded market far outweigh the benefits of being able to fix the price at a high level. In addition, their success has caused a storm of research on the part of other camera manufacturers, which has caused the development of numerous innovations that help them to siphon off a considerable portion of the expanding snapshot market. Thus, Polaroid's monopoly, far from hurting the public, has provided them with exceptional product variety at an ever-declining cost.

The example of Polaroid should serve to dispell the idea that when one firm absorbs a competitor, the product price will therefore rise in the marketplace. Raise the price, and the market for the product diminishes. Since the merging of two firms frequently means lower overhead and lower production costs, the surviving firm is more likely to lower the product price and thereby further expand the sales of the product.

Besides, to raise the price is to invite new competition to
enter the market.

After a firm gets big enough, and assuming that the cost of
setting up a manufacturing facility for a given product is
substantial, wouldn't the established firm have little fear of
competition? Of course not. The world is full of risk capital
just looking for opportunities to compete for profits. Not
only are people already in the business a threat, other
businesses are always looking for ways to diversify, and there
are hoards of entreprenuers looking for opportunities. Even
the auto makers like General Motors and Ford, who are
among the biggest companies in the world, must wage a
constant struggle for markets. Their costs of plant, advertising, and extensive dealer networks offer no real protection
against better product, or comparable product at lower cost.
Thus Volkswagen, Toyota, Datsun, Fiat, Mercedes, and
Mazda can all enter the market and be viable competitors.

Is Small Good?

Anti-trust advocates seem to be protectors of the small
businessman. Yet the question is, why? On the one hand,
they justify the anti-monopoly statutes on the basis of
keeping prices to consumers at the lowest level, yet by
keeping small business men small (by preventing mergers,
take-overs, etc.), they really keep price levels artificially high.
In the Von's Grocery Co. case in 1966, the court ruled that
the merger of Von's with Shopping Bag Markets would result
in fewer markets and would affect the mom-and-pop operators in the area. This decision ignored the fact that prices of
groceries would have gone down and the consumers would
have been benefited by the economics of scale. As Justice
Stewart said in the dissenting opinion, it was an indirect
attempt "to roll back the supermarket revolution."

Although one company may dominate a market, in a free
system it can only do this as long as it meets the quality and
price of its smallest competitors. By growing larger through

mergers, acquisitions, or simply market penetration, a company is usually able to offer better products for less. This is certainly to the benefit of all.

The Cartel—Threat or Illusion?

Why can't all the companies in an industry collude to fix prices at artificially high levels? Two examples of this theory would be the electrical equipment manufacturers' price conspiracy case decided in 1961, and a look at the OPEC oil cartel. In the electrical equipment case, the nation's largest manufacturers of electrical equipment (circuit breakers, meters, etc.) were convicted of conspiring to fix prices, and seven executives were sent to jail, twenty-three others were given suspended sentences, and the firms were fined $2 million. Anti-trust defenders say that the case proves the point, in that prices for this equipment fell dramatically after the conviction.

The truth was that the companies had *attempted* to fix prices at high levels, and had agreed to do so, and their catalogs reflected these prices. But in practice, they had all busily been breaking these agreements by undercutting their "agreed upon" prices to any and all customers. The collusion simply didn't work because the companies were intensely competitive, as are most companies, and were always ready to cheat if the opportunity presented itself. Prices didn't fall after the conviction; the new catalog prices merely reflected the true prices that had been offered under the table all along.

The OPEC nations, likewise, have created consternation in the oil consuming nations by their price fixing tactics. But behind the scenes they are doing the same shenanigans the electrical equipment companies were doing. Those member nations that have a need for cash want maximum volume sales and low prices to stimulate demand. Those that have no need for cash want to keep more oil in the ground for future sale at higher prices. The back-stabbing and secret price cutting is the result. It's doubtful that the cartel can hold together much longer under this strain.

Where Monopoly Hurts

In today's world there is one kind of monopoly power that is really working to the detriment of society. It is the only monopoly that can exist at all: the state-enforced monopoly.

It seems incredible that the state can say that monopoly power causes artificially higher prices and inferior products to the consumer and yet justify the creation of *government-controlled monopolies* by saying they are necessary to keep prices low and service up!

Currently the state (federal, state, or local) grants monopoly power to the U.S. Postal Service, the telephone company, public transportation, public utilities, taxi-cab companies, etc. using the argument that it's all in the public interest. In these areas, monopoly does function to the individual's detriment. With no competition to force them to offer better quality or price, your service goes down while prices go up. When you can't threaten to buy from another source, you, as a consumer, are helpless. You either pay the price or forego the product. When this monopoly power is coupled with a nonprofit system, such as the U.S. Postal Service, the result is even more devastating. Then there is no longer any way of measuring the efficiency of the operation and consumer satisfaction ceases to be a lever to improve the quality of the product.

Monopoly power is an illusion in any system in which free competition is allowed. Size of industry, concentration of market, or production notwithstanding, the consumer is best served when the businessman is completely free to pursue his profit goals. Only in situations where competition is illegal will competition not act naturally to bring the best product at the lowest price to the consumer. In our society, the history of anti-trust action has been to ignore the underlying market realities and to penalize the monopoly situation without regard to the end effect that that action might have on the well-being of the individual consumer. As D. T. Armentano so ably points out in his book, *The Myths of Anti-Trust,*[12] anti-trust is a giant hoax; public monopoly has never been proven to work to the disadvantage of the society or the individual. The truth is that "certain elements in the business community have never desired 'free competition' and the uncertainties and irrationalities often associated with it. They have sought and gained economic subsidy and protection through the political system. They have been anxious to use the government to 'regulate competition' because it was supposedly tending towards monopoly." All the court cases in anti-trust history bear out this thesis.

In addition to the immense harm that this type of government interference does to the productive output of the businesses involved, the cost to the taxpayer is substantial; he pays for the courts, the Federal Trade Commission (who investigates and enforces), the Congressional investigating committees, and for all the legal and reporting costs of the affected companies in the form of higher prices.

Where will anti-trust action lead in the future? As inflation heats up, monopolies will come under more criticism as causes of inflation. No doubt there will be increasing pressure to stiffen the anti-trust laws and to break up any situations in which market control can be imagined. The right of an individual company to make a profit at all will eventually come under question. Current anti-trust advocates are even arguing that patents are unreasonable—they would limit them to five years instead of the current seventeen and force the owners to license all competitors, while the state determines the royalty rate. In other words, it all leads to state control of the property rights of individuals; an abolition of your right to control the disposition of your property, whether it is a product you invent, or a product you produce. The result has to be a lower level of production, and thus a lower standard of living for all.

DEVALUATION

One piece that we can hardly overlook in this economic puzzle is the cause and effect of devaluation. To understand it, let's go back to the banker who issues more receipts for gold than he has in his vault. When the time comes that people realize this and come forward to claim their gold (before it's all gone), the banker is faced with two alternatives. He can refuse to give them the gold at all, or he can offer to give them less gold per receipt than they had originally been promised. He also has the option of trying to collect the gold from all the people to whom he lent the receipts. (That is, he could demand payment of all outstanding notes, but assuming that those people had not yet produced a product but had merely consumed the loan, collection would be impossible.)

If the banker refuses to redeem the receipts, they would become worthless as they could represent nothing. If he redeems them for a partial value, they have been "de"-valued. In the United States in the 1920's there was a tremendous expansion of bank credit.[13] When the Federal Reserve began to constrict credit in 1929 the stock market collapsed and consequently individuals and businesses were unable to meet their loan commitments. The depositors of the banks tried to redeem their banknotes for gold, found there wasn't enough gold to meet redemptions and the panic began. The government under President Roosevelt realized that if everyone came in and claimed the gold that was rightfully his, there would be far more receipts turned in than there was gold available. This would quickly cause the banks involved (and they were all involved) to go bankrupt, along with the federal government. In addition, he wanted to embark on a program of spending in order to "stimulate" the economy.

To save the banking system and stimulate the economy, two things were necessary. First, the people could not drain the gold from the system and in so doing prove the bankruptcy to be true; second, new "money" must be

created without the public being able to redeem gold for
their new money substitutes. The answer was exactly the
same as that tried by the French legislature in the 1780's. He
made it illegal to own gold and called in all the gold which
was being held in private hands. This was an absolute fraud
on those producers who had produced a product, exchanged
it for gold and then taken a receipt for the gold. Now, they
were told that in the "national interest" they could not have
their gold back, nor could they own gold at all. In the future,
they must be content to accept paper money as their sole
measure of wealth. With this accomplished, the government
had a free road toward printing all the money substitutes
they might want.

Only one problem still presented itself. While the President
could deny Americans the right to own gold, he couldn't
extend that prohibition to foreigners. If trade was to
continue between America and other countries, those countries would demand to be paid for their products in some
form of currency that was convertible into gold. Therefore,
he created a situation in which Americans couldn't redeem
dollars for gold but foreign banks could. The obvious result
was that while prices of American products and services
began to rise, foreign goods did not. The foreign car and the
foreign vacation became more and more a bargain. Why;
Because when you bought a Volkswagen from Germany, the
German manufacturer knew he could take that dollar and
convert it into gold at any time. He was essentially being paid
in gold, and gold being a commodity, there could be no
inflation of that supply. As long as the U.S. was willing to
redeem American Dollars in gold, the foreign producers were
able to essentially avoid inflation when selling to American
buyers. Those dollars that went overseas were replaced by
products here in our economy. We rid our money supply of
$2,000.00 and got a Volkswagen in return.

What did this mean to us? That we were able to maintain
lower prices domestically. Because price is a function of the

money supply versus the supply of all other commodities, when you increase the supply of commodities and decrease the supply of money (or money substitutes), the general prices are lower. By shipping billions of paper dollars abroad and bringing in exchange billions of usable, consumable products, we had a higher standard of living and lower prices. But anyone with a sense of real economics should have been able to predict the ultimate outcome. Soon the number of dollars abroad would build up beyond the supply of gold in the Treasury, just as earlier the supply of paper dollars in the U.S. had built up beyond the supply of gold. Then the government would be in exactly the same boat that it was in when the American people began to try to redeem their dollars for gold. There was a run on the gold supply and the government had to choose between continuing to redeem at its earlier agreed-upon price ($35.00 per troy ounce), and quickly running out of gold, thus admitting its bankruptcy; or redeeming for less than it had agreed upon, or refusing to redeem at all.

By 1971 the total outstanding claims on gold held overseas were almost $100 billion. Yet the total supply of gold in the U.S. Treasury was only 291 million ounces; at $35 an ounce, $10.2 billion. The stock was sufficiently low that it could have been wiped out in one day, and rather than let that happen, on August 15, 1971, President Nixon suspended the convertibility of dollars held by foreigners into gold the same as Roosevelt had done for American citizens some 38 years earlier. On December 18, 1971 he devalued the dollar in relation to gold from $35 per ounce to $38 per ounce.

The devaluation had a significant effect on the money supply of the U.S. as it increased the official dollar value of treasury gold holdings by $800 million and thus allowed the treasury to buy $800 million of goods and services from the private sector of the economy. This $800 million, once in the banking system, supported a $2 billion higher level of the money stock.[14]

After the suspension of redemption and the first devaluation, the price of gold in the free market jumped from $35 per ounce to about $65 per ounce. In February of 1973 Nixon again was faced with massive balance of payments deficits and a declining dollar value on world money markets. He chose to devalue again, this time pegging the price of gold at $42.22 (a fictitious price only applicable to central banks). This again resulted in a bonanza for the treasury, giving them $1.2 billion of new spending power and again supporting a huge $3 billion increase in the money stock.

Now step back and think about this refusal to redeem foreign dollar claims for gold from the foreigner's point of view. For example, the Germans sold us a Volkswagen. They, in good faith, took back two thousand American dollars, with the understanding that they could convert this amount to gold at $35.00 per ounce. We were happy enough to have the Volkswagen at that price, and they were pleased to have the gold. Now we renig. We say "Sorry, old chums. We changed our minds. You can't have the gold." Where does that leave them? They entered into the contract in good faith, and by anyone's standards, they've been cheated. Well, immediately the price of the Volkswagen must jump to its true value in relation to other products, and the foreigners are stuck with buying products with those American dollars which no longer can be converted into gold. By now, the price of gold has begun to jump on the free market, since the U.S. has stopped selling at $35.00 an ounce. If they want gold, they must pay $75.00, $100.00, or $150.00 an ounce. Their other alternative is to buy commodities other than gold, an option they have previously refused since gold was a much better buy. Now, they must come back into the American economy and buy commodities at the prices Americans have had to pay. They have lost.

What about us? Well, Secretary of the Treasury Schultz said that the devaluation of the dollar and the suspension of gold sales really wouldn't affect the American worker too much. On the *Today Show,* just after the first devaluation, he indicated that perhaps French wines would go up in price, but other than that we would be helped. For example, he indicated there would be a great surge in employment as foreigners became customers for American goods which would now be more attractively priced for them. That certainly sounded good. With California wines equal to French wines anyway, there wouldn't be much of a loss, and we could use those new jobs. What a boon to America, this devaluation!

But look again. Look at the real economics involved. What's happening now is that we're all paying for the years of low-priced products we've all enjoyed. We're about to make up for all that time that prices didn't rise as they should have because we were shipping dollars overseas and taking products back in their place. Now, those paper dollars will flow back into the economy, buying up products, bidding higher than you can bid for American production. They'll take the products out of the marketplace and replace them with paper money. And you know what happens: increase the money supply and simultaneously decrease the consumable goods, and you have a potentially disasterous rise in prices facing you. We will see higher rates of price increases in the future than we had ever dreamed possible. It's already happening.

Have you heard about the Japanese buying up real estate in California, or about the Arabs buying hotels in Florida, or about the "grain drain?" These things aren't coincidental; they aren't coming about as a matter of chance or because these foreigners are trying to destroy us. They want their money's worth for the products we bought from them. And they deserve their money's worth. I can't think of a more immoral stand than that suggested by some "economists" who say that we should pass laws to prevent them from buying our property. Nonsense. We took their products and gave them a claim check on our goods. Now it's time to honor our contract and let them buy whatever they want. It's bad enough that we refused them the original thing we promised (the gold). Let's not show ourselves to be totally immoral and not take the claim checks back at all!

Suppose you built a chair, went to the farmer and traded with him for six bushels of apples. But rather than taking them with you, you asked him if you could pick them up later. "Sure," he says, and gives you a claim check good for the six bushels. Later, you return with the claim check, and he says, "Sorry, I can't honor that claim check any more." Perhaps he offers you half as many apples, or perhaps no apples at all, but instead a dozen beets. Would you consider this man to be moral? More than likely, you'd either demand your chair back or insist that he honor his word; and you might even decide to get a gun to make him do it. In other words, this is the kind of immorality that leads to war.

GOLD

More and more over the last forty years, we have heard the politicians and spokesmen for politicians tell us that gold is outmoded as a medium of exchange. Lord Keynes called it a "barbaric metal." George Schultz said,

> "The rigidities of such a system [gold] subject to the uncertainties of gold production, speculation and demand for industrial uses cannot meet the needs of today."[15]

We hear a lot of talk about international solutions to the currency problem; demonetizing gold, using Special Drawing Rights (SDR's), and some miracle that will be pulled off by the International Monetary Fund. What one must realize is that when you trade the product you produce for any "money" that is in itself a money substitute, if that money substitute is issued by an entity that can inflate the supply at whim, you are going to be worse off. Between the time you take that receipt for money and the time you trade it for something you want, its value will go down. The farther removed those receipts become from being related to physical production, the more likely it is that you will suffer a very real loss of purchasing power.

There is only one reason that the international bankers and governments want to sever the ties between currencies and gold, and it's not because gold would not handle the problems of trade. It is because they cannot inflate the supply of money if that money is tied to gold. And if they cannot inflate the supply of money, they cannot take the production from you that they would like without your knowledge. The concept that we don't need to tie money to gold (or any other real commodity) because the dollar is backed by the productive capacity of the nation sounds good but is pure nonsense. It's only realistic if you are able at any time in the future to take the money and exchange it for the same amount of production that you gave away when you took the money in trade originally. Unless the money is tied to a commodity such as gold, this will never happen.

Why Gold? There is nothing magical about gold.

When you see a bumper sticker that says STOP IN-FLATION, DEMAND GOLD, it is correct. If we used gold as the backing for all currency, there would be no inflation, but the same holds true if you say, STOP INFLATION, DE-MAND POTATOES. It is the concept of backing the money substitutes with a real commodity, the supply of which can't be expanded at the whim of the politicians or bankers. Most commodities don't meet the requirements. Potatoes wouldn't keep. Furthermore, if they became the medium of exchange, the supply is too elastic and might increase drastically because everyone would start growing them and, therefore, their value would fall in relation to other commodities. Secondly, they are a real problem to store and transport, and they are far from uniform in quality. They would, however, be better than paper. Since we're looking for something that is recognizable by everyone, desired, divisible, durable and of relatively limited quantity, gold seems to fill the bill. Silver would too, as well as copper, platinum and diamonds, but as you think about it, gold might be the best.

THE IDEAL MONEY

In a correct natural exchange system, one not subjected to counterfeit currency from either government or private sources, the medium of exchange would initially take the form of some commodity, and the society would be on a commodity-money system.

The question is frequently asked, "How could the supply of money increase as demanded by an increasing population, without fiat money?" Let's suppose there were four people in the society and gold was the medium of exchange. If the quantity of gold in the community remained constant, but a fifth person moved into the system, the total production of goods would increase by the amount the new person produced. This would result in the production of the community rising relative to the supply of gold. When the quantity of goods increases relative to the quantity of the good used as money, then the value of the money commodity rises. Prices would fall in the community. Each unit of gold would be worth more. But the standard of living in the community would remain the same, *ceteris paribus.*

In other words, in a commodity-money society, an increasing population would not have an adverse effect on the standard of living of the community, since the new inhabitants would tend to be productive and would create as much or more than they consumed. Prices in terms of the money commodity would tend to fall, and so in order to supply enough of the exchange medium to facilitate trade, there would be a tendency to split the units of the commodity into smaller and smaller pieces. First the smallest gold coin might be worth one unit, then the coin would be ½ that size, then ¼, etc. We see the same thing happening now, but in the reverse direction. Larger and larger denominations of bills are becoming common in trade, while the smaller coins will gradually fall out of use. A penny is now worth what a mill used to be, so mills are no longer in use. Soon pennies won't be, then nickels, and so on.

In the case of a commodity money, as the value of the money increased due to increasing productivity of the society there would be a tendency for people to produce more of that commodity. Just as when the price of gold rises today we see an increasing amount of mining activity, so it would be with any commodity money. The supply of money would thus expand naturally as the demand of society for that money increased.

The ultimate money, it is believed, is not a commodity money at all. Eventually all exchanges will be automatic credit-debit entries to the accounts of individuals and companies without the need for physical currency. In this situation wealth would still be accumulated in whatever form people might find convenient to store (such as grain, steel, lumber, etc.), but the form of measurement of the value of any object would be some unit of measurement that would show the supply-demand ratio between that product and all other products. In this manner it would not be necessary that there be a physical unit of money, and the need to expand or contract the quantity of units of money would no longer exist. Increasing production by one person or group would be automatically evaluated relative to other products and exchanged through the mechanism of electronic transfer of credits.

It should be understood that a stable price level is not the objective of any economic system. In fact it is next to impossible to accomplish. What should be the objective is a system wherein it is impossible for anyone to steal through the mechanism of counterfeiting the money, whether that money be gold or paper. Fiat money is, by definition, money created by edict—that is, therefore, pure theft.

Many hard money advocates have worked to have gold returned to its role as a monetary metal, arguing that if the United States would return to a gold standard, its economic problems would be effectively solved, as would most of the social problems of the world. With a gold standard politicians would no longer be able to inflate the money supply at whim, and this would in turn eliminate the intensity of business cycles. It's true that some trading medium must be in use that cannot be arbitrarily increased before any society will long endure. Hard money, however, is not the basis for a sound society, but rather the result of a sound society. If a simple return to the gold standard is the answer, then why did it not work before? Remember, we were on the gold standard for 150 years until public pressure destroyed it. There is no doubt in my mind that the same thing would happen again. The lasting answer will start with a solution to the problems that destroyed hard money to begin with.

"THERE AIN'T NO SUCH THING AS A FREE LUNCH"

Somewhere about 75 pages ago, we began to talk about economics and you; hopefully, the realization has come that there is no such thing as something for nothing. If a product is to be eaten, it first must be produced. Yet, throughout history the politicians have tried to prove the contrary and have been so eloquent in their arguments that they've lulled society after society into expecting miraculous abundance from sleight of hand—borrowing from ourselves, creating money when none exists, plundering the future. These are not answers to a more abundant life. It is unlikely, however, that politicians will ever change; nor is it the intent of this book to try to alter the system. My entire purpose in writing the preceding chapter is to make you aware of the real nature of the system. You as an individual will have little hope of changing it, but there is one thing you can do. Armed with this knowledge, you can now begin to protect yourself and your wealth against the inevitable results of the actions going on within the system.

CHAPTER TWO

Plans and Strategies

Retaining part of the efforts of your labor is called the accumulation of wealth. If you can't understand what is likely to happen in the economy of the nation and the world, it would be impossible to adequately protect your stored wealth against loss. At this point, you should have an understanding of real economics, and so armed, you should be on your way to predicting the future. The next step in developing a rational strategy for accumulating wealth is to develop your goals. This is something that most never do, and the few that do, frequently go about it improperly.

GOALS

It's hard to imagine that you would set sail in a boat without a firm destination in mind. It's also hard to imagine that you would begin construction of a house without knowing what kind you intended to complete or what size you wanted. Yet, this is precisely what you are doing when you start to accumulate wealth without knowing how much you are after, and when you want to reach the goal. In every facet of our lives, we seem to know the value of planning. We plan our destination when we leave on vacation; we plan an inventory when we stock our business; we plan the menu before preparing dinner. But in the most difficult of all achievements, that of becoming independently wealthy, we assume that planning is unnecessary and we never give it a thought. Oh, for sure you might decide that you'd like to have a million dollars, or that you might like to make as much as you can. But that's not planning. You're about as likely to achieve reasonable success that way as you are if you set sail for Hawaii without a compass.

How does one set goals in an economy that is as erratic as ours, and what should a goal be in the first place? To start with, think about wealth itself, and your primary needs in life. We work to survive: to eat, provide shelter, and clothes. After survival is assured, we work to provide comfort and luxuries. Right now you are enjoying the consumption and use of a certain amount of products and services every year. If you added up the food you and your family eat, the clothes you buy, the use of the home you live in, the vacations you take and all the other commodities and services you enjoy, this would be your standard of living. It could be measured in the amount of dollars it would take to purchase these items. Circumstances may occur in your life wherein you will no longer wish to continue to produce a product for trade, or may no longer be able to. But the need to eat, be sheltered and clothed will continue, so your needs will have to come from your stored wealth. How much wealth you need to store away will depend on two things: how much do you consume each year (standard of living), and how many years will you still be consuming.

There are three situations in which you need to live off stored wealth:

RETIREMENT

If you live, you may decide not to work any more in order to do something you value more, i.e., fish, travel, go back to school, devote your time to charity or politics, etc. Statistically, it is most likely that you'll live a relatively healthy life until sometime between age 70 and 80. Assuming you will tire of pursuing your profession somewhere between age 50 and 65, there is an unknown span of years (perhaps as few as fifteen; perhaps as many as forty) during which you'll want to maintain a comfortable living standard without being pressed to regularly produce and sell a service or product. The only replacement for your regular working income must be your wealth, so you must either store up enough to last, or store up enough so that the income from this wealth will replace the income you received from working.

PREMATURE DEATH

You may die before you accumulate enough wealth to replace your income. In this case, the question arises, "who will be affected if your income doesn't continue?" If you're the breadwinner, married, and supporting a family, that family will now be without support. Assuming the spouse is not equipped to provide support, then the accumulated wealth must provide that support. If there is not enough of that, then there is one other solution; life insurance. Life insurance can provide the lump sum of capital necessary to continue the income stream uninterrupted, and it can replace the sum of capital you would have accumulated if you had lived, worked, and saved. In the chapter on life insurance I'll thoroughly explain how to integrate your life insurance requirements with your over-all planning and how to buy the right policy.

DISABILITY

You may become unable to produce income due to a disabling sickness or accident. In this case, the income from your present accumulated assets may not be enough to maintain your standard of living and you may be forced to quickly consume those assets and wind up relying on charity for sustenance. A serious risk, without question. Here again disability income insurance can help to cover this risk until you are able to accumulate enough wealth to replace your income. In the chapter on Disability Insurance, I'll cover the why, when, and how of its purchase.

INDEPENDENT WEALTH

Since in all three situations (retirement, death, and disability) the need is for a continuing income, step one in setting a financial goal is to determine what standard of living you feel is adequate, measured by *today's* dollars. To do this, make out a monthly budget. Figure 6 is an example of a budget form that could be used. The first objective is to determine the permanent monthly income that will satisfy your needs. *You can consider yourself independently wealthy when you have enough capital so that the income from the capital will meet these needs.*

If someone told you that they were willing to send you a check every month for the rest of your life, and they would adjust the amount of the check to the cost of living increase every year, what would the amount of that check have to be to cover your living expenses? The sample monthly budget tallies current expenses, expenses in the event of death of the breadwinner, and expenses in the event of his disability. You'll find a blank for your use in the Appendix. As you determine what your present expenses are, you should realize that certain expenses would cease if you suddenly had a permanent income. For example, you would no longer need life insurance, for the purpose of life insurance is really just to replace the breadwinner's earning power anyway. Furthermore, you would no longer need disability insurance, either. Payments on investment property, dollar cost averaging into stocks, and retirement plan deductions from your income would no longer be necessary. You would still have to pay income taxes, of course, but don't consider them at this point as there is a way to adjust for them later. You should figure in a reserve for replacement of "wasting" assets, that is a fund to replace things that wear out, such as automobiles, clothes, furniture, etc. Figure out your budget and determine the total amount of income you'll need every month.

SAMPLE MONTHLY BUDGET

	Current	After Death of Spouse	If Disabled
Regular Expenses			
Mortgage or Rent	$ 230	$ 230	$ 230
Utilities	50	40	40
Maid, Gardener, Pool Service, etc.	30	50	40
Groceries, Milk, Liquor	275	200	275
Lunches	40	20	20
Entertainment, Meals, Shows, etc.	80	50	80
Recreation (Skiing, Boating, etc.)	50	40	40
Clothes	150	100	150
Laundry, Cleaning, Shoe Repair	20	20	20
Personal (Haircuts & Allowances)	100	50	100
Auto Operation (Gas, Tires, Repairs)	100	50	50
Tuitions, Lessons	20	20	20
Donations	20	10	10
Support of Others, Alimony, etc.	—	—	—
Auto Loans (Or Amortization)	100	80	80
Other Loans	135	—	135
Total Regular Expenses	$1,400	$ 960	$1,300
Periodic Expenses			
Real Estate Taxes	$ 60	$ 60	$ 60
Household Maintenance & Repair	50	75	75
New Household Purchases	50	50	50
Casualty Insurance (Auto, Home)	40	30	30
Life Insurance	50	—	50
Disability, Medical Insurance	70	40	40
Vacations	100	75	100
Gifts (Birthdays, Anniv., Xmas)	50	30	50
Income Taxes, State & Federal	350	100	100
Legal, Accounting	10	10	10
Medical, Dental, Veterinarian	20	20	—
Total Periodic Expenses	$ 850	$ 490	$ 585
Savings & Investments			
Real Estate	$ 40	$ —	$ 40
Securities	100	—	100
Miscellaneous	25	—	25
Total Savings & Investments	$ 165	$ —	$ 165
Total Monthly Expenses	$2,415	$1,450	$2,050

Figure 6

For the sake of discussion, let's assume that you decide
$1,500 per month of today's dollars is adequate to maintain
a comfortable standard of living.

The question is, how much capital would be needed to
provide that income? It will depend, of course, on the rate of
return you receive on the invested capital. $1,500 per month
is $18,000 per year. A little simple arithmetic will tell you
that if you had $360,000 in a bank account and the bank was
paying you 5% per year interest, then that interest would
amount to $18,000 per year. You'd be sadly disappointed if
you stopped there, however. The government would step in
and take a portion of the $18,000 for taxes (probably around
$3,000) and you would wind up with only $15,000 to live
on. Next year prices would go up also. You would find that
what costs $18,000 today might cost $19,000 or $20,000
next year. So between taxes and inflation, you'd quickly find
that $360,000 yielding 5% would not meet your needs. Your
choices would be to:

1. Increase the rate of return;
2. Increase the amount of capital;
3. Use up some of the capital each year.

TRUE RATE OF RETURN

This brings us into a discussion of what I call true rate of
return. When a bank pays interest on normal passbook
savings accounts, it currently pays about 5% per annum. This
is an apparent rate of return, for although the bank may pay
you 5%, the government is going to tax that interest. The
percentage they'll take depends on the level of your income.
In addition to this, your capital will be losing its purchasing
power at the rate of inflation, whatever that may be. The
true rate of return then would be the apparent rate of return
multiplied by the percentage of income you keep after taxes,
and less the current rate of inflation. Thus if the tax rate on
your investment income is 30%, you would keep 70% of that

income. In addition your capital would decline in purchasing power by the rate of inflation.

Assuming you'd like to accumulate sufficient capital to provide yourself with an income of $18,000 per year (adjusted for inflation), you can calculate the amount of capital you'll need, provided you know the apparent rate of return you'd be getting on your investments. One thing becomes quickly evident. If the rate of inflation is 10% and your tax bracket is 30%, then you're going to have to get a pretty hefty 14.3% *apparent* rate of return before you'll be able to realize *any* positive true rate of return. You are now being exposed to one of the great fallacies of the investment industry; the idea that compound interest will make you rich. How many times have I heard investment salesmen tell their prospects that if they put away $100 a month from age 35 to 65 at some nominal rate of return like 10%, they'll wind up rich. The salesman will show you a compound interest table and point out that just $100 per month will accumulate to be $217,000 at that rate. What will it be on a true scale? If your combined tax bracket were only 30% and inflation averaged 4%, then you would accumulate purchasing power of only $58,000, a far cry from the amount promised; and if your bracket is 60% (which only requires a $32,000 taxable income for a single resident of California) and if the inflation rate is 10% (and I'll be amazed if it can be held to that) you'll wind up at age 65 with enough purchasing power to buy only $16,700 worth of goods and services by today's standards. That's less purchasing power than the amount saved! You not only won't get wealthy using compound interest coupled with regular savings, you'll probably lose money!

Unfortunately, the miscalculation perpetrated by the investment salesman will not be noticed until years and years later, and even then it's unlikely that the victim will relate his economic plight to the original error in strategy. He'll just realize it didn't work out, and he can't make it in retirement. Nothing more aptly illustrates this than rereading the

insurance ad that used to run in national magazines. It
showed a picture of a smiling man holding aloft a freshly
caught fish. "My wife and I retired in Florida on $129.00 a
month, thanks to our Phoenix Mutual Insurance Policy." A
vivid reminder of the devastation of inflation that must
surely haunt the people at Phoenix Mutual.

In today's economy I would think any person both shrewd
and fortunate who can achieve a positive true rate of return
on capital which is passively invested. Inflation ran at an
annual rate of 12% during 1974. This means anyone in a 50%
tax bracked would have to have earned at least 24% on his
investments just to break even! Even trying to project what
inflation might be in the future is futile. In planning for
retirement, suppose I assume that inflation will be 10% per
year 20 years from now when I want to begin drawing off my
wealth, and I adjust my goal accordingly. What if the rate
winds up at 15%, or 30%? All my planning has been
worthless. Somehow it's necessary to develop a strategy that
does not depend on projecting the rate of inflation, and that
is done by using true rate of return. Here's a sample
calculation:

Retirement Income Needed $18,000
Number of Years of Retirement .... .25
True Rate of Return Assumed Possible .. 0%

$18,000 x 25 years = $450,000

Your goal then will be reached when you have accumulated $450,000 in dollars by today's standards. If you had
$450,000 this year and you could get 0% true rate of return,
you could stop working now and have a permanent income
of $18,000 per year *of today's dollars* for the next 25 years.
Since dollars next year or ten years from now will have less
purchasing power, it will be necessary to have more of them
to have the equivalent of $450,000. You may find that prices
go up so much that you might need $5 million, and at 4%
that would yield $200,000 per year, but inflation may have

caused prices to rise so much that it would cost that
$200,000 per year to buy the same goods and services that
$18,000 will buy today. Since you are making the as-
sumption that you can earn 0% true, your total capital will
be going up even though its purchasing power isn't. Does it
sound fantastic that your living expenses could go to
$200,000 per year? Impossible? Remember when bread cost
5 cents a loaf? Did it seem possible that it could ever cost 50
cents? Don't kid yourself. It could go to $5 a loaf. It could
go to $50 a loaf. It could go to $5,000 a loaf.

*A rational financial goal, then, is one in which the amount
of capital accumulated will provide a continuation of an
acceptable standard of living for as long as you may live.*
Since most people will be very fortunate to break even on
their investments, let alone get any positive true rate of
return, you might as well figure on accumulating enough
wealth to last for the amount of time you figure on living.
For example, if you think you'll live twenty years past
retirement, and your current living expenses are $15,000 per
year, figure on accumulating 20 years x $15,000 or
$300,000. Then if your return on the capital is enough to
meet inflation and taxes, your money will last you the length
of time you expect to live. If you're fortunate enough to get
a true rate of return of 2%, then you'll wind up at the end of
twenty years with a little left over for your heirs.

RISK VS REWARD

The purpose of putting your money to work is two-fold:
first, to preserve the capital for future use; second, to
hopefully make that capital increase in size. To examine
these two purposes let's take them one at a time. The
question of preservation is one of risk. Will my capital be
there and be available when I want to consume it five years
or twenty years from now? Or will it be lost due to some
risk? The increase of the capital possible through loaning it or
investing it also brings up the question of reward. What rate

of return can be expected from different types of investments? In other words, what are the risks and what are the
rewards?

Most authors writing on the subject of investments tie the
two concepts together in what might be called a risk-reward
ratio, generally conceding that the higher the reward sought,
the higher must be the risk endured.

The reasoning is clear. Money has a value. When you offer
your money in the marketplace, a number of people will bid
for it. The more risky the venture, the more that an entre-
prenuer will have to pay for the use of your money. A person
bidding for your money will want to get it as cheaply as he
can; he'll want to give away as little of his future profit from
his business venture as possible in return for the use of the
capital. If he could borrow the money on the credit of his
venture with a promise to repay at the minimum interest
available, that's what he would do. Barring his ability to do
this, then he'll raise the amount of interest he's willing to pay
higher and higher until at last he "bids" your capital away
from the other venturers who are offering their investments
and loans in the market. He may offer to borrow your money
with a promise to repay at some later date, with interest. Or
he may actually sell you an interest in his business, which
would include a share of the profits and losses as well as an
ownership in present assets. He might combine the two by
offering a loan and the opportunity to convert the loan into a
share of the business later. In any case, he won't bid any
more for your money than absolutely necessary, and you'll
shop the market to determine that his is the best offer
around. This is what gives rise to the concept that risk
increases as reward increases.

A word that has come up over and over again in our
discussion is *risk*. Risk means exposure to loss. You'll never
have a good grasp of handling money and accumulating
wealth unless you can isolate and identify the variety of risks
that face you. To most of us, the primary risk that we

consider when making investment decisions is the risk of loss due to the market value of our investment falling. Many "conservative" older folks who suffered the market crash of 1929 won't have anything to do with investing in stocks due to the risk of another depression. This is far from the most important or the only risk that must be avoided. I break risks down into two categories. The first are what I call *economic* risks, or those risks of loss due to general economic conditions outside the control of myself or the management of the companies in which I invest. The second group of risks are what I term *financial* risks, or those risks of loss due to poor selection, timing, or planning on my part. Risks that fall into the economic category are as follows:

INFLATION—the risk that a general rise in prices will decrease my purchasing power.

RUNAWAY INFLATION—Same as inflation, only the rise in prices gets out of control, as it did in France in 1789, and in Germany in 1913-1923.

RECESSION—The risk that my assets will lose value due to a slow down in business activity and lower profits for industry.

DEPRESSION—The risk that my assets will lose value because of widespread industrial collapse and unemployment.

SOCIALISM—The risk that my assets will lose value due to confiscation by the government or by restrictions on the use or transfer of those assets.

WAR—Risk of physical destruction or capture.

Risks that fall in the financial category are as follows:

BUSINESS FAILURE—The risk that I will invest in a business that fails due to bad management or other internal miscalculations.

FRAUD—The risk that I will be defrauded of my assets.

NATURAL DISASTER—The risk that my assets will be wiped out by a natural disaster such as flood, fire, accident, sickness, premature death, etc.

POOR TIMING—The risk that I'll lose due to buying my investments at the high point on the price cycle, and being forced to sell them after they've dropped.

THEFT—The risk that my assets will be stolen.

You may be able to think of other risks that face you in handling your assets. Those above are, in my opinion, the most critical. Unfortunately, there is no one way to protect against all the risks, but we can break protection against loss down into a couple of categories: methods of physically protecting the assets, and methods of selecting the appropriate asset that inherently protects against a given risk. Different types of assets protect against different risks, which is an obvious reason for diversification. Common stocks are generally accepted protection against the risk of loss of purchasing power due to creeping inflation, but a poor protection against the risk of depression. Cash in the bank would be a good protection against theft, but a poor protection against inflation. Figure 7 will give some organization to the way that the different investments relate to the different risks.

Recognizing the elements of risk is absolutely essential to constructing a sound strategy for accumulating wealth. You will be the ultimate judge of which risks are most imminent, and which, therefore, to defend against most strongly. One general rule is to always remain as liquid as is consistent with achievement of your goals. If a choice presents itself between acquiring an asset that has a wide and immediate market, and another that would take time and effort to sell, choose the most readily marketable. Economic, as well as financial conditions can change rapidly, and as they do it's necessary to shift your portfolio accordingly. If we head rapidly into runaway inflation or a depression, you may be unable to find buyers for certain nonliquid assets such as income real estate, art, stock of closely held companies, limited partnerships, etc. The chances of growth from these types of investments must be weighed against the risks inherent in their lack of liquidity.

Risk/Protection

	RISKS TO WEALTH	PROTECTION				
		STORES OF VALUE	LOANS	EQUITIES	Speculations	OTHER
ECONOMIC	Inflation	2	3	2	3	Liquidity.
	Hyper-Inflation	1	4	3	2-3	Liquidity.
	Recession	2	2	3	3	Liquidity.
	Depression	2	3	4	4	Liquidity.
	Socialism	2	3	3		Liquidity; Concealed Foreign Accounts.
FINANCIAL	Business Failure	1	2	3	4	Diversification; Conservatism.
	Fraud	1	2	3	3	Knowledge; Control; Conservatism.
	Taxation	1	3	2	2	Form of Ownership.
	Poor Timing	1	2	3	3	Dollar-Cost Averaging.
	Spendthrift	3	2	2		Discipline.
	Personal Catastrophe	1	2	2	3	Liquidity; Insurance.
KEY: 1 VERY GOOD 2 GOOD 3 BAD 4 VERY BAD						

Figure 7

WHEN IS A "SAVINGS ACCOUNT"
REALLY A LOAN?

A proper understanding of investment theory must start with definitions and categories. Throughout your life you've been exposed to investment terminology, but I wonder if you've ever had a clear understanding of what the words meant, or how they related to one another. Loans, equities, speculations, gambles. The confusion about the meanings of these words has resulted in a lot of misdirected programs; much of the confusion comes directly from the financial world in the form of camouflage. For example, one tends to put "saving" in a lower risk category than "lending." Consequently, the banker will tell you to "save" at his bank rather than ask you to "lend" him your money, even though loaning him your money is exactly what you're doing when you deposit it in his "savings account." The commodities broker will ask you to "invest" in commodities futures, feeling that if he asked you to "speculate" it wouldn't seem so secure. The life insurance company will ask you to "invest" in cash value life insurance, or "buy a piece of the rock," insinuating that you have equity ownership in the company itself, or that you in some way participate in the profits they receive from their investments. In reality, it's not an investment at all, but a straight loan to the life insurance company. It's no wonder that there is confusion over the investment terminology when the industry itself works so hard at altering the image of its products.

The first step in organizing your investment program is to be able to recognize the true nature of any asset that is offered you. There are four things that you can do with your money. All types of offerings fall into one of these categories.

> Store of Value: The first thing you can do
> with your excess production is to *store* it. If
> you're an apple farmer you can keep your

extra apples in the cellar, for use at a later time. Or you can trade them for hides, wheat, chairs, or whatever other commodity you think will be usable later, and store that. A store-of-value asset is a *usable commodity* that is held by the owner for later trade or consumption. Any commodity, therefore, could be a store-of-value asset, but certainly some commodities would be more practical to store and thus would be more useful for this purpose. Fertilizer would be too bulky to store; bananas would spoil; and automobiles would go out of style. The best store-of-value assets are also those assets that would best serve as money. For example, gold and silver are practical store-of-value assets. So are diamonds, art, and raw land. All usable stores of value.

Loans: The second thing you can do with your excess production is to lend it to someone else for their use. The apple farmer could lend the tailor five bushels of apples, with the understanding that next year the tailor would pay him back (with a few apples extra for interest on the use of the money). Most so-called "conservative" investors use loans as their primary vehicle for accumulating wealth. You can lend your money to a friend, to a bank, to a savings and loan company, to a life insurance company, to a corporation, and to a state. In all these cases, you are given a promise of repayment, called a *note* or *bond*. That is, a promise to repay with interest at a specified future date, or on demand. Different loans carry different rates of interest, and of course, different degrees of

risk, based on the financial integrity of the
borrower.

Equities: The third thing that you can do
with your money is to buy ownership or part
ownership of some type of a business enterprise. You could buy a service station or a
grocery store, alone or in partnership with
others. This use of money would include
owning shares of stock in corporations and
owning income-producing real estate. An
apartment building, for example, is (hopefully) a profit-making business, as are a
vineyard and a warehouse. Most equities
include some of the attributes of store-of-value assets in that almost always a business
must own some commodities; i.e., income
producing real estate usually includes land,
the grocery store includes groceries, and
industrial corporations include equipment.

Gambling: The fourth and last thing that
can be done with your wealth is to gamble
with it. Gambling simply means placing a
wager that a certain event will happen. It
differs from the other categories in that no
ownership is involved; the event will be purely
a matter of chance, and you can therefore
have no foreknowledge of its occurrence.

SPECULATION

No discussion of money use would be complete without
covering that usually fuzzy area called "speculation." The
dictionary defines speculation as "buying and selling with a
view to making profits from future price changes." Unfortunately, this definition would mean that all investments, as
we've defined them, would be speculations, and for our
purposes, this isn't necessarily correct. When used in this

book, speculation is defined as the purchase of any thing in the belief that the *supply/demand forces* in the market will cause its price to rise. Thus, if I buy a stock not with the intention of holding that stock in order to profit from the future growth of the company or the current earnings of the company, but solely because I believe that the stock is currently underpriced and soon the market will discover this and the price will rise accordingly, then I am speculating. In the same way, if I buy any commodity, like gold for example, with the idea that the demand for gold is going to increase and thus bid up the price, then I am speculating on the future supply/demand factors for that commodity, not buying it simply as a store of value. You can even speculate with loans by buying bonds, not with the intention of holding those bonds for the income, but because you believe that interest rates will drop and make your bonds more valuable.

Throughout the investment industry, market values of all commodities and investments are driven up and down by the forces of speculation; but the underlying values of store-of-value assets, equities, and loans are what must ultimately be looked to when developing a rational strategy for accumulating wealth. The speculative market is a big poker game with each player hoping to profit from the other players' mistakes. The rational market, on the other hand, is a market in which one person's profit is not dependent on another person's mistakes. The thing that should be realized is that the speculative market is superimposed over the rational market. There is a level at which the price of commodities and businesses should rest. That is, they should be priced at what they could be duplicated for by the efforts of other labor, capital, and thought. In the commodities and stock markets you can watch the prices of commodities and stocks fluctuate above and below the price they will eventually bring on the real market as they are successively under-priced and over-priced by speculators. Most of us are not equipped

to be speculators anymore than most of us are equipped to
sit down with professional poker players and walk away
winners. We should try to find the natural levels, and place
our funds into store-of-value, loans, and equities based on a
long run conservative strategy and a sound knowledge of the
underlying economic conditions.

Speculation then, is not the thing that you're buying, but
the way that you're buying it. Raw land purchased because
you think land will become more valuable due to increasing
population is purchased as a speculation. Raw land purchased
because you want to put your money in a commodity that
will retain its relative value in the face of depreciating
purchasing power of dollars is a store-of-value asset. Gold
purchased because you believe a devaluation is imminent is a
speculation. Gold purchased because you think it will be a
commodity that will hold its trading value in the face of
inflation is a store-of-value asset. These distinctions are going
to be extremely important as we get into the chapters on
selecting types of assets for your portfolio, and it is well that
you understand them.

MARGINING OR MORTGAGING

It's a sad fact of life that almost all human decisions are
based on either emotion or hearsay. This is never more true
than in the question of borrowing money to invest. Should I
pay off my home mortgage? Should I buy silver on margin?
If I buy an apartment house for income, how large a
mortgage should I seek? Should stocks be margined? Should I
pay cash for new equipment for my plant or office?

You have been confronted with this question time after
time and your answer was probably based on some personal
prejudice (stories or experiences from the depression, for
example). Stanford University economist G.L. Bach points
out that young families who never experienced the de-

pression have large debts, payable later in cheaper dollars.[16]
The old, remembering the trauma of the 30's, have few debts
and comparatively large holdings in such low interest
monetary assets as savings accounts. The decision to borrow
should be based on something more than prejudice.

There are two situations in which a person might borrow
money. First, if you haven't yet produced enough to allow
you to trade for something you want, then you may go on
the line for your future earnings in order to have that desired
item now. An example would be a young couple who can't
afford to pay cash for a car, so they borrow the money to
buy one and pay off the loan a few dollars every month.
Second, you may borrow to purchase investment assets; these
are not consumed but are bought to increase your wealth.

Borrowing for Consumption

When you borrow money to buy a higher standard of
living (i.e., a new refrigerator, etc.), you are merely sen-
tencing yourself to a lower standard of living in the long run.
While you may enjoy the use of the refrigerator, the interest
you pay will not be available to buy other items that would
additionally increase your comfort. The person who waits to
buy his conveniences until he can pay cash is always better
off. In addition, borrowing for consumption robs you of
your freedom of choice. Not only do you wind up with a
lower standard of living, once in debt, you must make all
decisions based on whether or not the choice will interfere
with your ability to repay your loans. Your creditors sit in on
every decision you make. You may want to move to a new
environment, take a more interesting but lower paying job, or
take time for leisure, but your creditors prohibit it. We are a
nation built, supposedly, on consumer credit, yet I maintain
it has done more to hold back the standard of the nation
than anything else except the government. My advice on
consumption items is simple: pay cash.

Borrowing for Investment

There are a variety of reasons one might give for borrowing for investment. If you borrow money to buy a car in order to get a job that requires a car, then there is reason. If I'm a dentist and have no money to equip my office unless I borrow, then I'll borrow in order to earn. These are forms of borrowing to increase the capacity to earn, and are done on a massive scale by both individuals and industry. Your decision on whether to borrow for investment, whether it be in your own business or in some other asset, should be weighed against two considerations. First, economics: is it financially profitable? That can be fairly easily determined by comparing the after-tax cost of the financed product with the after-tax return of the dollars invested. It will depend on your tax bracket, the cost of financing the product, and the type and amount of projected return on your invested funds.

The second and often overlooked consideration is risk. How sure are you that you can continue to receive the stated income on your investment during the length of time you'll be paying off the loan? How sure can you be that you'll be in a position to continue to make the principal payments on the loan? If something goes wrong and you're unable to continue making the payments, will you be able to liquidate your investment to pay off the loan? If so, would you possibly have to liquidate at a loss to prevent foreclosure? Take a hypothetical example: you have ten thousand dollars. You would like to buy a boat, and plan to charter it for income. Instead of buying for cash, you finance on a five year note at 6% add-on interest, and put your money in a savings and loan and draw 6% interest, drawing on the principal to make the payments. If your economic situation doesn't change, everything can be predicted. But what would happen if the country slid into a depression six months after you made the deal? Well, you probably wouldn't be able to get your money out of the savings and loan. They have taken your money and put it into long term trust deeds and might not be able to retrieve it. Your lender, however, would insist that you continue to make your payments on the boat. If you couldn't charter it, you'd have to turn to your personal income, which may or may not be available, to make the payments. The right set of circumstances could mean you'd lose the boat.

The risk is there, and if it doesn't seem real, talk to the hundreds of thousands of people who went bankrupt during the last depression when they watched their assets melt away in building and loans, or banks that went bankrupt, while they themselves were unable to meet the mortgages they were carrying. Money in the bank isn't all as safe as one might think. The reason people borrow for investments is to increase the rate of return over what they could get if they paid cash. Only in the case where the increased return is due to tax savings will you find your risk not increased, and even then it could be. Margining is risky. In a depression, prices of all commodities fall, including the commodities you hold or produce, but loan balances do not fall.

An example of this risk is the recent experience of many investors in the real estate market. In 1969, there was a general drop in stock prices, and consequently, many investors were scared out of the stock market. There were very low vacancy factors at the time in the residential housing market so many turned towards apartment house syndications for tax savings and growth. By putting down as low as 10% of the purchase price, they could buy an apartment building (most pooled their money in large syndications). Assuming a 5% vacancy factor, the income from the project would be enough to carry the mortgages, expenses of operation, and pay a small cash flow to the owner. Everything was fine until the economy slumped and vacancies began to increase. Suddenly there wasn't enough cash from rentals to cover mortgage payments and operating costs, and unless the investors were financially prepared to subsidize the apartments on a monthly basis, it was foreclosure time. Thousands of real estate projects went into foreclosure during the period from 1970 to 1973, and it wasn't because of a general depression. A normal slump in real estate occupancy did the trick.

The same considerations hold true in the stock market as in the real estate market, with a couple of exceptions. In real estate, loans are generally made for a long term at a fixed monthly payment; if the price of real estate falls, the banker can't suddenly call his loan or ask for more margin. In stocks the price is quoted daily on the exchange and consequently a banker can look at his margin loan at any time and determine whether there is sufficient equity in the account to cover his risk. If the value of a stock falls, he may ask for more collateral (known as a margin call). If you don't have the capital to meet the margin calls, you lose your equity. The purpose of margining in the market is to leverage your capital to increase your profits. If you're wrong, you increase your losses by the same leverage by which you would have increased your gains.

A second risk that exists in margining stocks is that when you buy on margin you don't have the stock certificates in your hands. Even if the stocks did appreciate, you still have to rely on the financial integrity of the brokerage house. Considering the number of firms that have failed in the last few years, this must be a significant risk.

There is little difference between margining stocks and margining commodities. I might buy stocks, silver, gold coins, wheat, or pork bellies and the factors of margining don't change. In either case I get only a receipt so I must rely on the integrity of the broker; I'm subject to margin calls; I increase my reward if I'm right, and my loss if I'm wrong.

The ultimate question is, "*what rate of return do you need to get on your investments?*" Why go after the higher rates and subject yourself to the increased risks, if you don't really need that increased rate of return to meet your goals? There we are back to goals again. The *goal* is the determining factor.

CHAPTER THREE

Selecting a Rational Portfolio

This chapter will familiarize you with most of the things you can buy as a method of storing or increasing your wealth. The purpose is not to make specific recommendations but rather to define the advantages and disadvantages of each asset in relation to your particular goals and relative to the risks, both economic and financial. There is no investment that can be guaranteed to preserve or increase your wealth; but in given economic conditions, some investments are *more likely* to enable you to reach your goals than others. Never look for a panacea; recognize that you must diversify, and that you must be prepared to change your portfolio completely as times and conditions change.

STORE-OF-VALUE

Earlier I defined store-of-value assets as usable commodities that are held by the owner for later trade or consumption, and pointed out that any commodity could be used for this purpose. Now you should begin to see a definite correlation between a store-of-value asset and what was earlier defined as *money*. Money, as you may recall, was any commodity that was taken in exchange with the intention of holding it and later trading it for something that was to be consumed. A store-of-value asset is almost identical. Almost, but not exactly. With money the real idea is the "exchange" idea, and the length of time the commodity is held is of minor significance. With store-of-value assets, the primary consideration is the time factor. How long is it to be held before being traded? A week? Twenty years? Two hundred years? Money's attributes are divisibility, durability, recognized value, and constant supply. Store-of-value assets, on the other hand, do not necessarily have to be divisible (raw land, for example), but they should have all the other attributes of money. They should retain their value relative to other commodities for long periods (which money substitutes never do), and should be recognized for their value (although not necessarily by everyone, because not everyone, for example, would recognize the value of a great work of art). Their supply should not suddenly increase, leading to a loss of trading power in relation to other commodities. In order to minimize storage costs it would be helpful for a small amount of the asset to be worth a great deal.

The purpose of holding store-of-value assets is to preserve the purchasing power of accumulated surplus. An apple farmer may have two bushels of apples left at the end of the season. By trading them for store-of-value assets he should be able to trade back for the two bushels of apples ten years in the future when he decides that it's time to consume those apples. If you could only recognize the immense difficulty of this feat you'd come a lot closer to accomplishing it.

All store-of-value assets are affected in a similar way by economic conditions. In a slowly inflating economy they tend to rise slowly in value, keeping pace with inflation. In a hyper-inflating society they again tend to hold their value, as they are the yardstick by which the declining value of the currency is being measured. In a recession they tend to hold their value relative to each other. In a depression they hold their value relative to other commodities, but may lose their value relative to money or money substitutes. I said *may*, for depending on what is happening to the money supply at the time, they may still be rising in price.

Storing your excess production for consumption at a later time is the name of the game. It's most logical to start by accumulating those commodities that you'll personally consume. Unfortunately there are severe limitations in this area.

In the case of food, it's perishable. A person can store away a quantity of certain kinds of dried or canned food, and over a reasonably short length of time expect to be able to consume it. But how about long periods of time, like ten years? Most of the food value, or at least the appeal, regardless of the method used for preserving, will have been leached away. Long term storage of food under present technology is just not too practical. This should not deter you from purchasing the maximum amount you can conveniently store and consume over short periods. I certainly recommend keeping a full larder. A year's supply of all staple products used around the home will mean fewer trips to the store and a substantial savings as inflation rolls along.

Other things that might eventually be consumed are energy products (oil, coal, etc.), housing, clothing, means of transportation, and appliances. Most manufactured articles suffer from two kinds of loss; functional obsolescence, and physical deterioration. Thus an automobile purchased in 1956 and stored for use in 1976 would lose value due to deterioration of certain of its parts, whether it was used or not, and additionally would lose value due to design improvements on newer models. Another drawback to advance purchasing is the cost of storage. A lifetime supply of automobiles would take a significant amount of storage space; hardly practical.

When we look for commodities to use to store value, we look for the following attributes:

1. Durability (no functional or physical obsolescence).
2. Limited supply.
3. Consistent demand (regardless of world economic situation).

4. Ease of storage.
5. Protectable against individual or government theft.

In light of these criteria, it's easy to see why gold and silver have become standards of wealth and obvious store-of-value mechanisms.

GOLD

Gold has been used as a store of value and a medium of exchange in most nations throughout recorded history. As new nations come into existence, gold usually becomes one of the standard forms of exchange, if not the only official medium. As these nations mature, it always suffers debasement. As nations decline, it disappears from open trade, only to reemerge once again as another new nation is founded on the ashes of the old.

Today we are experiencing the advanced stages of economic deterioration, thus financial instability, so that the individual must try to determine what store-of-value assets might best protect wealth through the transition. The subject of gold has become so fraught with misconceptions and propaganda during this period of turmoil that it is necessary to review the fundamentals once again to predict what gold's value might be in the future.

Supply

The supply of gold in the world consists of that gold already mined and in the possession of individuals, banks, and governments; and the supply of newly mined gold produced each year. It is estimated that there are about 58,000 metric tons of gold held in the free world, which translates to some 1,900 million ounces. This is distributed approximately as follows:

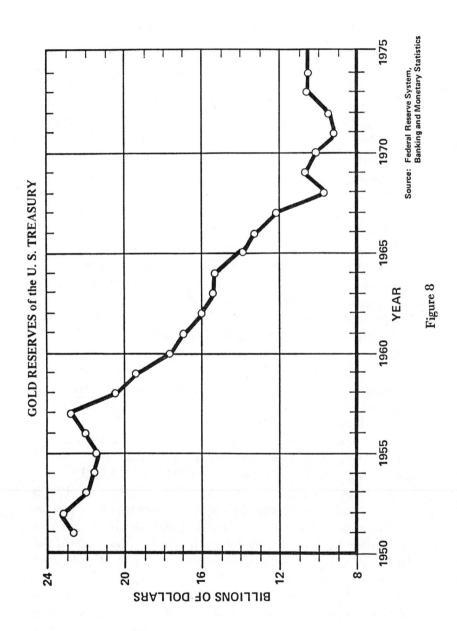

Figure 8

U.S. Government	275 million ounces
International Monetary Fund	153 million ounces
Other Free World Governments	744 million ounces
Private Gold Holders	700 million ounces

Current gold production of the free world is estimated at about 35 million ounces annually, while communist countries probably produce about 7 million ounces. Production of any commodity, gold included, is dependent on the price of that commodity; therefore, as the price of gold rises, the production will probably increase.

Demand

The demand side of the ledger must take into account two types of purchaser: those who consume the metal, and those who simply hold it in storage. Industrial consumption has been running fairly close to production for the past few years, and is currently about 30 million ounces (down from 40 million in 1968). Technology, including the sophisticated electronics and space industries, has found many new uses for gold over the past decade, and probably new uses will continue to be found. 1 would expect the demand attributed to consumption to continue to grow at least as fast as production could increase.

The demand for gold by those who would hold it as a store of value is more complicated to estimate. It consists of demand by individuals and corporations who hoard for the long term, speculators who buy and sell for short-term profits, and governments and central banks who hold gold as reserves. We'll discount the purchases and sales by speculators in this discussion, as their long-run effect on the price of the metal is negligible; we'll concentrate on the potential demand by individuals and governments.

The physical properties of the yellow metal including beauty, durability, and divisibility—have long made it a sought after and esteemed form of wealth for individuals. But the main thing that an individual looks for when attempting to preserve the value of accumulated wealth is convenience. Paper currency is a far more convenient form of storing wealth than is holding gold. Paper certificates take up little room, can be carried in the pocket, and are easily exchanged. Furthermore, the physical currency is not even needed in modern society, as holdings can simply be entered in bookkeeping systems in the form of credits, and assets can be transferred through a system of debits. The only reason that individuals would prefer to hold and exchange a metal such as gold rather than paper currency is if the value of that currency cannot be trusted. In other words, when paper becomes worthless, individuals will demand gold.

Why do governments collect and hold gold? Why is there currently half again more gold in the vaults of the central banks than in the hands of private individuals? Simply because it is the preferred medium of exchange of individuals. If individuals did not prefer it, neither would government. Gold becomes the backing for currency because, originally, it was the currency. But as soon as the government takes control of the issuance of money, forces are at work that try to dislodge gold as the foundation of the system. Currency inflation begins, paper begins to depreciate in value, and people begin to try to trade directly in gold once more. The politician must then combat this by passing laws to prevent it. Outlawing gold ownership, and prohibiting the making of contracts payable in gold, are known as "gold clause" laws and are accompanied by legal tender laws that force individuals to accept payment of debts in the paper currency issued by the government.

Individuals have a keen sense of self-preservation, however, so that money manipulations by governments can only go on for so long before ways will be found to circumvent the laws. It becomes a contest to see who is the most clever, the government or the private citizens.

The demand for gold, therefore, will depend to a great

extent on the inflation level in society. In the early 1970's inflation of paper currencies around the world hit worrisome levels. An article in *The Economist* viewed this problem as the world emerged from the inflationary surge of 1974:

> "Around most of the world, inflation is slowing. . . In February, the world inflation rate was 14% [that is the average of the rises in consumer prices over 12 months earlier in 96 countries in the International Monetary Fund, weighted by population] . . . this is the lowest figure since February, 1974, and well below the 16.2% peak last October. . . Here are some sample rates: Canada, 11%; United States 10.2%; Mexico, 16%; Bolivia, 59%; Brazil, 28%; Argentina, 79%; Uruguay, 92%; France, 12%; Britain, 25%; Iceland, 53%; Portugal, 17%; South Africa, 15%. . . Some Latin Americans are still doing very badly. Chile's inflation has risen 18-fold in four years. . . Last year Chile's junta said that its target was to bring the annual rate down to 250% in 1975 from 1974's rate of 500%. In April, the rise in prices was equivalent to 790% per year. . ."[17]

A world-wide recession cooled those inflation rates dramatically during 1975 and 1976, but the source of the inflation, deficit spending by governments, not only continued unabated, but increased at a terrifying rate as the public demanded more government spending as a cure for the recession.

Now that governments are faced with growing demand for assets that do not depreciate, they must again try to discourage individuals from turning away from paper money to gold. U.S. politicians, for example, hold office by promising the public maximum free social benefits, while at the same time minimizing the amount of economic turmoil in the nation. A rush to gold by U.S. citizens would have very negative effects from the administration's point of view. Since little gold is produced in this country, while much is consumed, gold is a negative item in the balance of trade. Money flowing overseas to buy gold is not here to buy stocks, bonds, and the products of American industry. This is bad for the administration, and the plan, therefore, has to be one of discouraging investors from turning to gold as a hedge. To prevent the public's rushing to gold, the government took steps to bring gold into disfavor.

In an editorial in the Wall Street Journal, in June, 1975, then Secretary of the Treasury, William Simon, noted that he was militating for a system in which the role of gold is reduced to lessen its destabilizing effects on the world monetary system. He noted that the IMF's Interim Committee has formally arranged to seek ways to "insure that the role of gold in the international monetary system is gradually reduced."[18] Almost simultaneously the New York Times noted that "the United States, with the support of most developing countries, wants gold to be a less attractive asset. One way it has sought to achieve this is to keep steady pressure on the price through periodic gold sales by the Treasury. . ."[19]

Mr. Simon pursued this plan by both a propaganda campaign and gold sales. The first Treasury auction resulted in the sale of 753,600 ounces at an average price of $165.67 an ounce. The second sale in June, 1975, saw another 499,500 ounces go for $165.05 an ounce.

Hard on the heels of the Treasury sales came the announcement by the International Monetary Fund that it would auction off 25,000,000 ounces of gold over a four-year period, and use the proceeds as a fund to help developing nations. The U.S. is the strongest voice in the IMF, and it is clear that Mr. Simon's wishes were being followed. Four years must certainly have been set by plan to put extended downward pressure on the gold market. Before the sales by the IMF were underway, the gold market was responding to other forces as well. The world had fallen into its worst recession since the Second World War, thus dampening commodity demand while simultaneously camouflaging the real money-supply inflation that was occurring. Meanwhile, the Russians, hit by drought and a need for foreign exchange with which to buy grain, became sellers of large quantities of gold. The first IMF sale in June of 1976 resulted in the auctioning off of 780,000 ounces at $126 an ounce, and the second sale in July brought $122.05 an ounce for another 780,000 ounces.

Clearly the strategy was working. With economists saying that inflation had been licked, and with the expectation of continuing large gold sales by both the IMF and Washington, gold fever had been subdued. After the second auction, the price on the free market moved relentlessly toward $100 an ounce.

Will the government be successful in this effort? Were they successful in pegging gold at $20.22 an ounce in 1900? At $35.00 an ounce in 1933? Were they successful in holding the price of silver at $1.29 an ounce in 1965? The answer in all cases is *no*. In the end governments will again be forced to accept reality: the printing of fiat money causes people to demand real goods in place of worthless paper. As our current inflation heats up again, this old truth will reappear. Meanwhile, the sales by the Treasury and IMF must be shortlived, since their supplies are limited. The 25,000,000 ounces that the IMF has planned to sell would be worth only $2.5 billion at $100 an ounce, or $5 billion at $200 an ounce. In today's world of megawealth, $5 billion is a drop in the bucket. Any significant move toward store-of-value assets by the world's citizens could easily absorb every ounce of gold that the IMF holds at prices far above $200 an ounce.

Inflationists have worked for well over 50 years in this country to eliminate hard currency by disparaging both gold and silver as mediums of exchange. These final sales by government are merely the struggles at the end of the rope.

In summary, I believe that the demand for gold from private holders will increase dramatically in the next few years as currency inflation accelerates. The next major upward thrusts will come when the signs of serious inflation reappear. Along the way the price will fluctuate violently, of course, but the trend will be upwards. Gold is not the only store-of-value asset that should be held by prudent investors, but it is definitely a must as a part of a diversified portfolio.

Buying Gold

There are three ways a person can hold gold: placer gold, bullion, or coins. Placer gold is simply raw, unprocessed gold direct from nature. It is in the form of nuggets and small particles. It can be held legally by citizens of the United States, and can be purchased through various brokers. Unfortunately, it's difficult to determine the quality and exact quantity of this type of gold until it is refined. Unless you're an expert in the field, you might find yourself stuck with less than you paid for it. An additional problem is that at some point you're going to want to sell your gold, and you must assume that the person who sold it to you won't be around to buy it back. Placer gold might present a problem in that you would have to find someone who would take your word for its value.

Now that gold bullion is legal for Americans to own, it can be purchased through a variety of outlets, including some banks, coin dealers, and bullion exchanges. Bullion can be purchased in wafers and bars from less than an ounce up to 1,000 ounces (almost 90 pounds). It will generally bear the hallmark of the refiner and will have the weight and fineness stamped on the bar. Obviously gold bullion could be adulterated, so when buying, make sure you buy from reliable sources or have the gold assayed.

The third method of buying gold is to purchase gold coins. Earlier regulations against gold ownership exempted coins held for their numismatic value, thus there has been a brisk traffic in gold coins in the U.S. prior to the legalization of gold ownership. Coins have an advantage over bullion in that they are a known weight and fineness. The gold content of common coins can be found in any collectors handbook. Figure 9 lists a few examples of coins and their gold content.

Usually coins will sell at somewhat of a premium over the value of their gold content.

GOLD CONTENT OF TEN COMMON COINS

COIN	TROY OZ. (PURE)
United States $20	.9675
United States $10	.48375
Mexican 50 Pesos	1.2056
Mexican 20 Pesos	.4823
Austrian 100 Corona	.9802
Austrian 20 Corona	.1960
British 1 Pound (Sovereign)	.2354
Netherlands 10 Guilders	.1947
South African 2 Rand	.2354
Switzerland 20 Francs	.1867

Figure 9

It's a rare situation when you'll be able to buy these coins for the value of the gold content alone. To start with, when a government mints a coin it charges a premium (called seigniorage) over and above the cost of manufacture. The U.S. twenty dollar gold piece has .9695 ounces of pure (.999 fine) gold in it. Gold was selling at $20.22 an ounce at the time that these coins were being minted, and thus the coin that the government sold for twenty dollars actually contained only $19.56 in gold. South Africa is currently minting about 10% of its gold production into Krugerrands, which it markets at a price about 8% above the gold value of the coins. Seigniorage tends to stay with the coin, and other factors can increase the coins' "numismatic premium", including scarcity of a particular coin, market demand for coins in general, commission charged by the person selling the coins, etc.

There has been a good deal of counterfeiting of gold coins, and it would be wise to either buy from a reputable source, or have each coin checked. It is relatively easy, using modern equipment, to determine the authenticity of a coin.

You may find yourself getting interested in numismatics in general if you handle many gold coins, as the appeal of their beauty transcends logic. Then you can begin to become a serious collector with an eye for the date of the coin, its condition, it rarity, etc. For the nonnumismatically inclined investor, you'll be buying bulk coins. These coins are not particularly rare and are in average condition for that particular coin and date. If you buy American gold coins or British Sovereigns in bulk, you will probably be buying circulated coins because these coins were used for exchange in the early part of the century.

In recent years gold coins, even if freshly minted, are hardly ever exchanged for other commodities in direct barter. They are still minting Mexican 50-Peso coins in Mexico (they're no longer worth 50 pesos, however), but you'll never get one in change when you cash a large bill at a restaurant. They're purchased exclusively by collectors or people who want to use them as store-of-value assets, and consequently will not be circulated. Their condition will probably be U (Uncirculated) or BU (Brilliant Uncirculated). Even when buying in bulk you'll expect that type of condition.

The premium for average coins of a particular mintage over the value of the gold in the coin will vary from day to day. They are, after all, a commodity like any other commodity. Their price will depend on supply and demand for that coin plus the current price of gold. While the coin price tends to follow closely the gold price, the numismatic premium does vary.

Where do you buy gold coins? Pick up your yellow pages and look under "Coin Dealers." Most of them will have a stock of coins, and many will have teletype services that link them with coin dealers throughout the United States. They'll be able to check prices all over the country, much as the stock broker can check stock prices, and order anything you want. Caution: prices will vary considerably from dealer to dealer, for although they may all have access to similar wholesale prices, they are free to mark up the coins to whatever they think the traffic will bear.

While most coin shops cater primarily to the numismatist and feel themselves lucky when they can snare a well heeled investor, there has recently been an upsurge in coin "exchanges," new companies that have sprung up to satisfy the desire of the investor who wishes to invest substantial amounts of his assets in gold or silver. In addition it's possible to purchase gold coins through various foreign banks, such as through the Swiss Credit Bank, or the Swiss Bank Corporation.

There are three ways in which you can buy gold coins from these retailers. First, you can pay cash and take delivery of the coins. You then have physical possession and must find a way to safely store the coins to protect against the risk of theft. Second, you can pay cash but not take delivery, by asking the dealer you buy from to store them for you. If you're dealing with a Swiss bank I'd think the risk of storing with them is minimal. If you're dealing with anyone else I'd be very cautious. Once you've asked anyone to store your gold, you're relying on the integrity of that party to honor the paper receipt he gives you for your gold. Historically, people who give paper receipts for stored gold have tended to give out more receipts than they have gold on deposit. Isn't that exactly what happened in the case of the U.S. Government? So beware. The third method of buying gold coins is to buy on margin. You purchase a given quantity of coins at the prevailing market price, but put only a small down payment (10% to 20%) on them. You can pick up the coins anytime in the future simply by paying off the balance due, in the meantime paying interest at slightly above the prime rate on the outstanding balance.

The benefits of buying on margin? If the price of gold goes up, your coins increase in value. Since you can buy more coins on margin with a given amount of cash than you can buy for delivery, your profit is magnified. Remember the chapter on margining? Using leverage in buying gold coins is not much different from using leverage in the purchase of any other investment. Also, when buying on margin you don't have to worry about taking possession and storing the coins.

What are the risks of buying on margin? First, if the coins go down in value you magnify your loss. Depending on the extent of your leverage, it's easy to have your equity wiped out with a minor downward move in the price of gold. Leveraging or margining is completely inconsistent with the purpose of buying gold, providing your purpose is to hold a store-of-value asset. Secondly, and by far the worst danger, is that the dealer may not put any coins away for you. Suppose I'm a dealer and you buy $10,000 worth of coins from me, paying $1,000 down and agreeing to finance the balance at 8% interest. I give you a contract promising to deliver the coins when the balance is paid off, but who knows whether I really put the coins away or not? If I don't, I now have your $1,000, you pay me interest at the rate of $720 per year, and my cost is nothing. If I'm a "gamblin' man" I might have the feeling that coin prices are going down and plan to buy the coins to cover my obligation to you at some lower price. If the price goes down, I could call for more money from you, as a ten percent drop in price of the coins would wipe out your equity. The profit to me could be substantial. The danger for me and you is that the price of gold could take a substantial jump upwards. In that case I would have to go out and buy the coins I owe you and come up with the difference between what you paid and the new purchase price out of my pocket. On a $10,000 order, if the price of gold jumps 10% then I'll be out of pocket a thousand dollars. A dealer who is trading heavily in coins may process $250,000 worth

of orders every week. The temptation to solve short run
financial problems by resorting to this tactic is tremendous,
and a dealer who succumbs can quickly run up debts in the
hundreds of thousands of dollars once any major price move
begins. Investors who get caught in this trap find they not
only don't have the profits they thought they had, but
they've lost their original capital as well.

Margining coins is highly speculative. Know your dealer,
and make him prove his claims that he has the gold to back
up his contract. But beware again. The fact that he can show
you a receipt for gold in the depository isn't enough. What
you must know is that he has as much gold as he has receipts
outstanding at any time.

A simple remedy for the above discussed dangers is to
always buy for cash and take delivery. The profits might not
be as high, but neither are the potential losses as great.

Storing Gold

After you have purchased your bullion or coins, you must
find a place to keep them. The alternatives are:
1. A bank safe deposit box.
2. A wall safe or other hiding place in the home.
3. A foreign bank safe deposit box.
4. A depository other than a bank.

Your decision should be based on your assessment of the
relative risks of each. The possible risks are theft, business
failure, and government confiscation. While bank safe-deposit
boxes are relatively theft free they do have a couple of
drawbacks. First, the bank could close its doors, in which
case it could be awhile before you'd have access to the
contents of your box; but even if the bank went through
bankruptcy they couldn't get at the contents of your box.
Another possibility is that government regulatory agencies
such as the IRS or the FBI could gain access to your
safe-deposit box without your consent. These agencies have
access to all bank records, and a person who fears the
confiscatory powers of the state should certainly be aware of

the vulnerability of a bank safe-deposit box. Also, in the event of your death the bank is bound by law to notify the taxing authorities of the existence of the box. They'll demand to be present when it's opened in order to tally the value of the contents. If you feel that the state is a potential threat to your wealth, think twice about the use of a bank safe-deposit box for coin storage.

There are depositories that could serve as alternatives to a banking institution. In most major cities you'll find them listed in the phone book. Typically they are private corporations that own vaults and rent out space in the vaults, usually in the form of lockable boxes, to anyone who wants it. They're usually bonded against theft by the owners, and insured against theft or other loss. Inasmuch as they aren't required to file reports listing their depositors and aren't required to open their vaults to government agents (unless a court order is involved), you have a greater degree of privacy with such an establishment. Foreign banks also rent safe-deposit boxes, and generally Swiss Banks are considered to be safe havens from the prying eyes of neighbors and federal agents.

The final solution is to keep your coins in your own possession. You might bury them in the backyard, build a wall safe into your home (not behind a painting, please!), or simply hide them in some inconspicuous place. The risks you take here are simple; they could be discovered and stolen by a thief, melted down from a fire, or possibly scattered to the winds in a tornado. I know of one couple who kept bags of silver coins hidden in their home. They found out to their dismay several months later that neighborhood kids, with whom they were friendly, had discovered the bags and gradually pilfered away the coins. Another collector, fearful of the government, had buried his in the backyard. The coins survived fine, but he made the mistake of burying several hundred dollars in Federal Reserve Notes along with them. When he dug them up he found it was just in the nick of time, because worms had gotten into his box and were busily devouring the tasty paper. Needless to say, if you're going to stash gold, silver, or any other valuables on your property, don't talk about it to anyone. Professional thieves have their ears to the ground at all times, and they're amazingly adept at discovering the most unlikely hiding places. So be clever and quiet.

Gold Mining Shares

A fourth method of investing in gold, although somewhat indirect, is buying shares in gold mining companies. Gold is a commodity whose price will fluctuate depending on supply, demand, and government edict. Since the profits of companies that mine gold depends directly on the price they can get for their product, it stands to reason that they would benefit from an increased price for the metal. History bears this out, of course. Since 1971 the leading gold mining stocks have experienced a breathtaking boom-and-bust cycle, as the price of gold went from $35 to $190 and back again to around $100.

In 1976 these stocks were being sold at prices that must be considered bargains by anyone who understands the nature of the world's financial dilemma. The temporarily depressed price of gold, coupled with racial unrest in South Africa, have disenchanted most of the investors who turned to the golds a few years ago. For those who want to take advantage of this method of holding interests in gold, I would recommend reading Donald J. Hoppe's excellent book *How to Invest In Gold Stocks and Avoid the Pitfalls*.[20]

If you still don't feel comfortable about following the stocks on a day-to-day basis, choose one of the mutual funds that specialize in gold mining shares. The two most prominent funds are International Investors, Inc. (the first major gold fund), and Research Capital Fund (one of the Franklin group).

In summary, gold should be part of every intelligent investor's portfolio. Coins or bullion should be purchased for cash and stored in as risk-free a situation as possible. If would certainly be wise to diversify into both the actual commodity and the gold stocks, as they both have advantages and are a fine complement to each other.

SILVER

While many of the comments about gold in the preceding section apply to silver as well, it's necessary for an investor to have a clear understanding that there are substantial differences between the two metals. Silver, like gold, has been esteemed for centuries for both its utility and its beauty. Because of its scarcity, weight, durability, and divisibility, it could serve and has served the function of money in many societies.

Bimetallism

C.V. Myers in his booklet "Silver" pointed out that as far back as the Dynasty of Pharaoh Menges (3,500 B.C.) silver was in use as money alongside gold. Its value set by decree, one part of gold was equal to two and one half parts of silver. What value they put on gold in relation to other commodities I don't know, but in all probability the price ratio of silver to gold was the result of the relative abundance of the two metals. Since silver has functioned as a form of money alongside gold in many societies, there have been repeated attempts to enforce a bimetallic standard. Bimetallism simply means that both metals are legal currency in a country and, as did Pharaoh Menges, the government establishes the price ratio between them.

In the first coinage act of 1792 the congress of the United States set up two units of value: a gold dollar containing 24.75 grains of pure gold and a silver dollar containing 371.25 grains of pure silver. Since there are 480 grains in an ounce, the "monetary" value of silver was therefore established at $1.2929 per ounce and the "monetary" value of gold was established at $19.3939 per ounce; or a 15-1 ratio between silver and gold.

The impossibility of maintaining this ratio might be better understood if we go back to our simple society and use other barter commodities in place of silver and gold. One unit of Farmer's production equals one unit of Tailor's production equals one unit of Carpenter's production. If the three producers were to decide that this ratio of A equals B equals C must always hold true, then what would happen if the production of one of the three increased (or decreased)? If apples became easier to produce and Farmer had twice as many, yet the value were to remain constant, either he would have more purchasing power than the other producers and could buy up all their production and they would be left with nothing but apples, or they would refuse to sell their production, preferring to hoard it. In fact, they would all try to use the abundant commodity to buy up the less abundant commodities.

The real value of a commodity depends on the quantity and usefulness of that commodity relative to the quantity and usefulness of the other commodities in the marketplace. To say that silver will always bear the same value relationship to gold is to assume that each will always be constant in supply and demand. No single commodity is constant in supply and demand. Thus, when the U.S. instituted a bimetallic standard and attempted to legislate a constant ratio, they were doomed to defeat.

Gresham's Law* went into force. Bad money drives good money out of circulation. As gold became more plentiful,

---

*Sir Thomas Gresham, founder of the English Royal Exchange, explained the principal of his law to Queen Elizabeth in 1558. When two or more kinds of money of equal denomination but different intrinsic value are in circulation at the same time, the one of highest intrinsic value will be hoarded and the one of lower instrinsic value spent. When you find you have a silver quarter and a copper plated quarter, you'll naturally follow Gresham's Law by keeping the silver and spending the copper.

people would spend gold dollars and hoard silver dollars; as silver became more plentiful, people would hoard gold and spend silver. Even at the time of the original fixing of the ratio, gold was more valuable than the ratio suggested so it was hoarded and silver became the nation's circulating money.

Finally in the 1830's gold was revalued, the ratio was reset at 16-to-1 and the situation reversed; gold began to circulate again and silver disappeared. Whenever the free market price of silver rose above $1.29 per ounce on the open market, none was offered to the Treasury for coinage, and silver coins quickly disappeared from the market. When it dropped below $1.29 per ounce, it was sold to the Treasury and the dollars received were then redeemed in gold. Even though it should have been obvious by this time that bimetallism wouldn't work, various forces were lobbying strongly in Congress to keep silver on as money.

After the civil war there was a depression during which prices fell to their prewar levels. Those who had contracted debts during the war found it difficult to earn the dollars necessary to repay these debts and pushed for inflationary policies, which included expanding the money supply by injecting silver into the currency system at inflated prices. Later on in the century, when the use of silver tapered off in Europe and new mines were opened in the west, the mining interests in the U.S. found the price of silver dropping and pressured Congress into passing the Sherman Silver Purchase Act of 1890, which directed the Treasury to buy 4.5 million ounces of silver every month.

All these purchases of silver didn't really save the price of silver, but did result in a drain in the Treasury's gold supply and eventually led to the panic of 1893. Faced with declining gold reserves, the government eventually repealed the Sherman Act and also devalued gold slightly (from 24.75 grains to the dollar to 25.8 grains per dollar). Thus, in 1900 the value of gold was set at $20.22 an ounce. Events, including discovery of new gold fields in South Africa, new processes for refining gold from ore, and increasing urban populations, caused increasing prices in general (remember, an increase in the supply of a commodity, in this case gold, causes a decrease in its value relative to other commodities). The increases in prices satisfied the farmers (or "Populists" as they were called) and they stopped pressuring congress to inflate with silver. Silver varied between 65 cents an ounce in 1900 and $1.10 at the peak of the First World War, then drifted downward again. The depression caused the industrial and artistic uses of silver to dry up and by 1932 its free market price hit a low of 29 cents an ounce. At this time the government stepped in again and passed laws to purchase silver.[21]

To understand the government's in-and-out position, it's necessary to think about their objectives. The federal bureaucracy survives by confiscating the wealth of the citizens. When the state is able to buy a commodity for one price, monetize it, and pass it back to the public at a higher price, it makes a profit. If it can buy silver at 64 cents an ounce, stamp it into silver dollars, and pass those dollars back to the public at $1.29 an ounce, it profits to the extent of 65 cents an ounce. The free market wouldn't pay $1.29 an ounce for silver. It placed a value of about 40 cents an ounce on it. The silver interests were delighted to be able to sell at the higher price to Uncle Sam, and Uncle Sam was delighted to pass it on to the gullible public at a price they wouldn't pay if given free choice. Thus, the state could inflate the money supply in a subtle way and keep the difference.

It was politically expeditious during the depression to appear to be creating new jobs and at the same time preventing prices from falling, thus keeping wages and profits up. The method used was to create jobs by creating make-work projects and create the dollars to pay the salaries by inflating the supply of money. Naturally, the state could not get the money to pay these wages from taxing the population, as the people wouldn't have been able or willing to pay the taxes. So the state simply inflated the money supply by whatever means were convenient. First, they had to release the pressure on the gold supplies by severing the dollar ties to gold, which they did by devaluing to $35.00 an ounce from $20.22. This effectively increased the gold reserves of the federal government by $3 billion. They then sold federal Treasury notes, bonds, and bills to the Federal Reserve Bank to the extent allowed by the then existing gold reserve requirements (you see, by devaluing to $35 an ounce they substantially increased their borrowing power). Additionally, they manipulated silver to help increase the supply of money. They bought silver at 64 cents an ounce and monetized it by issuing Silver Certificates redeemable at $1.29 an ounce. A neat trick not at all understood by the public.

From that time on, and no doubt to the disappointment of the politicians, silver began to become more valuable. The Second World War created a great demand for the metal, and after the war the boom in electronics and photography caused industrial consumption to rise dramatically. The free market price of silver then began to climb toward the official government price of $1.2929. As it rose, it became less and less profitable for the state to buy the metal and mint it into coins. Soon silver coins began to disappear from circulation, and the government's silver supply began to dwindle as new coins were minted, placed into circulation, and in turn hoarded.

Silver users preferred to purchase foreign silver to domestic silver until 1955, because before that the Treasury support price was higher than the market price. Thus, domestic suppliers could sell to the Treasury at a greater price than users were paying for foreign silver. The Treasury stocks increased by the amount of the purchases and decreased by the coinage. As far as the money supply was concerned, however, it was increased by the silver whether held in stockpile or issued in coinage.

After 1955, and until 1961, the market price approximated the Treasury support price and the trend reversed. It was as cheap to buy from domestic sources as from foreign sources; so users purchased from three sources; the Treasury, domestic producers, and foreign producers. From 1961 on, the Treasury supply began to dwindle rapidly because of new coinage and user purchases. The Treasury free silver stockpile reached its peak of 222 million ounces in 1959 (that was in addition to 1,700 million ounces used as backing for silver certificates). By 1960 the supply of free silver was down to 22 million ounces and the legislature was now ready to release the 1,700 million ounces.

The tables had completely turned. What originally was a bonanza to an inflation hungry bureaucracy now became a millstone. While originally they were able to inflate the money supply by buying silver cheaply and monetizing it; now that the price had risen, not only could they not continue to reap the benefits of the price differential, the very fact that they were bound to back the silver certificate and to mint silver coins prevented them from further inflation. Therefore, it was necessary to get rid of silver as a monetary metal completely. President Kennedy was in office when the crisis point was reached in 1961 and he made the decision to demonetize silver. But he really didn't have a choice, faced with the need of the state to increase the money supply in order to survive. Nor did Johnson have a choice when he made the decision in 1964 to stop minting silver coins. These were inevitable consequences of an inflating money supply and the need to be free of restrictions on that inflation.

The Future

The factors that will determine the future price will be supply and demand. The federal state is now out of the silver market almost completely. They still maintain a strategic

stockpile (which they could dump on the market at some
future date) but, since it is estimated at less than 200 million
ounces, it shouldn't have a prolonged effect. Of course, they
could step in at any time and confiscate silver, or fix the
price by selling or buying at some set price. The question is,
why would they? They did it in 1934 because they wanted to
inflate the money supply. But once the inflationary mechanism in any country has reached the state it has in this
country, where we have demonetized *all* metals and inflation
is accomplished merely by monetizing debt instead of production, there is no real reason to interfere with the pricing
of individual commodities.* The objective of the state is to
support its own survival and expansion by any means
possible, and since this can't be done through taxation alone,
the state will have to continue to do it through inflation.
Since the monetary metals are roadblocks to real inflation,
they'll have to be demonetized.

Formerly when a country wished to prevent the ownership
of gold and silver during inflationary periods, it was to
prevent the citizens from using these metals as mediums of
exchange. Now, with no countries any longer on a gold or
silver standard, a state doesn't have to worry that its citizens
will begin using the gold-backed currency of another country
for external trading. It is also unlikely that people will revert
to the inconvenience of the barter system, whether the
medium they're using is gold, silver, or potatoes. The power
of most countries to fix wages and prices in terms of their
own legal tender currency is a deterrant to bypassing that
currency by the population. The Federal Reserve Bank
controls the currency inflation in this country, and even if an
individual wanted to operate on a barter basis and bypass the
legal tender currency, he would be able to do this only on a

---

*This statement should be modified to take into consideration balance
of payment problems considered earlier, and wage price controls used
to make a show of fighting inflation or used to expand the power of
the bureaucracy.

small scale, since we are a nation that operates more and more on credit from bank borrowing.

Let's make the assumption that in the future the government will step out of the role of price controller of the monetary metals. These metals will be demonetized by all major nations, and prices will be functions solely of supply and demand. Demand will come from (1) industrial users, (2) hoarders, (3) speculators. Speculators can be more or less discounted over the long term because they don't consume, but merely buy from the market and resell to the market. Industrial use can be predicted over the short term, but may be unpredictable over the longer term. For example, substitutes can be developed for any material for almost any application given proper technological development. Uses as a store-of-value will depend on the need to place assets in secure positions. As economic conditions in the world become more precarious and as central banks continue to inflate their currencies, people everywhere will turn more and more to store-of-value assets and less and less to business investments. This will create a greater demand for gold and silver and they should rise in price.

All things being taken into consideration (current supply, industrial demand, etc.), is the market price of silver realistic or has it been driven artificially high by speculators? Assuming you answer that question, will industrial demand increase or decrease, and will supplies increase or decrease? We know for certain that if supply-demand forces were constant in the future, then the price of the metal would increase at whatever rate the money supply increased. If we are experiencing 15% a year inflation, the price of the commodity would go up that amount. Figure 10 shows the production and consumption of silver over the past 30 years. The future deficit should be covered by an increasing price of silver, and any further inflation of the money supply should carry the price up even higher.

In summary, silver still looks like a good long term

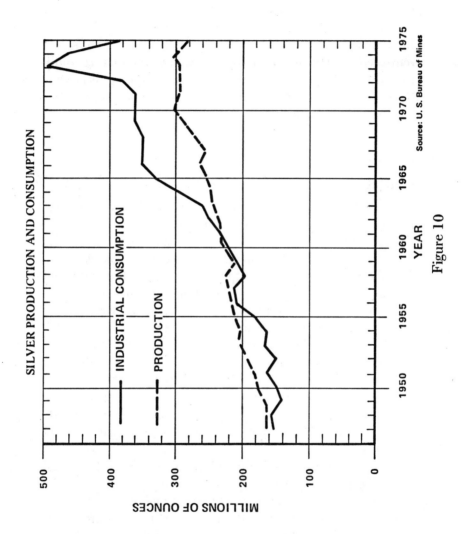

Figure 10

store-of-value asset. Unless you're a speculator, however, stay away from buying on margin. Buy for cash, take delivery, and store it in a safe place. Don't be rattled by price fluctuations. The silver market is volatile because it's currently controlled by speculators; it will be fluctuating wildly over the next few years. Remember that the long term view bodes for increasing inflation, and store-of-value commodities will increase in price.

OTHER METALS

Other metals can perform the same function, but in other metals we are looking at different characteristics. For one thing, few metals are really valued because of their beauty. For the most part other metals are industrial commodities, and the demand for them depends on the level of industrial production. The higher the cost-per-pound of a metal, the more practical it is as a store-of-value asset, providing other points are consistent. Platinum, for example, is more expensive than gold because of its rarity. Furthermore, it is unlikely that any substitute will be found that will cause demand for the metal to fall off. Industrially, it is used alone, or alloyed with other metals as a catalyst in the manufacture of acids, in electrical contacts and laboratory ware. Its properties and abundance make it cheaper than its next substitute.

From a storage standpoint, platinum would be the metal most likely to serve the purpose of storing wealth. It can be purchased in ingot form in weights from one ounce up.

Copper is relatively plentiful in the earth and its properties of conductivity, strength, and malleability make it particularly useful in wire, sheets, and bars that need to conduct electricity. When alloyed with zinc or tin it becomes brass or bronze and is extremely resistant to corrosion.

Supplies will fluctuate somewhat due to potential new

discoveries of the metal and recovery from scrap, while demand is unlikely to taper off. As a store-of-value it would be fine, except that it's bulky, and any significant amount of it could present storage problems. Some people have begun to save copper pennies, thinking they'll increase in value as copper moves up in price. There will be a penny's worth of copper in a penny when the price of copper reaches $1.37 per pound, and certainly copper could reach that in the near future. Still, the effort to collect and count a significant amount of pennies would probably eliminate the profits of hoarding them.

RAW COMMODITIES THROUGH THE FUTURES MARKET

There are two ways in which you can benefit from holding real goods. First, you can purchase them, take delivery, and store them yourself, just as you might buy towels at the department store when they're on sale and put them away in the closet for future use. Second, you can buy for future delivery, while letting the person you buy from hold the goods until the agreed upon delivery date. You do this when you put the towels on lay-a-way at the store, in which case you usually put down a small deposit, promising to pay the balance when you pick up the merchandise. In the commodities market the same options are available to the buyer. He can, for example, buy gold bars, pay for them, and place them in his safe deposit box; or he can put down a deposit, let the seller hold the bars, and take delivery on them in the future. This concept of buying now and taking delivery in the future is the foundation of the speculative market known as the commodities futures market.

Commodities futures markets have been around for hundreds of years, originating because of the need of merchants and manufacturers to make commitments to purchase raw materials and finished goods in advance of the date of delivery. In order to guarantee himself ample stocks, a miller

might contract to purchase wheat from the farmer far in
advance of the harvest, just as a manufacturer of automobiles
may contract to purchase steel from the mill months before
he actually needs the steel. Once the mechanism for advance
purchasing was established, it was natural that third parties—
speculators or financiers—would become involved. The speculator might buy a quantity of wheat from the coming fall
harvest in hopes that the miller may be willing to pay more
for the wheat when it becomes available than he is today.
When he buys (by putting down a deposit) he gets what
amounts to a warehouse receipt which states that there will
be, on such and such a date, the number of bushels of wheat
available in the warehouse on the demand of the receipt
holder. The speculator can hold the claim until delivery date
or sell it anytime prior to that date.

Commodities Futures Exchanges

To facilitate the trading of claims, exchanges are set up.
These are nothing more than places where buyers and sellers
get together to exchange claims. The major exchanges in the
United States are the Chicago Mercantile Exchange, the
Chicago Board of Trade, the New York Commodities
Exchange, the International Monetary Market of the Chicago
Mercantile Exchange, the New York Mercantile Exchange,
and the Kansas City Board of Trade. Many other exchanges
exist, some just for one or two products (like the New York
Coffee and Sugar Exchange).

Claims traded on these exchanges are called contracts. The
contracts specify the commodity, quality, quantity, and the
place and date of delivery. For example, on the Chicago
Mercantile Exchange a contract for potatoes will specify
80,000 pounds of USDA No. 1, size A, 2" diameter potatoes.
These contracts will be offered with delivery dates in
January, March, April, May, and November.

As in the case of stocks, not all commodities are traded on
these exchanges. To be traded, the contracts for a com-

modity must be in sufficient demand to make an active market. In addition, there are other trading rules and conditions for each type of contract.

Limit Moves

The exchange allows the price of a contract to fluctuate only within certain limits during each trading day. For example, the price of a pound of copper on the New York Commodities Exchange can fluctuate up or down a maximum of 3 cents a pound from the previous day's closing price. At that point the price is frozen until the next trading day.

This rule tends to dampen wild fluctuations and makes the market more orderly by giving traders the opportunity to digest the importance of news before acting. Secondly, and more important since most contracts are sold on high margin, it gives the brokerage houses time to collect more margin deposits from customers as the price moves up or down. The houses must collect margin in either case, because for every buyer there is a seller. When the price changes in either direction one or the other is losing money.

This limit-move condition can have the effect of locking a buyer into a falling position. If the buyer has purchased a contract for 5,000 bushels of wheat, the limit move is 25 cents a bushel per day. If adverse news enters the market, and the most that any buyer will bid for wheat is one dollar less per bushel than the contract owner paid, then the contract will begin moving down at 25 cents a day for four days, until it reaches the price offered by the next buyer. During this four-day period, the owner of the contract is 'locked-in'; he cannot sell, for there are no buyers at the mandatory price set by the exchange. He must just wait and absorb his loss.

Margin

In commodities futures trading, margin refers to the deposit made by a trader to insure that he will honor his

contract to buy the commodities involved at the expiration
of his contract. The amount of deposit or margin required on
a contract depends on the commodity and varies from
exchange to exchange. The amount depends on the potential
price fluctuation of a commodity during a day's trading. For
example, if you wanted to buy one contract of copper on the
New York Commodities Exchange, you would be contracting
for 25,000 pounds. If the price on the day of purchase is 70
cents a pound, you would be agreeing to pay $17,500 on the
delivery date. Initially you would be asked for margin of
$750. If the price of copper goes down 3 cents a pound, the
value of the entire contract would have dropped by $750. At
that point your deposit would have been wiped out and the
brokerage house would be in danger of going in the hole if
the price dropped further. Before that happened you would
be asked for additional money so that your margin would
never drop below 75% of the initial deposit. If you declined
to put up more margin at that time, your contract would be
sold (closed out). Maintenance margin is typically about 75%
of the initial margin requirement. Conversely, when the
amount of money in your margin account exceeds the
required maintenance margin, you can ask to receive a check
for the difference. Thus, if prices are moving up, you can
continuously draw your profits out of the account while still
owning the contract.

One feature of the margin account with most brokers is
that the margin does not have to be put up in cash. It's often
possible to buy Treasury bills or other securities and use
them as security rather than cash. Your margin deposit can
then be earning interest for you while it is guaranteeing you a
position in the commodity.

One of the risks in commodities trading, as opposed to the
stock market, is that it's possible to lose more money than
the initial deposit. In the event that the price of a contract
begins to fall the daily limit and no buyers are around at the
fixed price established by the exchange, your margin could

be wiped out quickly. If the broker calls for more margin, and you refused to put it up, he would be stuck, since he couldn't sell you out even if he wanted to. In order to protect themselves from this risk, the brokerage houses will usually ask you for some kind of security in addition to the margin deposit. This could mean hypothecating any other assets you have, including your home.

Let's see how a margin account might work in a copper contract. Contracts for future delivery of copper are sold on either the New York Commodities Exchange (Comex), or the International Monetary Market (IMM) of the Chicago Mercantile Exchange (CME). On the Comex, a contract is for 25,000 pounds of copper, the maximum daily price move is 3 cents per pound above or below the previous day's closing price, and the round trip commission is generally $45. As of Monday, April 19, 1976, the price of copper in the farthest contract month available (May 1977) was 73.8 cents a pound. Thus, the value of a 25,000-pound contract was $18,450. The spot price for copper the same day was 70.625 cents a pound, so that the difference between spot and a one-year future was 3.175 cents a pound or 4.5% higher than the current spot price. The trader has two options, he can place the minimum deposit with the broker to buy the contract, which in this case would be about $750, or he can place a greater deposit. If he places the minimum deposit, the broker will ask him to add more money to his margin account if the future price of copper drops to 73.0 cents, at which point the value of the contract would have fallen $187.50. If the trader decided not to meet the margin call, his position would be liquidated and, since the value of the contract had fallen by $187.50, his original margin deposit would have been reduced by that amount. He would close the account and receive back the remaining $562.50 less the commission cost of $45. On the other hand suppose the trader put the full price of the contract on deposit. In this case he would have deposited $18,450 with

the broker, on which amount he would probably be paid
interest. No matter how far the price of copper fell, he would
never need to deposit more money. When he decided to sell
his contract he would receive back the difference between
the selling price of the contract and his deposit, less
commission. He would essentially have owned the copper
during the entire holding period and made a profit or loss
equal to the price change during the period. Buying on the
futures market rather than buying the copper outright would
have also saved him the storage, shipping, and insurance
charges. Since he did not have the copper in his possession,
he would also avoid any personal property tax on the goods.
If copper moved up 25% in price during the period, the
trader would have earned 25% on his money less the 4.5%
price differential from spot to future, and less the commission. If it moved down 25% he would have lost 25% plus the
4.5% spot-future differential plus commission.

The point is that the risk to capital can be reduced by
increasing the margin deposit on any contract. This, of
course, also reduces the potential gain.

Commissions

In trading commodities there is a commission, just as in
trading stocks. In this case, however, you don't pay a
commission for each trade, but rather one commission for a
round-trip. Another difference is that the commission is paid
when the position is closed out, and therefore you don't have
less money working for you at the start. Commissions vary
from exchange to exchange, and from broker to broker. As in
the case of stocks, there are discounts for quantity purchases,
and even lower commissions if the entire round-trip is
handled in one trading day.

Commissions are nominal relative to the total value of the
contract, generally averaging about $45. Since the value of
the contract is probably around $18,000, the commission
rate is only 1/4%. This is misleading, however. If you

purchase a contract with the minimum margin, you'll put up only $1,000. Thus the commission becomes 4.5% of the money changing hands, which equates pretty well with the 2%- in, 2%-out commissions in the stock market.

Price Factors

There are a variety of factors that affect the price of any commodity. Two basic determinants are supply and demand, and these, in turn, can be affected by many things. In the case of a crop, the supply can go down due to bad weather, labor disputes, import or export controls, disease, reduction in plantings, or stockpiling by producers. Demand can be curtailed by economic recession, government regulations, competitive products, labor disputes in industries of purchasers, etc. As well as general supply-demand forces acting on prices, other factors apply as well. The location of goods (causing high shipping charges), government purchases, government regulations, currency exchange rates, taxation, and economic and political uncertainty all have a direct bearing on prices.

Prices of commodities for future delivery have additional complicating factors. Future prices may be higher than current cash (spot) prices due to costs of storage, insurance, interest rates, and the risk premium attached to an unknown future.

Trading Techniques

Over the years traders have developed numerous and complicated systems for playing the futures market. Some take a fundamental approach, analyzing supply and demand factors with the aid of supply and demand curves, elasticity equations, and forecasting models. Other traders rely more on the technical approach by following patterns on price charts, and by studying moving averages, volume, open interest, time cycles and wave theories. Many traders use

spreads and options to minimize taxes, as well as arbitrage to
secure profits. Needless to say, millions of dollars have been
spent as well as the labor of countless economists, mathe-
maticians, and theorists employed to find ways to beat the
commodities futures game. The stakes are high and the
competition fierce. Since there are always two sides to every
contract, a long and a short, for every winner there is a loser,
with the losers losing more than the winners because of the
commissions paid to the brokerage houses.

It's the job of the commodities speculator to analyze all
the incoming data regarding a commodity and to evaluate the
effect of that information on the future price. Since everyone
involved in the commodities market has access to essentially
equivalent information, and many of them have long and
intense experience in the various commodities, this is no
game for amateur gamblers.

Profiting From Inflation

My own approach to this market is to use it as a method of
profiting from an understanding of inflation and its effects
on commodities prices. While prices depend on supply-
demand factors, the public's expectations of future economic
conditions plays a big role in the longer-term price cycles.
When the inflation surge hit the economy in 1973 and 1974
the futures prices of most commodities surged as well, many
moving to all time highs. This didn't happen only with gold
and silver. Copper, sugar, platinum, oats, wheat, and many
other commodities reacted in the same way. When the
economy staggered from the high inflation rates, and the
government restricted credit in an attempt to control
inflation, down came the commodities prices, falling well
below what should be considered their stable levels. In one
case, the public overestimated the future rate of inflation as
they endured the double-digit rates of 1974; and then when
the recession followed it, they reacted the other way,
assuming that inflation had been permanently licked. For the

amateur speculator, the public's reaction to these economic cycles offers the best bet for profits.

Approaching the market in this light, it would seem most prudent to select commodities that have the fewest number of variables, and the greatest penchant for being affected by the economy and inflation. I prefer nonfood commodities for this reason. The metals, lumber, and debt securities have the advantage of not being affected by weather and disease, which reduces the number of variables that the trader must monitor. All moves in or out of these contracts would then be determined primarily by the level of interest rates, inflation, and the public sentiment. Of secondary importance will be an assessment of the supply and demand factors for each commodity. When inflation is high, interest rates high, and the Federal Reserve is obviously moving toward easier credit policies, contracts in these commodities would be sold short. When the inflation rate has fallen, interest rates are down, and the fed begins moving toward more restrictive monetary policy, contracts would be purchased long.

A Simple Strategy

For those individuals who wish simply to buy store-of-value assets and hold them for long-run appreciation, commodity futures contracts offer some advantages over actually buying and taking delivery of the commodities. You can take the full amount of the value of the contract ($18,450 in the case of the copper contract mentioned above), give $750 of it to the brokerage house as a deposit on the contract, and put the rest into a Treasury bill or savings account. If the commodity falls in price the margin calls can be met from the savings account, and when delivery time rolls around the contract can either be sold and the money rolled into a new contract, or delivery accepted. This system eliminates the problems of sales taxes, insurance, and storage. It does leave a person with the risks of only owning a paper claim to the commodity, however, and leaves any gains fully exposed to the taxing authorities.

For the speculator, the futures market allows the chance to margin to whatever extent desired. Many brokerage houses will allow you to put a certain amount of money into a Treasury bill ($30,000 is typical) and then use that bill as collateral for deposits on the contracts. Thus, you have no actual cash up as margin, but you are earning interest on your funds all the time. If you receive any margin calls after the initial margin, however, you must meet those with cash and not from the T-bill.

The simplest strategy is to buy far-away contracts in a diversified group of commodities, let's say gold, platinum, silver, and copper, and then determine what you think the downside price risk is over the period of the contract. By keeping enough cash in reserve to meet margin calls up to the extent of what you think your greatest potential loss is, you are protected against downside fluctuations and can sit back and hold the commodities until the inflation cycle drives the price up.

One word of caution! Your broker is probably going to tout you onto buying contracts that have delivery dates no more than 60 to 90 days away, by telling you that the market for far-away contracts is very thin. Don't be misled. Since you're going to hold the contract for several months, you'll find the market increasing, and in addition, you'll stand to make your gains qualify for long-term capital gains treatment. The broker will be unhappy, of course. He only profits when contracts are traded, and stands to make much more money if you roll contracts over every two or three months. Remember, short-term traders tend to be long-term losers.

RAW LAND

Another commodity that you can purchase to store value is raw land. It is in limited supply, constant demand, provides its own storage, and is reasonably durable (assuming you're not too close to the edge of a cliff or meandering river).

Increasing population makes it seem scarcer. Its value is more difficult to determine accurately than the values of the precious metals, for its quality is inconsistent. The variables of location, soil, population movement, and the lack of a wide auction market mean that a buyer can easily pay more than the land could be resold for, while in contrast gold is quoted daily on worldwide markets. Any novice can buy gold or silver and by checking a variety of sources be assured of a price reasonably close to the general market price, while buying raw land at the right price is really a job for a good negotiator who is knowledgeable about local real estate conditions.

The greatest disadvantage of land is that its ownership is a matter of public record, and its use is subject to the whim of the government. Zoning laws can restrict its use, environmental agencies can prevent its use, and the government can demand easements or simply confiscate it under the laws of eminent domain. It's impossible to hide it from the prying eyes of the tax collector, and confiscatory taxation by the state is an ever present threat, especially when the state is in economic trouble.

If you plan to use raw land as an investment vehicle, here are a few suggestions. Don't buy land from subdividers. Land that's split up and sold by TV or fancy brochures is meant for the unsophisticated, is sold on pure emotion, and usually results in profits only for the developer. These are generally large parcels of land in areas too far out to have current value that are divided up into small parcels of land and sold for a few dollars down and a few dollars a month. Most, if not all, the money you pay down goes into the salesman's pocket, and the syndicator gets his profit from the interest and principal payments you'll make. It's unusual for the syndicator not to have his investment back from your first few payments, even though you may be stuck with a ten year contract. If your land is fifty miles beyond the outback, and you're told that prices should double within a couple of years, make an estimate of the amount of land still in the syndicator's inventory that he'll be selling to next year's customers. Then figure out how likely he'll be to buy your land back at a higher price when he still has more land to sell. Also, figure out why a buyer might want your lot when he can buy a new lot at half the price from the syndicator.

If you've decided to buy raw land, buy it from a private party and be prepared to put some time and effort into its selection. Spend a lot of time checking comparable sales in the area, buy in a semi-developed area, and don't buy on margin unless you plan to use the asset as a speculation.

One possibility that shouldn't be overlooked is the operation of some type of business on the raw land while you're holding it. The land becomes the store-of-value and the business generates enough income to pay the taxes and hopefully a profit as well. Examples would be the operation of a mobile home park or a travel trailer park on a piece of suburban land. The improvements should be minimal in cost in relation to the value of the property and could be amortized over the holding period.

I'm not going to attempt to give you the information necessary to make you successful at buying raw land or most of the other vehicles mentioned in this book. The purpose here is to acquaint you with the characteristics of each of the assets and what the relative risks and advantages are to each. In other words, to help you organize and categorize and to make comprehensible the myriad of offerings available.

ART

Certain other commodities are always mentioned when it comes to store-of-value. Artists and art dealers have played very heavily on the idea that art is a great hedge against inflation, and should be part of everyone's portfolio. It's true that works of fine art, done by artists of widely established reputation, have appreciated dramatically in value during periods of inflation. Unfortunately most of the dramatic price rises that you hear about are for great works by world renowned and usually dead artists. These works are passing through the hands of extremely knowledgeable and dedicated art connoisseurs. The unknowledgeable investor will be buying less well-known works by less well-known artists, and will be paying retail prices through art galleries. Since most galleries are working on a markup of 40%, you'll have to have a 40% appreciation in the work in order to have a gallery interested in buying it back at what you paid for it.

The idea that the average person can select art works of new and promising artists, buy them, and hold them for long term appreciation is lunacy. There is no doubt that a few of the unknown artists who are today toiling behind hot paint brushes in dimlit garages around the world will someday be discovered, and their early works will command prices hundreds of times what they sell for today. The sheer quantity of new art being produced makes finding the budding Picasso a task far more difficult than finding the proverbial needle in the haystack. Even the super-pros of the art world; those prestigious dealers who comb the art fairs, galleries, and studios around the world; who have thousands of sources constantly supplying them with examples of fresh new talent and who really know talent when they see it; even they are rarely lucky enough to come across the diamond in the raw. Your chances of buying a work from an artist at the Laguna Art Festival, or any of the thousands of galleries in New York, Chicago, or Los Angeles, and having it ever appreciate enough to be worth what you paid for it are about zero. It can be done. But it's just about as reasonable an ambition as rolling five consecutive sevens on the crap table at Las Vegas.

If you want to make money at new art, become a dealer. Don't become a collector. If you want to become a collector, do it for the sheer pleasure of the art itself, not for the money.

For those with enough money and a taste for collecting

established master works, the risks and rewards are slightly different. Inflation will probably carry the value of the works up. You must still be cognizant of your potential market for resale, however. Selling back to the galleries will mean that you'll need to have the work appreciate at least high enough that they can make their normal profit by buying back from you and reselling. Otherwise you'll have to find a buyer outside the galleries, and that is almost unheard of. Any product is worth only as much as another person is willing to pay for it, and it stands to reason that it's going to cost money to find that buyer who's willing to pay.

You should also recall that inflation is not the only risk to one's capital. Depression is also a risk. What would happen to art in a depression? It's almost certain that the market would diminish considerably. When there isn't a lot of money floating around, all of the "luxury" industries fall off, and art is certainly a luxury industry.

DIAMONDS

"It repels poisons, it disperses fears, it is a formidable defense against sorcery. It quells quarrels, is a reliable cure for lunacy and a certain remedy against possession by devils. If worn on the left arm it leads to the conquering of enemies and enables one to tame wild beasts. It is a cure for nightmares. The wearer is made courageous and bold in battle."

Or so said Leonardus in 1502, as quoted in the International Diamond Annual of 1971. And if all this isn't enough reason for you to want to buy diamonds, then you might consider the fact that they've doubled in value between 1972 and 1975. With common stocks having lost their attraction from their wild price fluctuations, and apartment houses, citrus groves, and cattle feeding ventures having duly taken their turns at impoverishing the small investor, diamonds are a good bet to become the next investment craze. My guess is that there will be almost as many disappointed investors after the diamond rush is over as there were after the gold rush; but that doesn't mean there isn't money to be made.

What They Are

Diamonds are crystals of pure carbon, formed under tremendous pressures and temperatures in deep rock formations. They are the hardest substance known and thus are the basis for much of the world's cutting industry, being used to coat the cutting blades of all manner of tools, and often used as individual cutting stones. Beyond industrial use, diamonds have taken their proper place as the king of ornaments.

The diamond, like gold, is a mineral; it is also similar in that it is composed of a single element in the chemical table of elements. In the case of gold, the only measure of value is simply the purity of the gold. In the case of diamonds, however, the value comes not from the element carbon itself, but rather from the crystalline form that carbon takes. An ounce of pure gold is the same anywhere, and is valued the same. The value of an ounce of diamonds is variable, and depending on the perfection of the crystals could be worth anywhere from $1,000 to $2,000,000.

The Diamond Market

The world production of gem quality diamonds is running an an annual rate of about 12,000,000 carats, with the geographical distribution roughly as follows:

South Africa	23%
Other African Countries	53%
Russia	21%
South America	3%

There are some mines in India and Indonesia, but the production from them is negligible in comparison to the rest of the world.

The marketing of 80% of the world's raw diamonds is handled by a single organization, a DeBeers subsidiary called the Central Selling Organization. Formed back in 1930 after wild selling battles between rival producers had driven diamond prices disasterously low, the C.S.O. has become one of the strongest and most stable cartels in the world. It controls the prices of rough diamonds by becoming a buyer of rough when the market demand falls off, and selling when the demand increases. As it handles the production of all the major producing nations on a contract basis, it can set prices to suit its aims, and its aim is to stabilize the market and develop a gradually increasing price for its products.

About ten times each year, the C.S.O. holds sales of rough diamonds in London. It invites the major diamond merchants around the world to view "sights," which are packets of rough diamonds. Each sight is specially prepared with each merchant's particular needs in mind. Their value ranges from a low of about $50,000 to over a million, with the average sight probably selling in the neighborhood of $250,000. Each merchant is given the choice of buying at the C.S.O.'s price, or declining the sight. There is no bidding, and no sorting through the stones.

The purchaser of a sight is normally either a diamond cutter or a dealer who has his own cutters. The diamonds are cut into finished stones to meet the requirements of the dealer, and from there they move down the chain toward the ultimate consumer. Once a finished diamond is offered on the retail level, its price may vary by as much as 100% from one dealer to the next. DeBeers controls the price of the rough diamonds, but from there on the markup of each handler in the chain is completely variable, and since there are many levels of merchants ranging from the large cutting house that buys directly from the C.S.O. down to the small retail jeweler, the price of a stone will depend to a great extent on the source. To be offered diamonds at "wholesale" is meaningless, since unlike gold, there is no established wholesale price for cut stones.

Quality

The diamond industry grades diamonds according to four qualities, each quality having an effect on the value of the stone. First is clarity. Clarity refers to the absence of foreign material within the stone, as well as cleavages, cracks, or other defects that might interfere with the passage of light through the stone.

Although there are various clarity scales used in different areas of the world, the most common in the United States, and the scale which should be used by investors here, is the Gemological Institute of America Scale:

$$\left.\begin{matrix} FL \end{matrix}\right\} \; - \; \text{Flawless}$$

$$\left.\begin{matrix} VVS_1 \\ VVS_2 \end{matrix}\right\} - \; \text{Very Very Small Inclusions}$$

$$\left.\begin{matrix} VS_1 \\ VS_2 \end{matrix}\right\} \; - \; \text{Very Small Inclusions}$$

$$\left.\begin{matrix} SI_1 \\ SI_2 \end{matrix}\right\} \; - \; \text{Small Inclusions}$$

$$\left.\begin{matrix} I_1 \\ I_2 \\ I_3 \end{matrix}\right\} \; - \; \text{Imperfect}$$

The second quality that is taken into consideration in grading stones is color. As in the case of clarity grading scales, there are various color grading scales used around the world. The Gemological Institute of America has the most accurate grading scale which goes from completely colorless to yellow along a scale arranged alphabetically from D through X. A, B and C are not used.

Diamonds vary in color from white or completely colorless to yellow, green, or brown. Since pure white is the most rare, it is also the most valuable and thus at the top of the grading scale. The better gem quality stones are in the white to yellow group.

The third quality that is considered in valuing diamonds is weight. Diamonds are weighed in carats (originally from the carob bean, a bean used as a measure of weight). A carat is a metric unit equal to one-fiftieth of a gram. There are roughly 140 carats to an ounce. In as much as the cuts of diamonds are standard, it is also possible to measure a diamond and thereby calculate its weight within about 5%, this method being used most frequently when the stone is mounted.

The fourth quality examined when valuing a diamond is the cut of the stone. Over the years diamond cutters have designed numerous shapes and facettings to enhance the beauty of diamonds. Since the light entering the crystal from various directions is reflected from surface to surface within the stone, the exact angular relationship and number of facets will determine the way in which light is reflected back to the eye. A properly designed stone will appear to have much more brilliance and fire than a poorly designed stone.

The most popular design is the "brilliant" cut, a design originally calculated by Marcel Tolowsky in 1919 to arrive at the maximum brilliance. Many older diamonds are cut according to different, older designs, and even though they may weigh more than a similar brilliant cut, they are much less valuable due to their diminished beauty.

Older style diamonds are frequently recut into the newer more carefully calculated designs, and even though weight may be lost in the process, the value is increased. The cut of a diamond also takes on a fashion premium. Some cuts are simply out of vogue and so are less valuable because the demand is lower.

When placing a value on a diamond, an appraiser will take into account all of the above attributes: clarity, color, carat weight, and cut; the four 'c's as they are known in the diamond trade. Since clarity and color are somewhat subjective, as is an evaluation of the cut, diamond appraising is an imperfect science. The Gemological Institute of America has worked to take the human element out of diamond appraising as much as possible by setting up a rigid set of conditions under which a diamond is examined. To this end they have established schools for would be appraisers and a set of guidelines for each of the four qualities.

Buying diamonds at the right price presents two problems to the investor. First, how can you be certain that a particular stone is a given quality? Second, assuming that you can be assured that a stone is properly classified as to color, clarity, weight and cut, how can you be certain that the price you are paying for that stone is reasonable? If you were buying gold, both of these problems would be simplified. First, the quality of gold is standard, and a simple assay will confirm the purity. Second, gold is quoted daily on a world-wide auction market, so that a phone call will tell you what premium over the standard wholesale price you'll be paying that day. Both these advantages are missing when you deal in diamonds.

Determining Quality

If you buy a diamond at your local jewelry store, then take the same stone to another jeweler and ask him to appraise it, the difference may be dramatic. The jeweler you buy it from will often upgrade the appraisal, and the jeweler you take it to will usually downgrade the appraisal. One wants to sell you the stone at the maximum profit, and the other wants to disparage its quality so that in the future you'll buy from him. This practice (called "poisoning") is quite common, so never expect to take a stone you have purchased in one place to another jeweler, even if he is a good friend, and expect an accurate valuation.

Many of the organizations that sell diamonds will offer "certificates" stating that the stone you buy is of a certain GIA grade, as appraised by a graduate of the GIA school. This can be extremely misleading. If the company selling the stone also hires the appraiser to value it, the strong tendency is for the appraiser to overvalue.

There is only one way that I know of to insure that the diamond you might buy is properly graded: that is by taking it to the GIA and having it graded by them. The Institute has set up two laboratories, one in Los Angeles, and the other in New York. For a fee of about $50 these labs will examine a stone and grade it for clarity, cut, color, and weight and will issue a certificate for the stone. Furthermore, they will describe the characteristics of the stone in the certificate carefully enough that it would be nearly impossible for the stone to be switched without an expert being able to tell that the new stone was not the one described in the certificate. By using these labs, an investor can at least insure himself that the stone he is buying is correctly graded.

How to Buy

Once the quality of a stone is established, the problem is not over. A flawless one carat stone may vary 100% in price, depending on who is selling. Finding the lowest priced dealer is a matter of shopping. First, you should determine what grade of stones you're interested in buying. If the stones are for investment rather than for ornaments, the smart buyer will be interested only in the highest quality. These will be flawless, VVS_1 or VVS_2 stones of a color grade of D, E, or F and will probably be in weights of one to three carats, since these seem to be the most popular and therefore have the widest possible resale market. The next step will be to locate dealers that can supply these stones.

You will find diamond merchants listed in the Yellow Pages of the phone books, as well as advertised in most financial newspapers. Jewelers also can supply investment diamonds.

If you ask your local jeweler to sell you a VVS_1 gem, color grade D, E, or F, in a one carat weight, he'll be delighted to comply, and will probably quote you a reasonable price.

However, as soon as you ask that the stone carry a certificate from a GIA lab attesting to the grading he'll probably get evasive. Most retailers don't like to be forced to prove their valuations. Usually one will tell you that the certificate is an extra expense that's really unnecessary, that he or his supplier will attest to the grading, and that he or his supplier is a GIA graduate and fully capable of grading the stones. If you persist, however, and make it clear that the only thing you're interested in is something carrying the laboratory certificate, a strange thing will happen. He'll make a call or two, and suddenly you'll find that the price he quoted was low, that unbeknownst to him, these stones have become more rare, and the price is much higher. What has really happened? You've forced him to offer you a diamond that is really a VVS_1 rather than one that he tells you is VVS_1. In the end, the difference will show up in the resale price that you'll be able to command for your investment, and you'll most certainly be happy you persisted.

The Value of Diamonds

To evaluate the merits of holding diamonds as an investment, it is necessary to examine the underlying forces that act upon their value. Gem diamonds are owned for only two reasons. The first is for their ornamental value. Worn as an ornament they offer beauty and prestige, while having the advantage of being almost immune to wear. The second is for their store-of-value attributes. Since the demand for ornamental diamonds has been persistent, and because the supply has been limited, they have maintained a steady value. Their supply is so limited, in fact, that a single one-carat flawless diamond weighing only a one-hundred-and-fortieth of an ounce was selling retail for as much as $8,000 in mid-1976. This makes one-carat diamonds worth nearly $1,200,000 an ounce, and larger stones of equal quality bring even higher prices on a per-carat basis. Diamonds, therefore, are one of the most condensed forms of wealth in the world, and are attractive to investors who want to hide or transport their wealth with maximum ease.

The value of diamonds is a function of their supply and demand, as is the case with all goods.

Current world production of gem quality diamonds is running at about 11 million carats, or 3 tons annually, as compared with gold, which is running at about 2000 tons.

Of the 12 million ounces of diamonds now being mined annually, only a small fraction are larger, high-quality grades.

If there were an exact correlation between gold and diamonds as store-of-value assets, then the average size and quality of diamonds would be worth about 650 times the value of an equivalent weight of gold. With gold at about $150 an ounce, diamonds would be selling at about $100,000 an ounce or $700 a carat of average quality.

The future value of the diamond depends on the future supply versus the future demand. There is obviously a fixed supply of diamonds available yet to be mined, and at some point in the future this supply will be exhausted. Yet, I'm skeptical about the argument that the diamond mines will be exhausted in 30 years and thus prices will be bound to rise. In the early 60's, Oppenheimer, the head of DeBeers, said the diamond mines would be exhausted in 8 years at those levels of production; yet production has increased and we're now 30 years from estimated exhaustion. It's erroneous to make the assumption that the presently discovered sources are an indication of the total sources that might be discovered. As more sophisticated methods of geological exploration are developed it is possible, even probable, that whole new diamond sources may be found, either under the surface of the sea or at greater depths below the surface of the ground. Furthermore, it can hardly be imagined that all the continents have been thoroughly prospected for diamond deposits. China, for example, may one day become a leading diamond producer, and the Arctic and Antarctic have yet to be explored.

The production of synthetic diamonds is also a potential source, even though at present most synthetic production is going into industrial diamonds. It has been proven that nearly flawless stones can be produced by industrial processes, and, although the current techniques are only capable of producing smaller sizes of gem-quality stones, there is reason to believe that new techniques can be developed that would make the production of larger gemstones commercially feasible. In all, the supply of new diamonds seems reasonably assured, even though the processes for their extraction and manufacture will probably remain slow and costly.

The DeBeers organization is likely to retain control of the production of diamonds, so the supply brought to market is unlikely to fluctuate drastically over the next few years. The effect of the C.S.O.'s intervention in the market is to dampen out the normal fluctuations in supply that cause the price of most commodities to rise and fall. When demand for diamonds falls due to economic conditions, the C.S.O. withholds new production thus preventing price drops, and when the demand increases they feed their stockpiles into the market. While this dampening effect stabilizes the price, in the long run it does not keep it artificially high. In the end, the demand for diamonds comes from consumers, and at any level of prices that demand is going to be fixed. Since the diamond producers profit the most from the production of diamonds at some optimum level of operations, they will not be content to hold production at artificially low levels just to maintain higher prices. Even in this cartel situation, the price tends to seek a natural level wherein the supply meets the demand.

The demand for diamonds is greatly dependent on world economic conditions. Since diamonds are a luxury, prosperity brings a greater demand. During the great depression diamond prices fell substantially. In times of economic turmoil, apart from depressions, diamonds will show increases in value based on their store-of-value properties. I

would assume that the near future will bring increasing rates
of inflation to the world, which should encourage people to
seek store-of-value assets to protect the purchasing power of
their wealth. This would bode well for diamonds.

In my own opinion, diamonds offer a reasonable chance
for an investor to hold the purchasing power of part of his
wealth. I would never advise anyone to rely totally on
diamonds as a store of value, as there are too many factors
that could work against him. But as a reasonable diversification for a portion of your investable assets, they make sense.
Depending on the personal factors of age, total assets, need
for income, etc., it seems prudent for an individual to
consider putting somewhere between 10% and 30% of the
wealth that he intends to hold in store-of-value assets into
diamonds. That is, of course, assuming he has the ability to
buy them right, and hold them safely.

Your course of action if you're interested in buying
investment quality gems should be to request a price quote
from a number of diamond merchants. Tell them you want
flawless or VVS1 grade stones of a color grade of D, E, or F,
one carat in weight, and that the stone must have an
accompanying certificate from a GIA lab.

SUMMARY

The above is only a partial list of store-of value assets. The
important thing to realize is that in these tumultuous times
you must hold a significant percentage of your wealth in the
form of real, intrinsically valuable commodities. They present
as safe a haven as is possible against the risk of inflation, and
offer protection against most other risks as well. The type
you choose will depend on your facilities for storage, your
available capital, and your areas of expertise. So learn to
recognize a store-of-value asset when you see it, and stock up
while there's still time.

LENDING

The single most popular form of putting money to work is by lending it out. As of March, 1976, individuals, partnerships, and corporations had loaned the following sums to institutions in the U.S.[22]

Commercial Banks $456,000,000,000
Life Insurance Companies $296,000,000,000
Mutual Savings Banks $114,000,000,000
Savings & Loan Companies $302,000,000,000

Total $1,168,000,000,000

That figure doesn't include money loaned by purchase of corporate and government bonds. What's remarkable about this is that the people who have placed these funds in the loan market have done so because they want security and income. But let's take a close look at the facts.

Remember that in Chapter Two we discussed the concept of true rate of return. The net return you receive for the use of your capital is the advertised or apparent rate of return less the taxes and less the loss in purchasing power caused by rising prices. In some cases it's possible to postpone or eliminate state and federal taxes, but once money is loaned out and the contract calls for repayment to the lender in legal tender currency, there is no way to overcome erosion of purchasing power due to inflation. Figure 11 lists the more common types of loans you can make, their apparent rate of return (which will vary, of course), and a hypothetical loss due to taxes. Although the tax loss is estimated at 50% of the income received, your actual loss will depend on your tax bracket. Column 6 of the chart assumes that the income from the investment is funneled into a tax deferred or tax free trust, and is the apparent rate of return less only the rate of inflation.

The rate of inflation is presented in the chart as 12% per year. I realize this is an arbitrary choice, but it represents the highest rate of the last few years, that is, the rate in 1974. Although the rates in 1975 and 1976 were significantly lower, I believe that the future will bring us back into the double-digit range and beyond. The point the chart makes is that even if your gains are subject to no tax whatsoever, you still must earn a rate equal to at least the current rate of inflation just to break even. Looking at the chart, how much of the above mentioned $1.168 trillion currently invested in loans is earning a positive rate of return for its owners? Better yet, ask yourself this question: How much of *your* money is loaned out right now and how much of it is breaking even in purchasing power?* Let's look more closely at some of the common vehicles for lending money.

LIFE INSURANCE COMPANIES

Life insurance companies borrow money from policy holders in a variety of ways. First they sell cash value life insurance. That means you're buying a term insurance policy with a mandatory savings account attached (see Chapter Four for a more detailed explanation). The insurance company will pay you somewhere between 2% and 4% interest on that account, and the tax on the income will be deferred until the cash value is withdrawn from the policy. Even without considering tax, your net loss on capital is somewhere between -8% and -10% a year at a 12% inflation rate! The life insurance company will also ask you to leave your dividends with them to accumulate at interest. Here they'll pay 4% to 5% and again your loss, not considering taxes, is -7% to -8% a year. In this case, however, the interest is taxable as accrued, which could bring your loss up to -9% to -10% annually. Life insurance companies also ask that the death proceeds of a

---

*You should not necessarily figure that just because you have your money in a tax-deferred trust, like a corporate pension or profit sharing plan, that you can completely discount taxes. When that money comes out it will be taxable, and who knows what the rates will be then?

TRUE RATE OF RETURN ON LOANS					
LOAN	APPARENT RATE OF RETURN	INFLATION	TAXES	TRUE RATE OF RETURN	TRUE RATE OF RETURN IN TRUST
Cash Value Life Insurance	3%	12%	-0-	(9%)	(9%)
Bank, Checking	0%	12%	-0-	(12%)	(12%)
Bank, Savings	6%	12%	3%	(9%)	(6%)
Savings & Loan	7%	12%	3.5%	(8.5%)	(5%)
Municipal Bonds	6%	12%	-0-	(6%)	(6%)
Corporate Bonds	10%	12%	5%	(7%)	(2%)
1st Trust Deeds	9%	12%	4.5%	(7.5%)	(3%)
2nd Trust Deeds	12%	12%	6%	(6%)	-0-
Treasury Bills	9%	12%	4.5%	(7.5%)	(3%)
Annuities	4.5%	12%	2.25%	(9.75%)	N.A.
Floating Rate Securities	11%	12%	5.5%	(6.5%)	(1%)

Figure 11

policy be left with them and they'll pay the widow or other beneficiary a monthly income, that income being a fixed rate of interest plus a portion of the capital. The rate usually is 4% to 5%, again a serious loss to you.

BANKS

Banks pay a variety of interest rates, depending on federal and state laws. On checking accounts they pay nothing, so any currency you leave in that account will cost you the entire rate of inflation. Passbook savings accounts typically pay from 5% to 6%. Assuming this interest is fully taxable, you're losing 8% a year or more, depending on your tax bracket and the real rate of inflation. In the more lucrative time certificates of deposit, if you deposit a minimum amount of money and guarantee to leave it with the bank for longer periods of time, (6 months, 1 year, 5 years, etc.) you might currently get rates as high as 12%. But even then deducting the taxes and the loss of purchasing power, you'll still find yourself losing up to -6% a year. One sidelight about bank interest rates. Banks don't depend on the level of interest rates to make a profit, for their profit comes from the spread between what they have to pay for money and what they can lend it out for. If they must pay 5% to attract money, they can lend it out for 10% and profit by the difference. As the rate of inflation continues to climb, bank interest rates will get higher and higher, simply because they must pay enough interest to attract depositors and depositors won't be willing to leave money on deposit at a rate of return lower than the rate of inflation. At least not for long.

An example of this is seen in Brazil. In an interesting article in *The Journal of Money Credit and Banking*, Mr. Antonio M. Silviera pointed out that Brazil has had an average rate of inflation of over 30% a year for over 20 years![23] Interest rates likewise kept pace with inflation, climbing to an astronomical 35% a year. Interestingly, Brazil has usury laws as we have in the U.S., but they are easily circumvented:

"The explanation for the extremely low level of the stated prime rate in Brazil lies in two laws, the usury law and the gold clause law, both promulgated in 1933. The usury law fixed an upper bound of 12 percent per year on all interest rates. And the gold clause law "forbade contractual payments except in domestic currency at its legal value," i.e., monetary correction was outlawed. But the banks were able to circumvent the ceiling to a large extent. This was done mainly by charging a "service fee," a rate which in no way differs from the interest rate."

You can't expect to be able to borrow money in an inflating economy at less than the rate of inflation, unless you're borrowing from unsophisticated lenders, and lenders tend to gain sophistication as time goes on. The banks, savings and loans, and life insurance industries are borrowing now at ridiculous rates from a public unfamiliar with hyperinflation. This can't last. As you watch the interest rates go up at your neighborhood bank, don't be misled into thinking you're profiting because of the high rates. They're going up because the rate of inflation is going up, and you're in no more of a position to profit than you were when the rates were 2% or 3% a year.

SAVINGS AND LOANS

The $300 billion in savings and loan associations (formerly called "building and loans") indicates a strong trust in these institutions. Most people, however, don't understand how they work and how they make a profit, let alone what risks are involved in depositing money with them. Unlike banks, they are unable to leverage their deposits. If you deposit $10,000 in a savings and loan, that money will be loaned out on a long-term mortgage. They'll pay you about 5% to 8% on your money while it's on deposit and will try to earn 12% or more on that money by lending it to property owners.* Laws vary from state to state, but generally savings and loans must keep at least 5% of their net assets in liquid securities such as government bonds. The other 95% can be loaned out on mortgages. In their advertising on radio and television, they mention only their assets when talking of the safety and strength of their organization. "Four billion dollars strong" sounds mighty reassuring, until you find out that their liabilities are $4 billion also. Since almost all the money you deposit with them is loaned out on real estate mortgages, their position in the event of a serious recession is tenuous. If an economic collapse occurs, you'd better get to your local savings and loan before that 5% liquid capital is used up. In the event of a serious collapse it is likely many people will be unable to continue making mortgage payments. During the great depression thousands of building and loan companies closed their doors and depositors' losses amounted to hundreds of millions of dollars.

Even without considering the risks involved in the event of a depression, how about the rate of return on your capital? Figure 11 shows that if you're in a high tax bracket, your net annual *loss* on your capital will be about 8% at a 12% inflation rate. Not so good, everything considered.

U.S. GOVERNMENT SECURITIES

The United States Government and its various agencies issue a number of different types of securities. These fall under the category of bonds, although they are called by a variety of names. They include U.S. Treasury Bills, Notes, Bonds, and Certificates and Securities issued by instrumentalities of the U.S. Government such as Fanny Mae (Federal National Mortgage Association), FHDA (Farmers Home Administration), The Federal Land Bank, and Federal Home

---

*While the mortgage rate on a piece of real estate may only be 9%, the loan points, fees, and prepayment penalties bring up the net take substantially.

Loan Bank. These instrumentalities issue notes or debentures, or guarantee them for other issuers. The difference between these securities is primarily one of yield and duration.

If the choice is between a savings and loan account at 6% and a Treasury bill at 7% or 8%, then certainly the T-bill is better buy. It's far more secure and a better return. But it's still not good enough in hyperinflation. While the principle is secure, how can you afford the loss in purchasing power?

BONDS

When a corporation wants to borrow money, it issues corporate bonds. These are simply promises to repay a given amount of money at a given time in the future, and to pay interest at a specified rate until the bond is redeemed.

The price or value of a bond is a function of the strength of the issuing company and the general level of interest rates. For example, a Company sells you a $1,000 bond maturing in 20 years at a time when the general interest rate for that particular quality of bond is 8%. As interest rates rise a person looking for interest bearing securities would have a choice between a new bond issue yielding say 10%, and buying your bond from you which is only yielding 8%. To induce him to buy your bond, you'll have to offer it to him at a discount, and that discount will be calculated to make his investment yield him the 10% rate that the market is offering. Your bond might offer a couple of pluses however, one being that it is "seasoned," or has established a history of prompt payment of interest, and secondly, by buying at a discount, that is by paying only $800 for your bond, he is assured of a capital gain of $200 when the bond is redeemed at maturity. Usually the tax benefit of this potential capital gain is calculated into the discount on the bond and his current yield will be something less than the 10% that might be available on a new issue.

As to risk of loss of principal, it is unlikely that a well selected bond portfolio will suffer substantial losses due to the bankruptcy of the issuing companies. Companies do go bankrupt, of course, but even then the bondholders are first in line after the creditors and before the stockholders to benefit from the liquidation of the assets. A wide diversification and prudent selection of risks would make chances of loss of capital negligible. The real problems will come with runaway inflation, for history reveals that in the past bondholders have suffered the same fate as all holders of debt instruments; total loss of purchasing power of the principal. Even if we don't slide into runaway inflation the loss on 8% or 10% yields, especially if the yield is taxable, is enough to be significant. It takes the investment out of the category of "sound" or "prudent" and guarantees that if you keep it long enough, you'll be a sure loser.

Municipal Bonds

Municipal bonds differ only slightly from corporate or federal bonds. They are issued by states and municipalities and are backed either by the taxing authority of the municipality (general obligation bonds) or by the revenue from some project like a turnpike (revenue bonds). The single characteristic that differentiates them from other bonds is that the income is free of federal and sometimes state income tax. This means that the true rate of return is proportionately higher than on a corporate or federal bond. One of the more misleading advertisements regarding tax-free municipal bonds has to do with the rate of return realized by a high-tax-bracket investor. Sales organizations working with municipal bonds will frequently produce tables showing that if you're in a 70% tax bracket the yield of a 5% municipal bond is the equivalent of a 16.7% yield if that yield were taxable. Unfortunately you'll have a hard time compounding your money at 16.7% with these bonds even if you're in that tax bracket. The compounding will still take place at 5% (or whatever the bond is yielding), and the true rate of return will still be calculated by subtracting the current rate of inflation from the apparent rate of return. Municipal bonds generally have lower yields than corporate bonds of an equivalent quality, because the market is willing to pay more for them due to their tax-free qualities.

One further caution, although this might seem obvious to some. Never put municipal bonds into a tax-deferred pension, profit-sharing, or Keogh plan. If you did, the yield would eventually become taxable, as all gains in these plans are taxed on distribution. If you want bonds in a plan, buy the higher yielding corporate or federal securities.

Bond Funds

One vehicle for buying bonds is the bond fund. These are professionally managed portfolios of bonds, and they can be either open-end or closed-end type mutual funds. The advantages of buying bonds through these funds is as follows:

1. *A broader diversification of bonds can be purchased with a small amount of money.* The bond portfolio of the fund may contain two or three hundred different issues and each shareholder owns a proportionate share of each bond.
2. *There is no coupon clipping to do.* Managers of the fund take care of clipping the coupons and mailing away for the interest on each bond as the interest becomes due. Then they mail one monthly or quarterly check to each shareholder.
3. *You can conveniently reinvest the interest* you receive on your bonds in more shares of the bond fund, thus making the compounding of that interest simpler. It is difficult to take small interest checks from your individual bonds and buy more bonds.
4. *You don't have to worry about the custody of the bonds themselves.*

The disadvantage of the bond funds is that they charge a management fee (and in some cases an entrance fee) that you wouldn't pay if you were buying individual issues.

MORTGAGES AND TRUST DEEDS

Another method of lending out money at a high rate of return is by lending it to an individual or a company, and taking in return the deed to a piece of property as collateral for the loan. Since the deed is held in trust until the loan is repaid, it is said to be a trust deed. When an owner has borrowed against the property and signed over a first deed of trust, he may borrow again and issue a second deed of trust. The second trust deed is more risky and generally offers a higher yield in return for the increased risk. A trust deed can be sold at a discount by a holder who wishes to get rid of it rather than hold it to maturity. A buyer could thus get a higher yield by paying less than the face value of the trust deed. Mortgages or trust deeds are favorite investments of life insurance companies, as well as savings and loans. Inasmuch as these institutions collect points, prepayment penalties, and other fees, the effective rate of interest is higher than the rate indicated on the note.

REAL ESTATE INVESTMENT TRUSTS

An individual interested in lending money with property as collateral has the choice of buying trust deeds individually or investing in a pooling fund of trust deeds. These go under the name of mortgage Real Estate Investment Trusts (REITs), a relatively new vehicle whose assets have grown to about $20 billion from only $1 billion in the past few years.

There are two types of real estate investment trusts; equity and mortgage. Equity REITs invest directly in the ownership of real estate, while the mortgage REITs invest in mortgages on real estate. Typically the REIT will raise public funds, then borrow from commercial lending sources as heavily as possible and invest the entire amount in mortgages. The spread between the cost of the money they borrow and the return they receive from the higher yielding mortgages is added to the profit of the shareholders. Assuming this yield rises above what the market in general is paying for borrowed funds, the value of the shares of the REIT should rise in the market. This was the experience during the period from 1969 through 1972, but recently the picture has begun to change. A slump in the construction industry caused by tight money, inflation, and material shortages, coupled with business recession and tenant defaults, has caused havoc in the mortgage REIT community. Without the mortgage payments coming in to meet their own payments on the money they borrowed, many have been unable to meet their commitments when due, which in turn has led to suspended dividends to shareholders and plummeting share prices. When lured by the high returns offered by REITs, think carefully about the real risks involved in this type of leverage.

SUMMARY

The foregoing descriptions of places you can lend your money is not intended to be complete. You must be able to identify something as a loan, understand the risks involved, and calculate the true rate of return. Looked at rationally, there is little way a person can lend out money in an inflationary economy and come out ahead; it is almost a certain loss. The loss is gradual, almost unnoticed in many cases. If you lend out $1,000 and get back $1,500 later, it *seems* as though you're doing well, even if you have to give $250 to Uncle Sam. But the valid way to look at the transaction is not how many dollars do I have, but how much purchasing power. As time and the economy progress, you're going to find that purchasing power fading in frightening leaps. The rational position to take is that times have changed. What used to be conservative money management is today suicide. Stay away from debt securities. When you sell a piece of property and are tempted to take back a note for part of the purchase price, try another negotiation to get the cash, even if it's discounted. When someone tells you about the "fantastic" 10% yield on a bond or bank account, give him a short course in true rate of return technology. In other words, *get out of legal tender.*

EQUITIES

THE STOCK MARKET

You must have the impression by now that everything in your life that has to do with accumulating wealth relates to inflation. You'll continue to experience this truth; fiat money is the arch-enemy of financial security. As we begin to talk about the stock market, the spectre of inflation will again haunt every decision you make and influence the future of all the stocks you buy. Let's examine how the market-place, and thus the stocks of businesses that comprise the marketplace, react to the introduction of fiat money.

The market place is composed of the producers of goods, the distributors of goods, and the consumers of goods. In order to have a high standard of living, someone must produce the items that are to be consumed. Since the producer has only one reason for this production, and that is to make a profit, all his business decisions will be based on estimates of how his decisions will affect profits. In turn, the stockholder is relying on the correctness of the decisions of the operator of the company, owing to their effect on the price of the stock and the dividends.

With what factors must the businessman cope when making market decisions? There are three major inputs into the producer: *materials, labor,* and *capital.* Using these inputs, the producer assembles his product and offers it to the consumer on a supply-demand basis. If inflation is going to affect the producer and his profits (and thus the value of the shares of his business), it must come through one or all of the inputs mentioned.

Material

The companies and individuals supplying the raw materials and components to a producer are in themselves producers.

The effects of inflation on them are the same as on the producer, but still they pass on the effects once again. As the money supply is inflated, the costs of materials rise. This causes difficulties in planning for the producer and, consequently, his risk of failure increases. If he doesn't price his end product correctly he may find himself in red ink when the materials cost increases.

Labor

Labor is another form of material supplied to the producer. In an inflationary economy, the labor market demands higher and higher wages to offset increased living costs, without exchanging more time or efficiency in their operation. In a simple society the only reason wages would rise would be if the productive ability of the individual laborer increased. Consequently, he would never find it necessary to strike for higher wages. His standard of living would be increasing without an increase in wages, due to the ability of technology to produce more and more consumer goods with the same amount of human labor.

A society without labor strife would reward its citizens with a higher standard of living, since every day a laborer is off work due to a strike (or working at less than full capacity resulting from a feeling that he's not getting what he's worth), less goods are available. The disruption of the labor force by inflation leads to similar problems for the producer as those caused by rising costs and interrupted supplies from his materials suppliers.

Capital

The producer must go to the capital market to fund his business expansion. In an inflationary society the producer offsets many of the negative effects of increasing prices for supplies and labor by a higher degree of production efficiency, and this he achieves through an ever expanding investment in the improvement of his productive mechanism.

He absorbs a great deal of the increasing costs of materials and labor through this means so that he doesn't have to pass these costs on to the consumer. But somewhere along the line the cost of these improvements must be paid for, and this is done either through borrowing or by selling off part of the business. Even in a noninflationary society this process of expansion exists, and there is constant demand for money to supply the expansion of the producers. As inflation proceeds, it becomes more and more risky to be an entrepreneur and produce, it becomes more and more difficult to plan expansion and make it profitable, and more and more difficult to predict future sales and profits. Since the profits of business fluctuate due to inflation, the returns on capital fluctuate as well.

The investors, seeking to put their capital to work in a way that will overcome inflation, look at a business with more than an eye to the annual dividend. They want interest on the use of their money; but more than that, they want the value of their original capital to be protected against the depreciating effects of inflation. That the company continues to pay the same dividend every year becomes less important than that it begins to expand its operations and thus its *future potential earnings.* A company that simply earns 10% a year on its invested capital will not be attractive to the investor. His drive for growth is a result of subtle forces: like the inability to make an ever-increasing income raise his standard of living as much as it seems it should; or watching and hearing stories of great speculative successes. Even current tax laws, which tax dividends at a less favorable rate than capital appreciation, add to this search for "growth" companies. The producers, if they want to attract capital, must show an increasing expansion, a dynamic growth. This means taking risks and expanding into an unknown, unpredictable future.

Borrowing for investment is a logical phenomenon that accompanies all inflations. The investor, sensing the increasing prices of almost everything, recognizes that he can borrow money today at interest rates that seem to lag behind the pace of inflation, save half the cost of interest through taxes, and thus leverage his profits just on the basis of rising prices. Borrowing becomes psychologically easy because he knows his wages are going up, and that should give him the surplus to meet the new debts. More money feeding into the capital market must find a place to grow, and its availability creates a supply of entrepreneurs willing to start new businesses. Like a self-fulfilling prophecy, the search for growth companies stimulates the development of growth companies.

The periods of the 1920's and 1960's in this country are good examples of this phenomenon. The demand for growth stocks created a flood of new issues. Hardly was a new company formed with any name that indicated growth industry that the stock wasn't over-subscribed before it hit the street. The prices doubled and tripled on these new issues without the buyers as much as knowing the products the company would make, let alone the quality of the management or their ability to operate a long-term, profit-making enterprise. Just the word "new issue" was all that was necessary.

So the cycle runs on. The businessman, in order to get capital, must offer growth. The capital, in order to survive, must seek growth. Growth means risk, and the market seems to build in its own downfall. But while it's going on no one can seem to lose, and speculation becomes the craze. There is no better example of this inflation-caused sequence of events than the experience of France in the period immediately following the French revolution. Andrew Dickson White, in his book *Fiat Money Inflation in France*, described the phenomenon:

> "A still worse outgrowth [of the currency inflation] was the increase of speculation and gambling. With the plethora of paper currency in 1791 appeared the first evidences of that cancerous disease which always

> follows large issues of irredeemable currency—a di-
> sease more permanently injurious to a nation than
> war, pestilence or famine. For at the great metro-
> politan centers grew a luxurious, speculative, stock-
> gambling body, which like a malignant tumor,
> absorbed into itself the strength of the nation and
> sent out its cancerous fibres to the remotest hamlets.
> At these city centers abundant wealth seemed to be
> piled up: in the country at large there grew a dislike
> of steady labor and a contempt for moderate gains
> and simple living."[24]

As freshly printed money continues to flow into the capital
market, as well as into the hands of the consumers who
create the demand for the end products, a structure of
instability is created. The slightest constriction of credit and
the marginal businesses—those entrepreneurs that really
weren't suited and qualified to start businesses (and wouldn't
have been able to get the capital to do so in an economy
where those funds would have to come from the hard earned
savings of a producer)—will fall; consumer demand for all
products will taper off; and even the well-run businesses will
falter as their inflation-induced expansion plans become
unprofitable. Remember the go-go stocks of the sixties and
the growth-by-acquisition conglomerates? The whole thing
adds up to that misunderstood phenomenon called the
business cycle. Evidence is now almost overwhelming that
monetary inflation leads to the business cycle, and consequently to the cyclical nature of the stock market.
Inflation of the money supply leads to business boom, and
business recession; the amplitude of the market swings
increases as the inflation progresses. Since monetary inflation
cannot seem to reverse itself once the policy of fiat money is
established, greater and greater issues of currency are
required to sustain the distortions, much as greater and
greater amounts of a drug are needed to produce a high, until
the economy is totally hooked and the only way out is the
pain of withdrawal or death. Constantino Bresciana-Turroni

in his book *The Economics of Inflation*[25] described the consequences of a rapidly inflating money supply on the capital market in Germany in 1920 and 1921:

> "It was observed in Germany, as also, indeed, elsewhere, that the circle of speculators was greatly enlarged. Shares were held by speculators in a much larger measure than formerly, when they for the most part had been held longer by investors, who considered them as permanent investments. But in 1920 and 1921 shares passed rapidly from hand to hand, and oscillations of their prices were much more frequent and more violent than formerly . . . It was in the autumn of 1921 that business on the German Bourse reached such a condition as to put in the shade even the classical examples of the most violent fever of speculation."

Anyone who has been confused by the movements of stock prices on the U.S. exchanges over the past ten years could well understand them in light of the experiences of other countries that have undergone inflation.

We had a period of rather sustained upward growth in prices from 1959 to 1965. Now the oscillations have begun. No real forward movement any longer, just up and down to nowhere.

I think that one of the most damaging and most costly illusions that has ever been accepted by the American public is the concept that the stock market will go up and up forever. Almost all mutual fund sales literature has pushed graphs of the past, mountain charts as they call them, which showed the growth of the value of the shares of the mutual funds over the last twenty, thirty, or forty years. The insinuation was clear; that trends tend to continue and the great productive power of the United States industrial machine would cause stock prices to continue that upward spiral forever. Millions of people, believing the charts, and believing the fervent sales pitch of the brokerage industry, have been whiplashed into poverty by the violent market fluctuations of the past few years. Yet very few really understood why that growth trend did not continue, and many still have faith it will start again.

The Future

We are at a point where the past cannot repeat itself. The action of the stock market over the next twenty years will *not* be a repeat of the past: it will most certainly follow the classical lines of the capital market of every past society that has seen fit to plunder the future through inflation of the money supply.

What is the most probable course of market action over the next year? Over the next five years? Over the next 20 years? The market in general will be responsive to the real profitability of the companies whose stock makes up the market. And the profitability of these companies will depend on the economic course of the nation as a whole. If we make the assumption that the bureaucrats who make the laws and determine the extent to which the money supply is expanded will continue to make the same mistakes as in the past; that is, that they will continue to spend more money on social programs than they are able to collect in taxes, that they will continue to try to solve business recession by expansion of bank credit, that they will continue to react to inflation by blaming the businessman and the consuming public, and therefore slap more and greater controls on the producers to hold prices in line; then we can make some further assumptions about the future course of the capital market.

1. It will become difficult to isolate the true profits of the companies studied.
2. Profits will be harder to obtain due to increased costs of operation (i.e., increased accounting and legal costs as businessmen try to cope with mounting control programs). Although it will be more and more difficult to make real profits, many companies will appear to be making profits

when they are not. They'll be able to do that by camouflaging (perhaps unwittingly) the true costs of depreciating equipment, by not anticipating the future increased costs of supplies and labor, and by not properly anticipating the current effects of inflation.

3. Producers will find it harder and harder to predict obtainability of the supplies and materials they need.

4. Shortages, rationing, and black markets will be common byproducts of the bureaucratic interference with the producers' free market.

You might look at this whole mess something like a chicken coop full of laying hens. While they are supplied with the things they need (water and feed) and left alone, they produce at maximum efficiency. But let their supplies become sporadic; go in periodically and try to shake an extra egg out of one and stop another from laying; let a fox loose in the coop; and you'll have total chaos. Egg production will go down. The producers of the products we consume will be no different. Let the government bureaucrats threaten their very lives with antitrust suits, confiscatory taxes, mandatory racial mixes of employees, price controls, and wage controls; and you *must* have lower production, higher costs, and a lower standard of living for everyone.

To Market, To Market

Let's look at the alternative methods of investing in common stocks:

1. Buy stocks and hold them for the long pull.

2. Trade common stocks, selling those that stop performing as growth stocks and rebuying others. Try to outguess the market but stay invested in stocks.

3. Buy a portfolio of stocks as the market in general appears to be in a rising phase, and sell the entire

portfolio when the market appears ready to
decline.

You must, in cases one and two, be able to select the best
individual companies from the thousands available, and you
must believe in a long-term rising market. In case number
three you must have some system for determining when the
market is rising and falling. In other words, the *issue* and the
cycle.

Selecting the Issue

There are approximately 2000 stocks listed on the New
York Stock Exchange, 1250 on the American Exchange, and
2700 on the national over the counter. Add in the regional
exchanges and over-the-counter stocks and the total comes to
something over 10,000.

The prices of each of these stocks varies according to the
potential buyer's assessment of what other buyers might be
willing to pay in the future. Factors that go into determining
future worth are:

1. Financial condition of the company.
2. Ability of the management team.
3. Present and estimated future competitive position
    of the company's product in the market.
4. Future earnings of the company.
5. An estimate of the future course of the market in
    general.

One of the first considerations is the reliability of the inputs
used for selecting the stock. There is a tremendous bias
present throughout the industry. The owners and managers
of a corporation have a vested interest in seeing that the price
of that stock rises. All financial statements to whatever
extent possible will always be slanted toward the positive. All
news releases will be edited to be as favorable as possible.
Everyone involved has a direct monetary interest in making
that company and its future look good.

Next in line comes the brokerage house that sells the stock. How much of the stock is held by the brokerage firm for its own account? How much has been sold to favored customers in the past? How much is held by the officers and friends of officers in the firm? All these factors will most certainly influence the statements and recommendations made by a firm to its brokers, and after all, a broker working for a brokerage firm usually takes his recommendations from the people for whom he works. If he doesn't, then his recommendations must be the result of his own investigations into the value of the stock. What are his inputs? Has he the time to personally investigate the company, its management, the market for its products, etc.? Probably not.

I certainly don't believe that everyone involved is bound to pass on erroneous information to serve his own interests, but the bias that *must* be injected into this system by the personal interests of the people involved *tends* to lead the investor down the wrong paths. When looking for outside advice, there are two questions that must be answered (whether that advice is about a medical problem, an engineering problem, or an investment decision): is the advisor knowledgeable, and is the advisor self-interested. If he tends to profit more from giving one recommendation than another, the tendency will be to give the one that's most profitable. All the investment areas that might be profitable for the investor but aren't remunerative for the broker are left unexplored and undeveloped. Brokers aren't dishonest, they are blinded by self-interest; a natural human frailty.

If you're going to select an individual stock, whose advice do you take? My personal view, after having been involved directly in the capital market for many years, is that the average individual is not able to make rational informed decisions about individual stocks whether his advice comes from himself or his stock broker. To do so on his own would mean he would have to have access to reliable information about the affairs of the companies, the industries in which they operate, and the economic outlook as a whole.

From your standpoint as an investor, you must steer a course around these pitfalls, and the best way to do that is by taking your advice from someone who does not tend to profit from the investment he makes for you, but only from being right in that advice.

It's unfortunate that the regulatory bodies that are charged with protecting the public from the abuses of unethical practioners set up rules and regulations that preclude the ethical practitioner from being properly compensated. For example, if there is a mutual fund for sale and the commission rate that that fund pays to the salesman is 8%, the investment advisor either must take a fee for his services and forego the commission, or take a commission and forego the fee. He can't take a commission and rebate it to the buyer, which is what he should do. So if you want to pay a fee to an advisor, you'll wind up paying a commission to someone else, whether you like it or not. The result is that the investor avoids the fee advisor and takes his advice from the commissioned salesman. Once you start buying from him, how can he be objective about his advice if his entire income depends on the number of trades you make?

The point is clear. If you want advice, don't seek it from a salesman. He'll steer you to his own product. Seek it from an independent advisor, someone who will stand to benefit if the advice is sound and will stand to lose if the advice is unsound. About the only person you probably know who fills this bill is yourself, and more likely than not, you're unqualified to render the advice to yourself. You have the integrity to treat yourself honestly, but you may not have the knowledge. If you refuse to take the time to make yourself knowledgeable, then the next best step would be to find an advisor and arrange to pay him provided his advice is correct and collect damages from him if it's not.

The closest thing to both knowledgeability and coincidence of interest would be a managed account in which an

independent advisor, for a fee, advises which stocks to buy
and sell, and when to buy and sell. Make sure there is no
opportunity for that person to benefit by recommending one
stock over another or by churning the account. Furthermore,
there should be some relationship between the performance
of the recommended stocks and the income to the advisor
(the idea of having the advisor be penalized if performance is
not up to standard would be best, even though illegal).
Obviously positive or negative remuneration based on the
performance of the portfolio will not guarantee results, but
its effect would be to weed out the advisors that weren't
competent, as they wouldn't be able to make a living and
would quickly migrate to other occupations.

Managed Portfolios

Since one of the most logical (at least in my opinion)
methods of investing in the stock market is through hiring an
independent advisor and paying him for selecting individual
stock issues, the managed portfolio might be one of the more
practical avenues to consider. The theory behind a managed
portfolio is that a group of people with more or less similar
financial objectives pool their money and hire a portfolio
manager. Due to the large amount of money available, the
portfolio manager is able to hire a staff of people. These
might include financial analysts that would concentrate on
studying the various industry groups, chartists that would
plot the movements of individual securities, selling and
buying order specialists that would assure the best prices
once a stock selection was made.

Assuming that the manager was remunerated based on a
flat fee (most mutual funds charge their shareholders
somewhere between 1/10th of 1% and 1½% of the average
asset value of the fund per year as a management fee), then
his advice should be relatively objective. Without a doubt it's
far more objective than taking the same stock recommendations from someone who was compensated based on

the number of sales and purchases within the portfolio. Additionally, by pooling resources, a great deal more weight can be swung in the investment world. Doors open for access to inside information far more readily when an investor is representing $10,000,000 than when he's representing $10,000. Furthermore, access to the more sophisticated tools of stock analysis (such as computers) is certainly limited to the big spenders. Assuming you feel that you'd like to pool your funds with those of others and hire a portfolio manager, there are several alternatives available.

Bank Trusts: Bank trusts operate in a manner similar to mutual funds. The bank hires portfolio managers to buy and sell common stocks and other securities for its common trust fund. Many banks will set up several different funds, each catering to the particular needs of its clients, such as a growth fund, an income fund, etc. Unlike the mutual funds, the historical data about the performance of these funds is not as easy to come by, and is not available on a daily basis in your local newspaper. Additionally, by reason of their affiliation with the bank, these funds are attractive to unsophisticated widows and orphans whose money was left through wills naming the bank as trustee. The banks' byword is conservatism; they would far rather forego a potential profit than risk a loss. This may be prudent management in an economy that doesn't suffer from the inflation rampant in this country, but today, limiting oneself to preservation of the original capital means certain loss. The bank gets paid whether the individual makes a profit or not, and since the typical investor in a bank trust never pays much attention to the comparative results of the trust versus other managed portfolios, the banker feels the safest route is the route of no growth and no apparent loss. Bank trusts in general should be avoided.

Investment Advisors: There are quite a number of investment advisors who will manage money in the market for a fee. In these cases you commit a certain amount of capital (the minimums vary from advisor to advisor, with the lowest being about $10,000, but the average minimum being closer to $50,000), and the advisor then purchases stock for you in your name. Thus, you own a series of individual issues. In theory the advisor tailors the portfolio to suit your individual needs and preferences. He may submit recommendations to you for your approval prior to purchase, or may have discretion to buy and sell as he sees fit.

Technically, this concept is preferable to the idea of a bank trust, but the problems are that, unless you have a great deal of capital, you can't diversify very well, and there is usually no reliable record available to indicate how well the advisor has done in the past. It should be obvious that most advisors don't tailor accounts exactly to the specifications of the individuals involved, but must lump investors into categories such as need for growth, conservation of capital, etc. Calculating the fee an advisor would get from an account of say $25,000 (which might amount to $250 a year) would tell you that he really couldn't afford to pay too much attention to your particular problems. Since these accounts are not bound by as strict rules for accounting, record keeping, etc., as are more public vehicles like mutual funds, you will never know how badly he may have managed other clients' funds. Additionally, there is opportunity for an independent advisor to take under-the-table kickbacks from the brokers through which he places his buy and sell orders. This would create the conflict of interest that you are trying to avoid.

Mutual Funds: The third category of managed portfolios is the mutual fund. Today there are over 500 mutual funds in operation, including open-end funds, closed-end funds, and duo-funds. Since a mutual fund is a logical investment vehicle, I'm going to take some time to explain how they function, and how to avoid some of the more common pitfalls of investing in them.

An open-end mutual fund is a pool of shareholders' money

invested in a portfolio of securities at the discretion of the manager of the fund. The structure and sequence of events is diagrammed in Figure 12. Shareholders contribute to the pool and receive shares in return proportionate to their relative investment. In other words, if 1,000 investors each invested $1,000 there would be a total contribution of $1,000,000. If the fund initially decided to price its shares at $10 then they would issue 10,000 shares and each investor would receive 100 shares. As new shareholders were added new shares would be issued, but the addition or deletion of new shareholders *would not in itself change the share price of the fund.* For example, if another 1,000 investors contributed another $1,000 apiece the fund would simply issue an additional 10,000 shares at $10 a share and each shareholder would own the same proportionate share of the total assets of the fund.

The money is not sent directly to the manager of the fund, but rather the manager selects an independent trustee, usually a major bank or trust company, and this trustee receives and cares for the money, for which it is paid a fee, of course. The fund management has no immediate access to the funds and merely instructs the trustee as to the stocks it should buy and sell. When the trustee places a purchase order, the stock certificates are returned to it, and it holds them in safekeeping.

When dividends are received, the trustee deducts the costs of administration, as well as the management fee for the management company, and the balance is sent to the shareholders as a taxable distribution. When the management company directs the trustee to sell a stock held in the portfolio, that stock is sold and the proceeds are reinvested or held in interest-bearing securities at the direction of the managers of the fund. If a gain is realized on the sale of a stock held by the fund, that gain is distributed to the shareholders of the fund on a prorata basis. It is identified as a capital gain distribution and is reportable on the share-

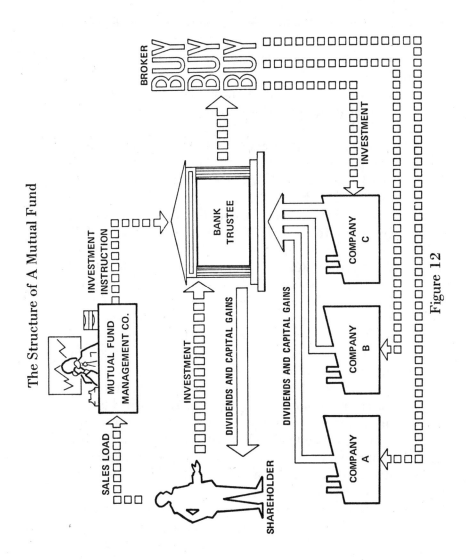

The Structure of A Mutual Fund

Figure 12

holders' tax returns as such. Usually a cash reserve is
maintained by the funds with which to meet shareholder
redemptions. When a shareholder wishes to cash out, he sends
in his certificates to the fund, they are retired, and he
receives a check for his proportionate share of the net assets
of the fund on the day of redemption.

There are several categories of mutual funds to choose
from.

1. Open-End Load Funds: These are standard
mutual funds that charge a fee for buying into the
fund. Usually this fee is 8½% of the total cost of the
fund shares, which amounts to 9.3% of the money
you pay to the fund. Thus if you buy a share that has
a net asset value of $10.00, you'll pay $10.93, with
the 93 cents being 8½% of the $10.93. This fee will
usually drop as larger amounts are invested until it
gets down to about 1% for investments of $1,000,000
or more.

2. No-Load Funds: These are funds which act just
like the load funds but charge little or no fee for
buying in. When you buy a share it is at net asset
value, which is determined by adding up the total
assets of the fund at the end of the trading day and
dividing by the number of shares outstanding. The
load paid to a load fund is normally disbursed to the
sales organization to compensate the commission
salesman. No-load funds have no salesmen, but rely
on newspaper and other advertising to sell shares.
Although they tend to be smaller in size than the load
funds, and there are fewer of them, their performance
does not seem to be adversely affected by their lack
of commissioned salesmen.

3. Closed-End Funds: Most of the funds on the
market are so-called open-end investment companies.
Open-end refers to the continuous sale and redemption of shares by the fund. A closed-end fund is

a pool of investors' money the same as the open-end fund, but in this case the fund issues a fixed number of shares and then closes off the sale. Nor does it redeem shares from shareholders should they desire to liquidate their holdings. A shareholder who wishes to sell must find an outside buyer, just as must the holder of shares in an individual corporation. Shares in closed-end funds, therefore, are sold through brokerage houses and these companies are usually listed as over-the-counter stocks.

Since sale of shares and purchase of shares after the fund has ceased selling is done at arm's length between two investors, the shares do not necessarily sell for net asset value but will normally sell at a premium or a discount. This means that if a fund holds shares of stock valued at $1,000,000 and is selling at a 15% discount, you could buy all the shares of the fund for $850,000. Closed-end funds frequently sell at discounts up to 30% of net asset value. Most brokers don't push closed-end funds because they carry commissions at the same rate that individual stocks do, rather than the more attractive load-fund rates.

4. **Dual Purpose Funds:** These are a variation on the closed-end funds in which there are two classes of shares. Initially half the shares of the fund are sold as preferred or income shares, and half sold as capital or equity shares. The income shares receive all the dividend income from the stocks held in the portfolio, and the capital shares receive all the capital gains. Thus, if the income investors put up half the capital, they get double the income they normally would, while the capital shares receive double the capital gains they normally would. These funds are usually set up to close out and redeem all shares at asset value at some predetermined date in the future.

Thus, even though the shares may be currently selling
at a discount, the buyer can be assured the discount
will be eliminated if he holds the shares to maturity.

Most actively traded mutual funds are listed daily in the
Wall Street Journal and most major newspapers around the
country. Open-End funds are listed under Mutual Funds, and
there are separate headings for Closed-End Funds and
Dual-Purpose Funds. No-load funds can be distinguished in
the open-end fund listing by looking at the two prices listed.
If the Net Asset Value (NAV) and the Asked or Purchase
(Prc.) price are the same, then it's a no-load.

If you believe that you're not qualified to select individual
issues, and that you probably can't find a broker that will
objectively handle that chore for you, yet you want to use
the stock market as a vehicle for your equity assets, then a
mutual fund is probably for you.

Strategies

Assuming you study the variety of funds available and
choose one that seems best suited, then you arrive at the
decision of what strategy you'll use—when to buy and when
to sell. As mentioned earlier, there are three basic strategies
that can be used.

**1. Buy and hold for the long pull, adding new
money as it becomes available:** This strategy would
have worked admirably for you had you started into
mutual funds thirty or forty years ago. Hardly a fund
in existence for that time would have done less than
12% a year compounded. Unfortunately history and
common sense economics would indicate that those
days are gone forever. The person who invests in this
manner today may find his total assets twenty years
from now less than the total money he has invested
along the way.

2. Try to find the "hot" fund. When it gets cold,
switch to another. This strategy implies that you can
find that hot fund, and that you can determine when

it's getting cold. There are a variety of theories that have been developed to do just that. Richardson and Roebuck put out a booklet called *Choosing a Mutual Fund for Maximum Growth.*[26] They developed four guideposts for this task as follows:

Guidepost No. 1: For maximum growth, invest in a mutual fund with total assets of only a few million dollars—preferably under $50 million and certainly no more than $150 million.

Guidepost No. 2: For maximum growth, invest in a mutual fund that's enjoying a substantial influx of new money.

Guidepost No. 3: For maximum growth, invest in a mutual fund with proven management.

Guidepost No. 4: For maximum growth, invest in a mutual fund that maintains an appropriate cash position.

One of the most obvious problems in this strategy is that even if you select from the top 10% of the funds in a rising market, you'll still be invested in funds when the market falls. If you believe that the overall long run trend of the market is not up, but rather sideways, then you have to do considerably better in up markets than in down markets to come out ahead.

3. Determine the market trends. Go into funds when the market is rising and get out and into cash or bonds when it is falling. If you believe that the market is a place in which to have a portion of your assets working, that you can't effectively select individual issues, and that the market will fluctuate up and down in cycles due to fiat-money inflation, this third strategy might be your best bet. The obvious difficulty in succeeding at this in-and-out technique is to be able to correctly predict the market swings. To say it's difficult is to magnificently understate the problem.

The Market Trend

Charting the market is one technique by which market swings can sometimes be predicted. The question is, is the past performance of the market a key to the future performance? Probably, but who has the magic glasses to read through the unimportant data and filter out the casual factors? Are the streets wet because it rained, or did it rain because the streets are wet? When two events seem to always accompany each other there can frequently be confusion about the cause and the effect. When you have hundreds of events, all intertwined, and all subjectively evaluated, it may be impossible. One of the most entertaining and enjoyable books on the whole subject of selecting stocks, and the methods of doing so is Burton G. Malkiel's *A Random Walk Down Wall Street*.[27] Before you subscribe to any method, be it charting, fundamental analysis, or hemline watching, you should read it.

My own preference for determining the probable direction of the stock market is through a study of money and inflation. Earlier I mentioned that fiat money has a significant and lasting effect on businesses, and therefore on the prices of the stocks of those businesses. Let's review these effects of inflation.

1. Stock prices are affected by the profits of the companies involved. When the public has more cash, it buys more products, and profits rise. When the public has less cash, it buys less and profits fall. Likewise, when the government spends more money the profits of companies rise, and when it spends less, the profits fall.

2. When interest rates, which are related to the inflation rate, rise, it costs companies more to borrow and profits fall. When rates are low, profits tend to rise.

3. When interest rates fall, or when the Federal Reserve lowers margin requirements on stocks,

there is more money around with which to purchase products as well as stocks.

4. When the public anticipates a high rate of future inflation, they tend to take their money out of stocks to purchase real goods, causing downward pressure on stock prices.

5. When interest rates go up, the yield on bonds makes them more attractive than stocks and money flows from stocks to bonds, depressing stock prices.

6. Inflation makes companies appear to have greater profits than they really have due to profits on inventory and inadequate depreciation allowances. In this way inflation is initially beneficial to stock prices, but later on, when these false profits are recognized for what they are, prices fall.

7. Inflation causes social unrest, and labor trouble. These factors are detrimental to the profits of companies, as well as the public confidence in the future that is necessary to stable or rising stock prices.

In summary, the initial increase in spending power caused by inflation of the money supply results in higher stock prices, while the subsequent effects of this flood of new money, including rising prices, higher interest rates and future uncertainty cause profits and stock prices to fall.

Profits From Stocks

There are several possibilities for using commons stocks for profits. You can buy long or sell short, pay cash or buy on margin, and buy or sell options.

Buying long simply means to buy shares of stock to hold for appreciation and income. A speculator normally isn't interested in income, and will probably be looking for more volatile stocks to achieve maximum profit in the minimum

amount of time. *Selling short* is a method of taking advantage
of a falling market. It means that you sell shares of stock that
you don't own at todays price, hoping to buy it back later at
a reduced price and thus profit by the difference. Long and
short selling cost the same commission, about 2% for each
trade, with the actual commission depending on the size of
the order. The risk is not the same, however. If you pay $100
for a share of stock, buying long, the most that you can lose
is $100 should the stock fall to zero. Even then, you'd still
own the share. Sell that same share short, though, and that
stock might go higher than $200. Before that happened
you'd be asked to put up more money, and if you chose not
to, your position would be automatically closed out.

Margin: Whether buying or selling, it's possible to use
margin. Currently margin requirements are 50%, meaning the
broker will loan you up to 50% of the value of the stock
when buying long or selling short. You must maintain a
minimum amount of equity in the stock, so if you're long
and the price drops, you'll get a call for more margin if your
equity drops to 25%. On a short position, you must maintain
30% equity. Currently, the exchange requires a minimum of
$2,000 to open a margin account.

Options: Buying an option is the way to achieve the
maximum leverage with your money. You're buying the right
to purchase stock at a fixed price for some specified time
period. For example, in 1976, when IBM was selling for
$257.50 per share, you could have purchased an option to
buy 100 shares at a price of $260 a share, exercizeable
anytime up to October 31, and the total cost of the option
would have been $2,175 plus commission. In order for you
make a profit, IBM would have to move above $275 a share
within that time period. At that time you would simply
exercise the option (that is, purchase the stock for $260 a
share), and then either hold it or resell it immediately. You
might also choose to sell your option, and since the value of
the option would have increased, you would make your
profit in that way.

Outguessing the Market: In the game of stocks, analysts look at either fundamental or technical indicators. Fundamentals have to do with company profits, inflation, and supply-demand factors for the products being sold. Technical indicators revolve around the psychology of the traders and include volume of shares traded, price movements, margin interest, odd-lot volume, etc. We'll be concerned almost totally with fundamentals here, with almost all decisions based on long-range factors of inflation, money supply, interest rates, and Federal Reserve actions.

What we'll be trying to do is anticipate when the public's judgement of the future is wrong. If the public thinks the inflation rate is going to be 5%, this will influence the value they place on stocks. If we believe it will be 8%, we assume that stocks are currently overpriced, of course. The same holds true for interest rates, which are more closely tied to inflation rates than most investors are aware.

Without attempting a quantitative analysis, let's study Figure 13, a chart of stock prices and interest rates.

Stocks hit a high in 1968, turned down in early 1969 and hit a low in mid-1970. They reversed again and rose until early 1971, made a six month correction, and then continued upward to a new high in January, 1973. They then promptly fell to a new low in the latter part of 1974, turned around and by mid-1976 were close to their 1973 highs.

Meanwhile, these moves were correlating closely to activities in the credit market. The economy had all the signs of overheating in 1968, and the Federal Reserve began a restrictive policy. The federal funds rate rose to 9% and remained there for almost a year. Meanwhile the T-bill rate rose steadily, peaking at 8% in early 1970. Economic activity was weakening, so at this point the Fed shifted to an easier policy and immediately interest rates turned. The federal funds rate fell to 3½% by the end of 1970. T-bill rates slid to a low of 3½% as well by the end of the first quarter of 1971,

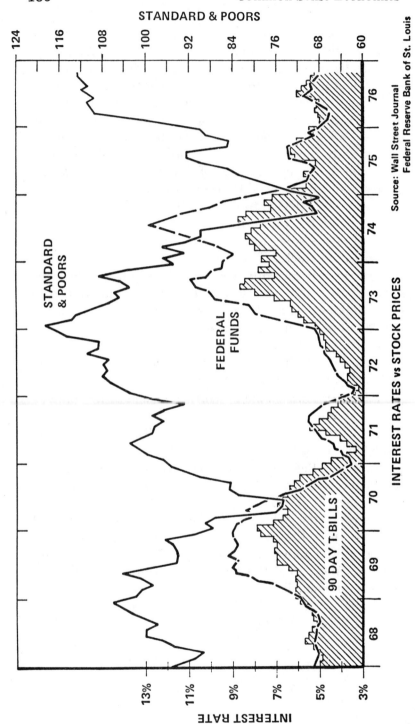

Figure 13

but by then the Fed reversed again and the federal fund rates went up to around 6%. It turned again in mid-1971 and dropped to a low of 3¼% in February of 1972.

The restrictive policy came on again in face of the mounting inflationary pressures, and both the T-bill rate and the federal funds rate rose to a peak in mid-1973. By this time the stock market had begun to tumble, pausing for a brief rally when the rates peaked out, but then when they did not fall substantially it continued down, and in the face of the double-digit inflation being experienced in 1974, the Fed continued to put pressure on interest rates until August, 1974, when rates finally began to drift downward. It should be noted that much of the upward pressure on interest rates during 1973-74 was a result of booming loan demand as businesses sought to stock up inventories in the face of inflation. Rates moved steadily downward from August, 1974, to May, 1975, then leveled out and finally in early 1976 drifted down to a low of below 5%.

The pattern of the stock market and the way it responded to these rates can be easily seen. Once headed down, it continued its momentum even after the rates began to move down. The only time it completely defied the direction of interest rates was when it continued up during the year of 1972, even though interest rates were rising steadily. It should be remembered that this was the era of price controls, and the market was probably responding to the mistaken belief that controls would work. Long before the rates started to fall, however, the market realized its mistake and began to plummet. After that, the correlation between market turns and interest rate changes was remarkably close.

The market crept cautiously upwards during all of 1975 in light of a continuing drop in the rate of inflation and a steady drop in interest rates. When interest rates again fell in January, it made its predictable advance to near its former highs.

What are the factors that cause the Federal Reserve to change its credit posture? They are in the position of trying to keep the money supply in line with stable economic growth, dampening it when inflationary pressures start to build, and stimulating its growth when the economy starts into a recession. To anticipate when they will restrict credit, you must anticipate when the inflation rate will begin to rise.

Signals of a Falling Market: The following will act as signals to the next bear market.

1. Interest rates, including the prime rate, T-bill rate, and the federal funds rate will begin to move upwards.
2. The Federal Reserve will be buying securities on the open market.
3. The Fed may raise the member bank reserve requirements.
4. The Fed may raise margin requirements on stock purchases.
5. The above actions may or may not be accompanied by a rise in the rate of inflation, but will probably occur after inflation has accelerated, or the signals indicating a probable increase in inflation have occurred.

When any or all of the above signals occur, the stock speculator should take any or all of the following actions:

1. Liquidate all common stocks except precious metals mining stocks.
2. Sell a diversified group of volatile stocks short.
3. Sell short on margin.
4. Sell naked call options.
5. Purchase put options.

The length of time that these positions are held will depend on certain personal and market factors.

If the speculator is highly leveraged and without much back-up capital, he may want to close out his short positions at any significant rise in the market. This could be done with stop-loss orders in most cases. If the market continues to fall, the aggressive speculator may want to parlay his profits by selling more options or using his margin build-up to sell more shorts, perhaps again placing buy-stop orders as his profits accumulate.

The conservative speculator will want to simply ride out the falling market, allowing his profits to build, and watching for the signals that the trend may reverse itself.

Signals of a Rising Market: A change in the down market will occur when the factors that originally caused that down market either change or investors anticipate that they are about to change. Signals for a bull market will be as follows:

1. The Federal Reserve will do some or all of the following:
   Lower the Federal Funds rate.
   Lower the member bank reserve requirements.
   Lower margin requirements.
   Purchase securities in the open market.

2. Interest rates will be falling, including the prime rate and T-bill rate.
3. The money supply rate-of-increase will be rising or will have already risen.
4. The rate of inflation will be falling and the public's expectation of the future rate will be low.

When some combination of the above signals is in effect, the speculator will take any or all of the following actions.

1. Cover all short positions.
2. Liquidate puts and cover naked calls.
3. Purchase individual common stocks.
4. Purchase mutual funds.
5. Purchase stocks on margin.
6. Buy calls.

Caution: If all this sounds obvious and relatively simple, fine. It isn't quite as simple or foolproof as it sounds, simply because the signals that are used to initiate actions are often confused. The Fed will do contradictory things, interest rates will reverse themselves and then do it again, inflation will move eratically, and the market will go through convulsions. The objective, always, is to try and spot the primary trends and to ignore the temporary and unimportant minor corrections.

The Federal Reserve Bank of St. Louis issues a number of monthly and quarterly publications that can provide the investor with the monetary data necessary for a proper interpretation of the growth of the money supply. Among them are U.S. *Financial Data,* a weekly series, *Monetary Trends* (monthly), and *National Economic Trends* (monthly). A letter to them requesting that you be added to their subscriber list for these publications is all that is necessary.

The key to profits is to realize that the long-term trend of the stock market is not up, but rather up and down. To take advantage of this inflationary phenomenon you must be ready to move in and out as the cycles occur, basing your timing on either a simple stop-loss formula like the 39-week moving average of a representative group of stocks, or on some broad economic indicator such as the monetary policy of the Fed. In any case, don't waste your time and endanger your assets unless you're willing to make yourself knowledgeable about what you're doing. Don't walk out and hope that some salesman, or even paid advisor will take the responsibility off your shoulders. You're the only one who has the integrity to handle your money carefully and responsibly. Now just gain the knowledge.

REAL ESTATE

Along with apple pie, democracy, and free education, belief in real estate ownership stands almost unquestioned. Yet, like all these other "basics," it's time the intelligent individual began to check fundamentals, before accepting the emotional appeal. As a matter of fact, it's too late for many to check. Thousands of investors have found already that real estate is not a one-way elevator to wealth.

Real estate syndications, for example, have cost hapless investors hundreds of millions of dollars in the past decade. Nor have the losses been limited to the unsophisticated investor, as evidenced by the tremendous losses incurred by the real estate investment trusts, and in turn by the banks and other financial institutions that financed them.

At the risk of being labelled un-American, I'd like to say that I think real estate, in general, is one of the most dangerous investments in the U.S. today. This comes from the fact that concepts of real estate are fraught with old-wives tales, fallacies, and misunderstandings. For example: "real estate doesn't fluctuate in value as do common stocks; real estate is where the 'big money' goes for safety; the government is bound to protect the real estate industry for the benefit of the nation; inflation always helps the real estate owner; increasing population will always mean an increasing demand for property, and thus the price is always uni-directional."

To understand the risks of real estate, let me first say that I forsee an increasing rate of inflation for the country. Not a gradual increase from the old 3% or 4% rates, but a significant increase from the new 10% and 15% rates. Further, this increasing inflation will be accompanied by certain inevitable political actions, including, but not limited to, rising taxes, increasing government expenditures, stricter controls on business (including wage, price, and rent controls), and a general movement toward what has come to be known in the world as socialism. Inflation and its side effects are the primary forces that any potential real estate investor must be aware of.

Residential Property

Owning a single family residence has been both good and bad during the past two decades. Many friends in my area have seen the value of their homes jump 50% in two or three years. In other nearby areas however, I've known people who have owned their homes for ten years and find them worth less today than when they bought them. It isn't always a one-way elevator. *Money Magazine* gave an overall 1% edge financially to ownership versus renting. As inflation increases, that edge might increase also.

New money must constantly be injected into the real estate market to justify the increasing valuation on houses. If you liken real estate to a closed poker game you'll see the reason. If seven players sit down to a game, each with one hundred dollars, and the dealer (or house) takes one dollar out of each pot, after 700 hands the house will have all the money. In real estate commissions vary, but probably average 6% of the selling price of a home. Since the average home sells about every five years, within the thirty-year life of that home 30% of the value goes into the pocket of the real estate agent. In addition, closing costs, prepayment penalties, etc. add another 2% or 3%, which means that the real cost has risen by as much as 50%. This is lost money—it adds nothing to the wealth of the property owner—and must come from outside the real estate market. In poker it's easy to see why there must be more losers than winners; in real estate it's not so obvious, but just as true.

Income Property

Income property, whether residential or commercial-industrial is the most dangerous to own today. Added on to the normal investment risks inherent in any investment, you have the over-riding threats of both inflation and socialism. When inflation begins to accelerate in any society, people naturally seek to protect their wealth by getting out of depreciating currency and into real assets. To businessmen this means ploughing money into new plant and equipment to protect the purchasing power of the capital. They realize that if they wait to build until they really need the space, costs will have soared. What better place to keep the profits than in

new building? This can only be effective for a limited time.
When the inflationary boom hits its peak they are left with
an excess of unneeded buildings. A good example is Germany
after the hyper-inflation that accompanied and followed
World War I. Constantino Bresciani-Turroni told of that
situation:

> "The outspoken words of an industrialist during that
> congress are worth quoting: 'We have some very
> extensive factories which are nothing but rubbish.
> Therefore it is not sufficient, if we wish to restore our
> business, to close these establishments, in the hope of
> reopening them later. Even factories not working cost
> money. Therefore our slogan must be: Demolition!
> We must consider as finally lost the capital unwisely
> invested in those factories. Certainly this is a unique
> occurrence in the industrial history of Germany; it is
> a recognition of very grave mistakes committed
> during the inflation' ... In the potash industry a
> good 118 mines were closed or definitely abandoned;
> 'now since the average cost of a mine is about five
> million marks, it may be seen what an enormous sum
> of national capital has been uselessly invested'... The
> cement syndicate of northern Germany closed and
> practically demolished seventeen factories..."[28]

I cannot help but observe the plethora of commercial-
industrial construction going on across the U.S.—the
shopping centers, high rise office buildings, industrial
parks—and think about the economic forces at work.
Investors with abundant but depreciating paper currency,
battered by the roller coaster stock market, interest rates on
bonds that don't meet even the inflation rate (let alone
taxes), and oppressive income tax rates, are flooding into the
real estate market in an attempt to preserve their wealth. The
building glut of 1970-73 still has not been absorbed and
millions of square feet of office space stands vacant. Yet, new
buildings are rising everywhere.

Of course the inflation has other characteristics which add
to the over-building. The tide of fresh money carries with it a
sense of speculation, a business recklessness that creates

thousands of new businesses, and these new entrepreneurs demand space. But when the money runs out and the ensuing recession quells the demand for their products, they just as quickly disappear, leaving behind bankruptcies, broken leases, and empty buildings. This overbuilding is not an isolated occurrence. It happens wherever inflation becomes a way of life. The *London Economist* carried this story:

> "Nobody wants to admit it, but it could take years to sort out the mess the British banking system is in over property. The figures speak for themselves. By the end of 1974, bank lending to the property and construction industry had reached five billion pounds. That's more than half the banks' commitment to all of British manufacturing although the ratio had been little more than one fifth early in 1970. What the banks are hoping is that the investment institutions—insurance companies and pension funds—will regain confidence enough to take over the property millstone.
>
> But the institutions, too, had a chastening experience in 1974 when the property market collapsed and their rental income was docked by rent control. Their time horizon has shortened. Even after the lifting of rent control early this year, they are reluctant to buy properties yielding a below-market rent when rent reviews and reversions are a long way off."[29]

That heavy lending to commercial and residential building was purely a result of the inflation inspired building boom. *The Economist* went on to point out that

> "the amount of empty office space in London now stands at 4 million feet, nearly six times the level of April, 1974."

Over-building is not the only danger to property owners in hyper-inflation. Property values suffer from the ancillary problems of rent controls and tenant protection laws, as well as rapidly rising taxes and expenses. Frank D. Graham in *Exchange, Prices, and Production in Hyper-Inflation: Germany, 1920-1923* chronicled the problem:

> "Tenants were protected from eviction so long as they paid rentals officially determined on the basis of pre-war charges. The amount collectible was occasionally raised as inflation proceeded but the increases always lagged far behind the existing depreciation of the currency and were quickly rendered nugatory by the further loss of value of the monetary unit. At all times after 1920 rentals were more or less nominal, and, in the period of hyper-inflation, housing was obtained practically free of charge. Except for a possible reversion when financial order should be restored, the property of the landlords was to all intents and purposes confiscated."[30]

Already in England the same problem has surfaced. Rent controls exert a severe downward pressure on property values, and periodic recessions with concomitant unemployment mean widespread vacancies. Another article in *The Economist* tells the story:

> "Banks are particularly cautious about financing developments, which is where the banks most need their help. Building costs are rising dramatically, but rents are not rising in line. In some areas, they are falling. Even if a developer has pre-rent his property to a good tenant, there is no guarantee that the institution will see an economic return on completion. During the boom most developers and their bankers were prepared to allow interest and other charges to exceed rental income on the assumption that property values would continue to go up and that the property could always be sold at a profit if cash was needed. Now they know better. Most development companies are either having to sell completed properties in order to meet interest charges and reduce borrowing—if they can find a buyer. A really dramatic improvement in the property market would probably be met by a wave of sales, just as the rise in the British stock market has been met by a wave of rights issues. The market in secondary property, as the valuers call it, is dead, and most property men think it will stay that way for a long time."[31]

Nor are the experiences during the German inflation and Britain's current situation isolated instances. Whenever there have been severe inflations, the same problems with property have existed.

Probably one of the few property areas that is not completely devastated by inflation is agricultural land. People keep buying food, even when unable to pay rent. The government will buy it for them if necessary. And price controls at the farm level are so immediately destructive of production that they can't be effectively imposed. So strong is the farm lobby in the U.S. that prices are more often held at artificially high levels than held down. Graham points out that in the German inflation, holders of agricultural land didn't fare as poorly as their urban counterparts.

A Simple Summary

What are the rules that should guide a potential real estate investor?

1. Realize that economic conditions have changed real estate from an investment to a speculation.
2. Don't buy for long term appreciation.
3. Don't buy in syndicates.
4. Beware of income property whether commercial, industrial, or residential. The exception is if you're the tenant.
5. Buy your own house, but don't expect to make money.
6. Beware—

And good luck:

CHAPTER FOUR

Insurance

Risk as I defined it in an earlier chapter means exposure to loss, and insurance represents pooled risk. It's a guarantee that the insured will be reimbursed for certain financial losses when and if they occur. In more primitive societies, when an individual suffers a major loss the neighbors pool their resources to aid that individual. When a farmer's barn burns down the neighbors will hold a "barn-raising." When he's too ill to till his fields they share the burden. Thus the people in the community pool their risks. This is a form of insurance with the premium being the obligation to do the same for others in the community. In today's society insurance is on a monetary basis. When we have an accident we no longer rely on the charity of our neighbors, but rather we contribute in advance to a pool of money, along with many thousands of other individuals, and when catastrophe does strike we are entitled to dip into that pool of money and recover part or all of our loss. An insurance company is in business to make a profit, and by offering you the chance to share your risk with others, it takes a profit for its role in the calculation of that risk.

The profits of the insurance company are determined by a number of factors:

1. How well its actuaries are able to calculate the number of losses that might occur in given situations and properly charge the subscriber for that risk.
2. How efficiently its operations are able to minimize overhead while properly servicing the client.
3. How successful it is in advertising and promotion and the training of its sales force, in order to sell its product to a great number of people.

WHAT LOSSES SHOULD BE COVERED?

If an unforeseen occurrence could cause you financial loss, then it is possible that this risk should be covered by insurance. To determine when it's necessary, look at the extent of the potential financial loss. If the loss would force you to alter your financial goals or change your standard of living, then you would be wise to cover that risk by insurance. Conversely, *if you can easily pay for the loss out of present assets or earnings without significantly affecting your economic position, then you should probably act as your own insurance company.* You should pay yourself the premiums and thus earn for yourself the salesman's commissions, overhead expense allowance, and profits.

An example of this is automobile *collision* insurance.* When you buy collision insurance, the insurance company will determine statistically the number of accidents you'll have and will charge enough to pay for the repairs on the accidents plus commissions. In addition the company will charge you overhead expense and profits. One of my clients, a successful doctor, has a net worth in excess of $500,000.

---

*In this example I'm not referring to public liability insurance on the auto. The loss from an injury to another person can be so enormous that few people can afford to cover the risk themselves. If you were sued for half a million dollars after causing an accident, could you pay without damage to your financial security? If not, then insure.

He drives an automobile worth about $9,000 and the automobile has been fully covered by collision insurance for a premium of $110.00 a year. Statistically he will have approximately 0.25 accidents this year and the cost of repairs will be about $50. The balance of the premium will pay the insurance company its operating costs and profits. Assuming that the doctor pays this premium for a period of fifty years (from age 20 to age 70) he will have tripled the cost of repairing his automobile.

The only reason he bothered to insure was habit. Since he could have afforded to pay for any damage without affecting his financial security, he should have done so. The only possible reasons for carrying collision insurance are: 1. You may be financing the car and thus the lending institution may require collision insurance, 2. You may not be able to afford to replace your car if it is damaged.

This logic regarding the reason to buy insurance applies throughout the field of insurance. *If you can afford to cover a loss yourself, don't pay an insurance company to cover it for you.* You'll probably be playing the insurance game for fifty years; buying it because you think you might "profit" from it is injudicious. You can't profit by buying insurance any more than you can profit by gambling at the roulette wheel at Las Vegas. You may play for a short time and come out a winner, but play long enough and the laws of probability will get you. You'll most certainly lose.

HOW MUCH SHOULD BE CARRIED?

After you determine that you need insurance to cover a risk, you must calculate the size of the potential loss, and thereby determine the amount of insurance needed. Some potential losses are so large it's impossible to insure against them. An example would be the loss caused by a disabling accident or illness. A highly-paid professional might be earning $200,000 a year and have twenty or thirty years of earning power ahead. There is no insurance company that I know that would be willing to completely cover that loss. In cases like this it's more practical to look not at the loss, but at the size of the *need* if the loss occurred. The true needs of the individual would normally be far less than the amount of his current income, and therefore it would be sensible to buy enough insurance to cover his needs, rather than his loss. Thus we have another rule that should always be followed: *buy only enough to satisfy the need.*

After you've determined the amount of insurance, you must shop the market to find the companies that offer the best contracts at the lowest price. Insurance contracts are written in carefully worded legal language and are based on past experience of the company and future assumptions of loss. While provisions of certain types of contracts are almost completely dictated by state laws, other types are at the discretion of the company. In life insurance, for example, the majority of the policy provisions are written to conform to the stringent requirements of state insurance codes, and thus the contracts of all companies will be essentially identical. In disability insurance, on the other hand, companies have a much wider latitude in wording and coverage. When the fine print of one disability policy says you are protected from *sickness contracted during the term of the policy*, and another says you are protected from *sickness which first manifests itself during the term of the policy*, you have to be both alert and knowledgeable to realize the significance of the change in wording.

The insurance problem summarized is:
1. Determine needs.
2. Compare contracts.
3. Shop price.

As I cover each area of insurance I'll give you information on how to handle these problems.

LIFE INSURANCE

The concept of life insurance has spawned one of the largest industries in the world. Assets of life insurance companies in the United States totaled $300 billion by mid-1976. There is about $1.75 trillion of coverage in force, which is the equivalent of $8,000 on every man, woman, and child in the country. Yet I would doubt that one insured in a hundred has the correct amount, and type, or is paying the lowest premium available to him. The life insurance industry *sells* insurance, people don't *buy* it. The product is so thoroughly camouflaged that few people ever understand what they own.

One clue to the industry lies in your local library. Peruse the books available on salesmanship; you'll find the vast majority were written by life insurance salesmen. Why? Because this is the biggest training ground for salesmen in the world. No industry has ever concentrated so much energy and money in the development of raw sales technique as has the life insurance industry. Whenever any industry relies that heavily on sales technique, you can be sure the customer will have little objective product information. The purpose of the salesman who'll be confronting you is to sell the maximum amount of insurance that you can be induced to buy and to make it the kind that will be the most profitable to him and his company. In very few cases is this the most profitable for you. If you want to buy insurance correctly the *last* person to contact is your life insurance agent. He has been brainwashed by the life insurance industry not to satisfy your need, but to satisfy theirs.

The correct approach to the purchase of life insurance is the same as for any other form of insurance. First determine what *financial* losses will occur upon death of the insured. Then determine what contracts are available and which companies offer the lowest rates for the type and size policy you need.

WHEN IS A "NEED" NOT A NEED?

Here are a few of your needs that the life insurance salesman will point out:

1. Capital to provide an income to the family.
2. Money with which to pay estate taxes.
3. Money to pay off the home mortgage.
4. Money to pay off the installment debts and notes.
5. Money to educate the children.
6. Money to buy out partners in your business.
7. Money for the business to replace your loss as an employee.
8. Money to retire on.
9. In the case of insuring a nonworking wife, money to pay the costs of a housekeeper and the increased income taxes due to the loss of the exemption.
10. If you're young, to insure your future insurability.
11. To capture the lower rates only available to younger people.
12. To fund your pension plan or Keogh plan.

Before you accept his word that these are valid needs you'd better examine your own situation thoroughly. In fact, before you even talk to an agent you should make your own calculations. What will be the financial loss to others in the event of your death? This, of course, depends on your situation.

INSURING CHILDREN

Let's assume you are considering insuring a child. At this point in the child's life it's probable that no one is dependent on it for support, so if it dies, no one will be deprived of income. The only financial consequences will be the costs of burial, and properly handled these will be minimal. Therefore, the only possible insurance need would be the funeral expenses, and then only if they can't be met from existing resources. "Yes" you say, "but the salesman pointed out that I could fund my children's education by buying insurance." Don't confuse insurance with investing even if they are combined by the insurance company. When I talk about insurance need I'm speaking solely of alleviating the *financial loss* of death through the payment of insurance premiums. I'll discuss the idea of using insurance as a vehicle for the accumulation of wealth later in this chapter.

O.K., but what about the idea that you can buy insurance at much lower rates when you're young? At age 5 the rate is only $7.00 per $1,000 of insurance. By the time the child reaches 25 it will have jumped to $12.00 per $1,000 of insurance. Yes it will, but believe it or not the cost *per thousand dollars of coverage* when you reach age 25 will be the same whether the policy is taken out at age 5 and kept until then, or taken out when needed. Since medical science is progressing and life expectancies are increasing, 20 years from now insurance premiums for a 25-year-old will probably be less than they are today. All you will have accomplished by taking out the insurance at age five is to guarantee the right to *have it* at age 25. Paying the full premiums for years when you don't need the insurance is a pretty high price to pay for the guarantee of insurability. I'll shortly prove the point that the cost will not go up if you wait until you're older to buy. The conclusion regarding buying life insurance on children is this: don't waste your money unless you can't afford the burial costs. It's senseless.

INSURING A NONINCOME-PRODUCING SPOUSE

How about buying insurance on a nonincome-producing member of the household whose economic value lies in their contribution to maintenance of the home and care of the family, like a nonworking wife? Again the test is simple. What is the economic result of the death of this member of the family? Can this loss be met from the assets or income of the remaining family members without undue strain? Typically the person we're referring to is the wife, although it might be a nonworking husband, father, mother or other person.

If a wife is lost, someone must take over the labor she performs. It might entail the hiring of a housekeeper, and babysitters, and could also mean the breadwinner might have to work less hours. It will certainly mean the loss of an income tax deduction, and could result in the payment of inheritance and estate taxes if the estate is sufficiently large. But let's not forget the financial gains which might offset part of these losses. The deceased spouse will no longer need to be fed, clothed, entertained, taken on vacations, cared for medically, furnished transportation, or lodging. It's doubtful that there are many cases in which the financial losses would really exceed the gains. Wives are expensive propositions, as is the carrying of any member of a household. And even if it were slightly more expensive to pay for the new costs of babysitters, housekeepers, etc., there is more than an even chance that the current income of the working, surviving spouse would be able to cope with the added expense.

How about the question of estate taxes? Suppose the couple's gross estate is $300,000. Under the community property laws, the wife already owns $150,000 worth of the property. The other $150,000 would be taxable but after the decedent's $60,000 personal estate tax exemption, only $90,000 would be subject to tax. This would result in federal estate taxes of about $18,000 plus administrative and probate costs (depending on the way in which title to the property had been held), and any state inheritance taxes. Any life insurance salesman worth his license would sell a whole life policy in this case to cover the entire amount. Yet the real question is, would the reduction of assets caused by payment of the taxes really diminish the survivor's wealth in a way that would make him or her unable to meet goals as scheduled? Probably not. Remember, the only reason to buy insurance is to cover a financial risk that you can't afford to cover any other way.

A family should carefully examine its need to insure the nonworking members. They'll usually come to the conclusion that it's unnecessary. Take the premium that would have been spent for that nonworking member, and invest it; the great probability is that that member won't die anyway, and the premium dollars will come in very handy at retirement.

INSURING THE BREADWINNER

The obvious purpose of life insurance is to provide funds with which to meet the obligations that normally would be paid out of income if the person producing that income dies. These include:
1. Debts.
2. The obligation of continuing support for dependents.
3. The costs of death, including taxes and burial.

Figure 14 is a sample calculation format for determining how much life insurance to carry. By filling in the "Needs" column and the "Assets" column, the net insurance required can be arrived at.

Covering the Debts: To determine the amount of insurance that should be carried, first determine the size of these obligations. Let's take them one at a time beginning with debts. Add up all outstanding notes and accounts. The mortgages on real estate may be excluded inasmuch as these are not debts in the same sense that an account at a department store is a debt. The home itself is an asset, even though it may have an outstanding mortgage, and shouldn't be considered a liability.

A decision should be made as to whether the surviving spouse will continue to live in the home. If the answer is no, then the *net equity* in the home should be listed under "Assets" and the assumption made that the home will be sold and the proceeds from the sale will become part of the general assets. If the survivor intends to buy another home, either for cash or with a down payment, the amount of cash required should be listed as a need. When calculating the income needed for the family, a provision would then be made for the annual cost of the dwelling.

If the wife is going to remain in the present home, she has the alternative of paying off the mortgage or continuing to make monthly payments. A payoff would be entered as a cash need. If she continues mortgage payments the amount of the payment is part of her need for income, and capital must be provided to meet that income need. From the standpoint of life insurance need, if the wife stays in the home it is inconsequential whether she pays off the mortgage or not. One way she needs the capital to pay it off, the other way she needs the capital to provide the income necessary to continue making the payments on the mortgage.

Final Expenses

Next comes the cost of estate taxes, burial, and other final expense. The estate tax table in the Appendix should assist you in calculating what these might be. As far as final expenses go, it's your funeral. Estimate how grand you want that last tribute to your mortal remains to be and enter that figure accordingly. Most dedicated insurance agents will always jack up this figure by throwing in a bit about final medical expenses. I don't agree with this. Your medical costs should be taken care of by medical insurance, not life insurance, and buying extra life insurance to take care of them just doesn't make sense. I suppose if a person were unable to get the kind of medical insurance he needed, it might be a last resort to cover some of this potential loss through life insurance, but you have to die in this case to pay the medical bills. Hardly an incentive for your doctor to cure you.

Family Income

The next, and by far the most difficult, determination to make is how much capital is required to support the dependents after the breadwinner is gone. Here we have to make assumptions about the need for income and the probability of certain future events occurring.

Income can be provided in three ways: From the efforts of work; from charity; or from capital. Either you work, your money works, or you look to charity. Since most people don't want to accept charity, let's look at the other possibilities. If the breadwinner dies, the wife or children could begin to provide income by working. Although this is an individual decision that each family must make, here are a few thoughts that may help. Does the wife have a skill? If not, she could probably develop one within a few years of the death of the spouse by entering some program of education. Will she want to work? If the children are young, perhaps not. Then the husband can simply provide the money to meet the family's income needs. Perhaps she will want to work simply to have something to occupy her time. Assuming a minimal income from this type of effort would be sensible. If the wife is young and childless she would probably remarry. In fact, most young marrieds who have no children should examine carefully the concept of life insurance, as there may be no logical reason to carry it at all. The wife survived some way prior to marriage, and could probably revert to that method of survival in the event of the death of her husband. Since the chances of his death are small, they would normally be better off by spending or saving those premiums.

Don't automatically assume that the wife will remarry or go to work in the event of the husband's death, before considering the chance that she might not be able to do either. For example, there could be an auto accident in which the husband is killed and the wife seriously crippled. Chances are small of this happening to any given family, but it does happen and is worth thinking about.

From your budget sheet you should be able to determine the amount of income that the dependents will need in the event of the breadwinner's death. Decide how much of that income can reasonably be expected to come from the efforts of the survivors; the balance must be provided by the money left by the deceased.*

A Hypothetical Case

Let's take a hypothetical case and work it through to help you get an idea of how to calculate your own need for insurance. Assume a family of four, husband's age is 35, wife's is 35, two children ages 8 and 10. There are approximately $8,500 in outstanding debts including an auto loan, some charge accounts, and a small loan against the husband's equipment. In addition, they figure they're about $1,000 behind at this point in the year as to what their total tax bill will be. They have estimated their final expenses if he were to die at $3,000 (which includes travel expenses to fly his parents to the funeral). Their estate taxes and probate-administration fees will probably come to about $2,000. They live in a home that's worth about $50,000 with a $32,000 mortgage against it, and if the husband were to die, the wife would stay in the home. In the event of the husband's death, the wife would need to pay off the loans, pay the final expenses, and meet her income needs, which would include the payment on the home plus the regular monthly living costs.

Since the children are young but in school, she'll work part time, taking a job during some of the hours the kids are away. They estimate her income might be $300 per month. Their monthly living expenses are as indicated in the sample budget on page 81. Notice how certain expenses are estimated to be lower if the husband is gone, while others, such as home maintenance, are estimated to rise. Certain amounts are indicated to replace items that wear out, such as the automobile and home furnishings. Income taxes are

*Social Security—One element that will reduce the income need is social security. Assuming the federal government doesn't go into bankruptcy, any wage earner who has been contributing to the social security pool should have some benefits coming to his family in the event of his death or disability. To find out what the payment would be in your situation, contact your local Social Security office and ask them to send you the information.

obviously lower, and insurance premiums have dropped significantly. Since the insurance and assets available on the husband's death are adequate to carry the wife and children as far as necessary, there is still no need for insurance on the mother. However, if she had planned to completely support the children after the death of her husband, some insurance to replace her working income would be indicated to provide for the children's continued support.

We've arrived at a monthly income necessary to support the surviving spouse and children until the kids are grown. After that the wife's needs will diminish, but this lowered need will be offset by the loss of the social security payment. The required income in our example is $1,450 per month, and the amount needed after deducting her income ($300 per month), and the estimated social security payment ($400 per month), is approximately $750 per month, which must be made up out of income from capital. Once we determine how long that income needs to last, we can calculate how much capital is necessary to provide it.

The typical approach taken by the insurance man is to simply capitalize the income at the rate of interest that the insurance company pays for policy proceeds left at interest. For example, if the life insurance company pays 5% interest, then the amount of capital required would be calculated: $750 times 12 months = $9,000 per year. Divide the $9,000 by the 5% and you get $180,000. Thus $180,000, if earning at the rate of 5%, would yield $9,000 per year.

The wife would then have a perpetual income of $9,000 per year and the capital would never be depleted. While this is apparently true, the problem would surface next year. She would have the $9,000 income, but she would find that next year it would buy her significantly less than it will buy this year. Her budget would suddenly jump by whatever the rate of inflation happened to be. If it's 20% this year, next year she'll need to have $10,800 to buy the same goods and services. And so on every year thereafter.

Compensating for Inflation

Since there is no way to predict very far in advance what the rate of inflation may be, the calculation must integrate an unknown rate of inflation in order to determine what amount of capital is necessary to meet her income needs. The only way I can see that this can be done is to assume a rate of earnings that is variable but somehow constant in relation to inflation. Since interest rates tend to rise in inflating economies, I think the way to estimate need in this area is to assume that the surviving spouse will attempt to invest the assets in a way that will keep pace with both taxes and inflation. If inflation grew at 8% then she would have to earn 8% (plus taxes) to break even for the year. If it runs at 20% she must earn 20% plus taxes. Now assuming she could do this, how much capital would she need? If her earnings were just equal to inflation and taxes, then it should be obvious that the income she consumes would have to come out of principal, and, therefore, the principal would be consumed. Many an investment advisor or stock salesman will tell you that you can do much better than this; that you'll be able to invest the money and not only meet inflation and taxes but make a profit as well. Think it over. Let's take 1974 as an example. According to the government figures the cost of living rose 12.2%. However, the things that your wife would have been spending money on, had she been in a widow's situation that year, might have increased much more. For example, food jumped almost 18%, and gasoline almost doubled. Clothes, automobiles, etc., likewise leaped at a pace that made 12.2% look like no inflation at all. So the fact is that her expenses might have gone up far more than the 12.2% overall average calculated by Uncle Sam.

Just for talking's sake, suppose her cost of living rose only 12.2%. Whatever she has her money invested in, other than tax-free municipal bonds, there's almost certain to be some tax to pay, but let's assume the lowest rate. Say that of her total income she pays only 10% out in state and federal taxes. She would need to be earning 12.2% to cover inflation, plus another 1.2% to cover the taxes on the income, meaning she would have to have her money growing at 13.4% per annum. And that was 1974! The probability is that in the coming years inflation will get worse. And taxes too. So how would you rate your wife's chances of getting a safe 15% to 20% return on her invested capital? She's going to have to be both very astute and very fortunate to realize it year after year. It's a tough world in today's money markets.

The conclusion is that unless you consider your wife to be sharper than average when it comes to handling money, you'd better put away enough assets to last her for whatever number of years you want her to have an independent income, and cross your fingers that she'll get at least a zero true rate of return.

In our example the couple decides that the wife should have this income until the children are through college, let's say until they're 23. That means another 15 years. Then she'll make a living on her own. Since the amount needed in today's dollars is $9,000 per year, that amount times the 15 years will equal $135,000. In other words, $135,000 will last the widow 15 years if it is invested at a rate of return that equals inflation and taxes, and she consumes it at the rate of $9,000 per year of today's dollars. The formula for determining the amount of capital required to meet the income needs of your dependents becomes simple: it is the amount per year in today's dollars times the number of years of support required. The only assumption you're making is they will be able to invest that capital at a rate that equals inflation plus taxes.

To finish the calculation of the amount of life insurance required, a couple of more steps are necessary. Total needs consist of the sum of the debts, an allowance for a home, a capital sum to provide income, money for final expenses and taxes, and perhaps a fund for the college education of the children.

The College Fund

In educational expenses we are again confronted with the problem of inflation. College costs have been rising at a rate even higher than general prices. The Life Insurance Institute

annually publishes a list of all the colleges in the U.S. along
with tuition costs and the cost of room and board.[32] In
1974-1975 the average cost of a state-supported college or
university, including room, board, and tuition for the year,
was about $3,000. That's how much it was them, but how
large a fund should be set up for a child whose college won't
start until ten or twenty years in the future? The solution is
to put away a lump sum equal to today's cost, and assume
that the money will grow at a rate equal to the rate of
inaltion. It's possible to avoid paying taxes on the income the
funds will be earning by putting them into a trust for the
children. The income would be taxed to them rather than the
widow, and since it's unlikely the children's income will be
great enough to be taxed, the income to the fund will be tax
free.

Whether or not to put money away for your children's
education is a subjective decision on your part. Some parents
feel they should provide the entire cost of four years of
college, and graduate school as well, while others feel that
partially assisting the children through the first four years is
more than adequate. After you decide the amount you want
to provide, add this amount to your total needs list.

In our example $177,500 is the total amount required to
provide a comfortable living for our hypothetical family, at
least through the college years of the children. If the widow
were fortunate in the way the money was put to work, or in
the amount she earned, or in keeping expenditures down,
then the original capital would carry her much farther in life
than the calculated 15 years.

Adding Back the Assets

The $177,500 of needs we've calculated in our example is
not the amount of insurance necessary, for the present assets
of the family will be owned by the wife on the death of the
husband, and can be used to reduce the need. As a matter of
fact, if the family at this point had $177,500 in assets there
would be no reason to carry life insurance at all. Effectively,

they would be their own insurance company. The premiums that would have gone for insurance could be spent or invested for the future.

In our example, our family has assets amounting to $116,100 that would be available to the survivors. When subtracted from the total needs, this leaves them with a total life insurance requirement of $61,400.

After you have determined what your survivors' needs will be, make a list of the assets currently owned that can be used to satisfy these needs. To be realistic ask what any given asset would be able to be sold for if the breadwinner was not around. A doctor, for example, might value his practice, including accounts receivable, at $100,000. On his death, however, his widow might be hard pressed to collect those receivables, and might find it difficult to find another doctor to buy the equipment and good will. She could wind up selling the practice for half of what the doctor himself might have been able to get for it if alive.

Other assets should be carefully evaluated as well. Many limited partnership interests are not liquid. If there is reasonable chance that they might turn out to be losers in the long run, they should be discounted when figuring the amount of capital available to meet her needs. Additionally, assets should be discounted by the income taxes that will be due on their liquidation. Income taxes due on the sale of an asset after the death of one of the owners will be partially determined by the way in which title is held. If for one reason or another you are holding title to property in a form that doesn't avoid income taxes, then the tax liability should be taken into consideration when your life insurance needs are calculated.

LIFE INSURANCE NEEDS ESTIMATE

Capital Requirements
Debts	$ 8,500	
Income Taxes	1,000	
Probate and Estate Tax	2,000	
Final Expenses	3,000	
Education Fund	28,000	
Family Income	135,000	
Total Capital Requirements		$177,500

Available Assets
Stocks, Bonds	$ 17,000	
Income Real Estate (Equity)	23,000	
Coin Collection	14,000	
Second Car	2,100	
Husband's Business	60,000	
Total Available Assets		116,100
Total Life Insurance Needed		$ 61,400

Figure 14

In summary, the amount of life insurance you need is the difference between the needs for capital of your surviving dependents, and the total assets they'll have available. Once you've established the size of the need, the next step is to decide on the correct type of insurance.

PERMANENT OR TERM?
WILL THE REAL BARGAIN PLEASE STAND UP?

At this point you should know how much life insurance you need, and on what members of the family. The next question is what kind? There have been many exposes of the insurance industry, yet it continues year after year to sell hundreds of millions of dollars worth of the wrong kind of insurance to the gullible public. When you finish this chapter, I would hope you'll never again fall victim to the sophisticated deceit of any insurance company.

There are two ways that you can buy life insurance. You can buy pure death protection, or you can buy pure death protection that includes a savings account. The first is called *term* insurance, the other is called *cash value* insurance. Term is a word contrived by the insurance industry to have a negative impression on the prospect. It means either "in force for a limited term," or "terminating" depending on which agent you talk to. Insurance that falls in the cash value category is referred to as "permanent," and thereby is contrasted with terminating insurance. Tell me, would you rather have something that is permanent or terminating? Permanent seems so much more stable and secure. But is it?

Term Insurance

Term insurance is sold as a simple wager with the insurance company. You want to cover the risk that you'll die this year. The insurance company is willing to make a wager with you that that event won't occur. They do it in much the same way that the casino in Las Vegas arranges the payoff on a bet on the roulette wheel. They make a wheel with 38 pockets in which the ball can fall. There is one chance in 38 that the ball will fall in any particular pocket. When you bet on one pocket, they will pay you only 36 to 1 if you win. Thus, if a one dollar bet were placed on each of the 38 pockets, the casino would make a net profit of $2 on each spin of the wheel.

So it is with an insurance company. They have mortality tables which are drawn from the number of people of any given age that die in any given year. These tables are expressed in number of deaths per thousand, and are periodically revised to reflect the increasing life expectancy of Americans. Figure 15 is a copy of the table that is currently being used by most insurance companies to calculate their rates. At age 35 this table predicts that 2.51 persons per thousand will die and that the remaining life expectancy of any 35 year old is 36.69 years. If every person in a group of 1,000 people went to the insurance company and asked to be insured for $1,000, the insurance company would know that it would probably have to pay claims totaling $2,510. In order to assure itself of a profit it would simply calculate its overhead costs for being in business, its commission costs for selling the policies, income taxes that would be due on its profits, and the profit it desired, and add them to the $2,510 it would have to pay out in claims, and divide the result up among the 1,000 applicants. In other words the policy should cost $2.51 per $1,000 worth of insurance plus the company's costs and profit.

The company goes one step further in assuring itself that it won't lose. It selects the best risks from among the applicants. It won't insure the 1,000 people at random and thus incur the 2.51 deaths that are the average. It will refuse to insure, or charge higher rates to anyone that shows a higher risk of dying by having some physical or moral handicap that places them in a higher risk category. Although I don't know how this affects the statistics, we might assume that if the 1,000 people represented by the mortality table only included people in good health, then the deaths per thousand might drop to 1.5 rather than the 2.51 who actually died. Thus the insurance company increases the odds even further in its favor. So if we look at the mortality table and estimate some expenses, commissions and profits, we might assume that for a reasonably healthy individual age 35 to buy $1,000 worth of insurance for one year he would probably have to pay around $2.00 to $3.00 per thousand. If you look at rate tables for one year term insurance at that age, you'll find the rates vary from about $2.50 to $5.00 per thousand. If the only thing you need is insurance one year, then pick the cheapest company and buy. Assuming that you

TABLE OF MORTALITY

Age	Deaths Per 1,000	Expectation of Life	Age	Deaths Per 1,000	Expectation of Life
0	7.08	68.30	50	8.32	23.63
1	1.76	67.78	51	9.11	22.82
2	1.52	66.90	52	9.96	22.03
3	1.46	66.00	53	10.89	21.25
4	1.40	65.10	54	11.90	20.47
5	1.35	64.19	55	13.00	19.71
6	1.30	63.27	56	14.21	18.97
7	1.26	62.35	57	15.54	18.23
8	1.23	61.43	58	17.00	17.51
9	1.21	60.51	59	18.59	16.81
10	1.21	59.58	60	20.34	16.12
11	1.23	58.65	61	22.24	15.44
12	1.26	57.72	62	24.31	14.78
13	1.32	56.80	63	26.57	14.14
14	1.39	55.87	64	29.04	13.51
15	1.46	54.95	65	31.75	12.90
16	1.54	54.03	66	34.74	12.31
17	1.62	53.11	67	38.04	11.73
18	1.69	52.19	68	41.68	11.17
19	1.74	51.28	69	45.61	10.64
20	1.79	50.37	70	49.79	10.12
21	1.83	49.46	71	54.15	9.63
22	1.86	48.55	72	58.65	9.15
23	1.89	47.64	73	63.26	8.69
24	1.91	46.73	74	68.12	8.24
25	1.93	45.82	75	73.37	7.81
26	1.96	44.90	76	79.18	7.39
27	1.99	43.99	77	85.70	6.98
28	2.03	43.08	78	93.06	6.59
29	2.08	42.16	79	101.19	6.21
30	2.13	41.25	80	109.98	5.85
31	2.19	40.34	81	119.35	5.51
32	2.25	39.43	82	129.17	5.19
33	2.32	38.51	83	139.38	4.89
34	2.40	37.60	84	150.01	4.60
35	2.51	36.69	85	161.14	4.32
36	2.64	35.78	86	172.82	4.06
37	2.80	34.88	87	185.13	3.80
38	3.01	33.97	88	198.25	3.55
39	3.25	33.07	89	212.46	3.31
40	3.53	32.18	90	228.14	3.06
41	3.84	31.29	91	245.77	2.82
42	4.17	30.41	92	265.93	2.58
43	4.53	29.54	93	289.30	2.33
44	4.92	28.67	94	316.66	2.07
45	5.35	27.81	95	351.24	1.80
46	5.83	26.95	96	400.56	1.51
47	6.36	26.11	97	488.42	1.18
48	6.95	25.27	98	668.15	.83
49	7.60	24.45	99	1000.00	.50

Figure 15

may want to be insured for longer than one year, there are other considerations.

The Rate Goes Up Every Year. Notice I said the rate, not the premium. The rate is the cost per thousand dollars of insurance. The premium is the amount you pay the insurance company every year. One thing the mortality table makes clear is that more people die each year as age increases. If the insurance company is going to continue making a profit, they'll have to charge more each year for each $1,000 worth of insurance, and there's no way around it. To the person paying the premium this isn't always obvious, for frequently the premium for a policy will remain constant. There are two ways in which the insurance company can continue to profit while keeping your costs constant. One is to decrease the amount of insurance each year based on the increasing mortality risk. This is normally referred to as "decreasing" or "declining" term. A policy that starts at $10,000 and drops to zero over ten years in $1,000 increments is called ten-year decreasing term. If it declines to zero over twenty years it's called twenty-year decreasing term, and so on. Most companies that sell this type of insurance have policies that decline over 10, 15, 20, 25, 30, and 40 years and some companies offer decreasing term to age 65 or age 100. When the agent shows you the cost per thousand on these policies you'll notice that the cost goes up as the length of the decline increases. This is your cost for the right to be guaranteed you can buy insurance in those future years.

Decreasing term insurance is logical for a number of needs: for example, if you have an installment debt and the amount of the debt is decreasing each year, you can buy a policy that will decline along with the debt. Mortgage insurance is nothing but decreasing term insurance, but since it's often sold by the lender and goes under the fancy name of mortgage insurance, you'll usually find it more expensive than the same product bought under the name of decreasing term (just like buying the generic name vs. the trade name in drugs).

Many investment salesmen recommend decreasing term on the assumption that your insurance need will go down every year as your investments increase in value. Look carefully at this concept and the figures involved. Even though your assets seem to be increasing every year, the rising costs of living may offset them and you may need more insurance rather than less.

I previously stated there were ways that the insurance company could keep your premium level while increasing the cost-per-thousand of your insurance. The first was to decrease the amount of insurance, the second is to make you prepay the increasing costs in the early years of the policy. This is called level term insurance, and goes under the names of 5-year renewable term, 10-year renewable term, term to age 65, etc. It's a level amount of death benefit and a level premium. In the case of 5-year renewable term, the company keeps your premium level for five years then jumps it to a new five year level. As opposed to annual renewable term in which the premium jumps up every year, the company will take the average premium over the five years and charge you that from the beginning. You're paying more the first two years than the term rate should be, and less the last two years, and thus the rate seems to be level. In term to age 65, the premiums are level from the date you take out the policy up to age 65.

Buying insurance where the premium is leveled over long periods just doesn't make good sense. In the end you're going to pay an increasing cost-per-thousand every year due to increasing mortality, so why pay in advance just to keep the premium level? You're just letting them use your money at no interest.

Rates for term will vary from company to company, and usually the companies with the biggest advertising budgets are the most expensive (as they prefer not to sell term at all). After you've decided what type of term insurance you want, get a variety of price quotes from companies. If you want some assistance in this task get hold of Consumer Union's

Guide to Life Insurance.[33] It contains a wealth of premium comparisons that should enable you to select the lowest cost company.

Cash Value Insurance

Suppose you decide to begin to save money on a regular investment plan. You have $100 per month that you're willing to put away regularly and you want a good deal of safety. So you walk down to your friendly savings and loan and talk with the new accounts man. The conversation goes something like this:

"Hi," you say, "my wife and I were thinking of opening a savings account and we'd like to deposit $100 every month toward our retirement."

"Oh, great," says he, "I have just the account for you. It offers security and growth. If you promise to put away $100 a month for thirty years you'll have . . ." glances down at a chart, "$54,000 when you reach age 65, that's thirty years from now. Not bad, right?"

"Great," you reply glancing at your wife "it really adds up, doesn't it?"

"It certainly does. Furthermore, if you want to borrow money from us any time along the way, we'll loan you up to the amount in your account for only 6% interest. Now where else can you borrow money for only 6%?"

"You mean you'll *loan me my own money* and I pay you 6%?"

"Well, of course you continue to earn interest on the money as though it were still in your account, so the net cost to you is only 3%," he smiles somewhat uneasily.

"By the way," you ask, "the account amounts to $54,000 at the end of the thirty years. What compound rate of interest is that?"

The banker fidgets "2½% per year, but I must point out that it's tax deferred until you actually draw it out, so that's not bad considering how high taxes are nowadays."

"Well, it doesn't sound too good to me," you reply, "but I guess maybe we'll start out and we can always move the account if we find a better rate somewhere else."

"Well, I must point out," he replies, "that our costs and overhead are such that if you wanted to close out your account at the end of the first year, we would have to keep the amount you've deposited to cover our expenses. However, if you didn't close out until the end of the second year then we'd give you back $600."

"But I would have deposited $2400 by that time."

"Well, we have expenses, you know!"

"Let me get this straight," your wife chimes in, "we open savings account, you pay us 2½% interest, nothing is credited to our account for the first year and a half, and after that if we want to use our money you'll loan it to us for 6%?"

"Well, don't forget the tax feature, and also other advantages I've failed to mention, like the fact that since you lose your first eighteen month's deposits, this tends to force you to continue to make regular deposits. A kind of forced savings plan."

"Any other 'benefits?' " she asks skeptically.

"Well yes, one more. We offer you a chance to buy decreasing-term life insurance at the same rates you could buy it outside. In fact, I should have mentioned that we require that you buy some proportionate to the amount of your savings. We have several different plans to offer."

By this time you have your coat in hand and you both rise and bid the "banker" adieu. Thanks, but no thanks, you snicker. You're too smart for this con artist; after all there are much better deals for saving your money at a dozen other banks, savings and loans, and thrift institutions within walking distance. What does he take you for, sucker of the week?

Are you really that smart? Do you now own any whole life, retirement income, or endowment life insurance policies? In other words have you ever bought cash value life insurance? Then you've already deposited money with this banker, and probably on worse terms than outlined above. He didn't come at you honestly and tell you what his real product was when he sold it to you. He told you you were buying permanent insurance and he was going to help you build a living estate as well as provide for your family in the event of your death. Life insurance companies in the United States have caused people to deposit over $200 billion under terms just as bad or worse than those outlined above, and not one policyholder in a hundred will ever know what is really happening.

The life insurance industry didn't build those massive monuments of concrete, steel, and glass from the profits of selling insurance. They built them from the profits realized by borrowing money from a gullible public at 1, 2 and 3% a year interest, and lending it back to the public in the form of mortgages on homes and office buildings at a rate of 6, 8, 10 and 12%. They are in the finance business, and insurance is merely a front.

So that you can inbed this fact clearly in your mind, without a chance of ever being brainwashed again by another well-intentioned insurance agent, let's go through and analyze a typical cash-value policy. Rather than take the most expensive policies on the market, such as those of the bigger more advertised companies like John Hancock, Mutual of New York, or Prudential, I'll take an actual policy of one of the less expensive nonparticipating companies. Following is an illustration of a policy sold by a company that is considered to be one of the best and least expensive companies on the market. It is a whole life policy sold to a man age 35, and is for an amount of $100,000. The rate-per-thousand of face amount is $16.93 and in addition there is an annual policy fee of $15.00 regardless of the size of the policy. The premium comes to $1,708 per year. Each year the company credits a certain amount to the cash value of the policy. The cash value table is shown in Figure 16. In other words, if the premium is paid every year until age 65, the policy can be dropped and the owner will receive $54,400 in cash. Since he will have paid in only $51,240, any good insurance agent will tell you that he has had $100,000 worth of insurance for 30 years for free, and made a profit of $3,160 to boot.

What Figure 16 points up is that the insurance company is not providing the insured with $100,000 worth of insurance during the term of the contract. The insurance benefit is decreasing every year by the amount of the cash value increase. Since the cash value always belongs to the policy owner, the insurance agent can't claim that it constitutes part of the "insurance."

In fact, the policy offers almost exactly the same amount of insurance as a decreasing-term-to-age-100 would offer. Suppose I went to the same insurance company and wanted to buy the same amount of term insurance each year that was actually provided under the death benefit of the whole life policy. The difference between the cost of the term and the cost of the whole life policy could be invested. Assuming a compound interest rate of 3% on the invested savings, you would accumulate $55,285 in your savings account at the end of 30 years. That's $885 more than you'd have in cash value in your policy. In other words, whole life is almost exactly the same as taking out a declining term policy and investing the difference at 3%. The cash value table also illustrates an earlier point: that you are paying a higher rate-per-thousand for insurance every year, whether your insurance agent will admit it or not. You're paying a level premium, the death benefit is going down, and the amount of savings you have on deposit is going up.

Cash value life insurance is simply a disguised form of term plus savings. What about the other types of cash value insurance? Like endowment, 20-pay life, or retirement income, for example. The only difference between these forms of insurance is the amount of premium that goes

CASH VALUE TABLE — WHOLE LIFE
MALE AGE 35 — $100,000
Annual Premium = $1708

End of Policy Year	Cash Value	+	Insurance	=	Death Benefit
1	$ 200		$99,800		$100,000
2	1,900		98,100		100,000
3	3,600		96,400		100,000
4	5,300		94,700		100,000
5	7,100		92,900		100,000
6	8,900		91,100		100,000
7	10,700		89,300		100,000
8	12,600		87,400		100,000
9	14,500		85,500		100,000
10	16,400		83,600		100,000
11	18,400		81,600		100,000
12	20,300		79,700		100,000
13	22,400		77,600		100,000
14	14,400		75,600		100,000
15	26,500		73,500		100,000
16	38,600		71,400		100,000
17	30,700		69,300		100,000
18	32,900		67,100		100,000
19	35,100		64,000		100,000
20	37,300		62,700		100,000
21	39,300		60,700		100,000
22	41,100		58,900		100,000
23	42,800		57,200		100,000
24	44,400		55,600		100,000
25	46,000		54,000		100,000
26	47,700		52,300		100,000
27	49,400		50,600		100,000
28	51,100		48,900		100,000
29	52,800		47,200		100,000
30	54,400		45,600		100,000

Figure 16

toward savings every year. If the ratio between the cost of the term insurance and the savings portion of the premium changes, the name of the policy changes. For example, endowment at age 65 means that at age 65 there is cash value in the policy equal to the face value of the policy. If you have a $10,000 endowment policy it will have $10,000 in cash value on the day it endows. To accomplish this you'll simply pay a higher premium each year, with more of your dollars going into savings and less into insurance. In an endowment policy the amount of insurance purchased declines rapidly to the date of the endowment. A whole life policy could be said to be an endowment policy that endows at approximately age 100.

Figure 17 is a rough illustration of three types of insurance a 35-year-old could buy, and the rates of decline of insurance protection versus cash value. No matter how you buy it, however, the cost of the pure insurance protection still declines, still costs more every year, and would still be replaceable by a simple term policy, leaving the opportunity to invest the difference at a rate hopefully higher than the 3% the insurance company offers.

If it is true that the insurance company is really a financing institution, and that cash value insurance is just term with a savings account, is there any reason why a person would want to buy cash-value insurance? Why don't the life insurance agents sell term instead? There are only two reasons a person would want to buy cash-value insurance. First, if they need some type of policemen hovering over them to force them to save, this is one to do it. The policyholder should know, however, that he can borrow that cash value out of the policy at any time; thus, his forced savings is really not forced. The cost for this discipline is so enormous and the psychology so ridiculous that it can hardly be considered a rational reason for buying whole life. The second reason that a person might buy cash-value insurance is if the tax advantages make it effectively cheaper than term.

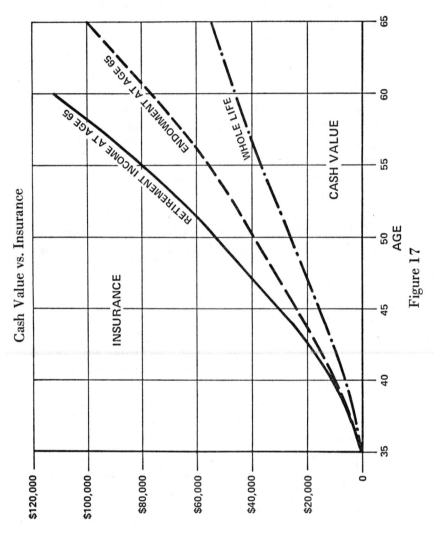

Cash Value vs. Insurance

Figure 17

Minimum Deposit Insurance: This can sometimes be done through what is known in the trade as *minimum deposit* insurance. Minimum deposit simply means that you buy regular cash value insurance, but every year you take out a maximum loan against the cash value of the policy. Thus no cash value builds up and you have the money to invest that would normally be sitting with the insurance company. The company pays you 3% interest on the savings portion of your policy. If you borrow against the policy the mechanics are something like borrowing against a savings account at the bank, wherein you use your savings passbook as collateral, and get a favorable rate of interest on the loan. The banker, knowing that you have $1,000 on deposit in a savings account, will loan you $1,000 and charge you something like 2 or 3% over what he is paying you on the savings account. He has no risk, and earns the spread between what he pays you and what you pay him. There may be reasons why a person might at some time want to do this. For example, you have a time deposit and if you drew the money out early you'd have an interest penalty. Usually it doesn't make sense. In a life insurance policy, however, it sometimes does make sense. The life insurance company treats a loan in the same way the banker does. They leave your savings untouched, still earning the magnificent 3% interest. But interest on the loan is charged to you at the rate of 6%. Thus they make the 3% difference as profit. They don't like to do this and you'll be constantly encouraged to repay the loan and bring your policy back up to "full death benefit," inasmuch as the loan reduces the amount that the company would pay your beneficiary in the event of your death. Why don't they want to make that 3% profit? Because if they lend your money to anyone else they can make two or three times as much profit.

Now comes the tax advantage to you. The company charges you 6% interest and this is deductible on your tax return as an interest expense. If you are in the happy state of being in a 50% tax bracket you'll save half the interest. In

other words, the net amount that you'll be paying to the
insurance company for the use of the money is 3%. Since
they are paying you 3% and under current tax laws that
amount *is not being currently taxed to you as income,* you
are in a break-even situation. You have the cash value out of
the policy and you can invest it and all you have left is the
term insurance portion of the contract. You have effectively
separated the cash value insurance into its two components,
and eliminated the savings element.

What's the advantage to this? Life insurance companies
heavily load their term policies in order to make them
profitable. Since profit from their cash value products is
realized from the use of the cash values, the term portion of
these policies is less expensive than it would be if purchased
separately. If you minimum deposit a cash-value policy, you
may find the net cost substantially less than a similar term
policy.

Qualifying for the Tax Deduction: The IRS says that
interest paid on a policy loan is not deductible if the
insurance was bought *under a plan of borrowing.* They call it
a plan of borrowing if the policy owner borrows more than
the amount of three full premiums out of the first seven
years of the policy. Anyone wishing to minimum deposit a
policy must be careful to pay in full four of the first seven
years and not borrow more than the amount of the premium
from the other three. After seven years he can strip the
policy every year. Also, you can lose that interest deduction
if you don't pay the interest each year in full and in cash.
Simply using a loan from the policy to pay the interest is not
enough; write a separate check for the interest.

High tax bracket policyholders should look carefully at old
cash value policies before deciding to drop them for term. It
might be possible to minimum deposit them and wind up
with a cost less than a new term policy.

Why You Can't Get the Truth: Why don't insurance agents
tell the client the truth about cash value insurance? Either

they don't know, or they find it so profitable to sell cash
value insurance that they don't want to know. On the
$100,000 policy discussed earlier, the agent will earn a
commission of $1110.20 or 65% of the first year premium.
Every year thereafter that the policy remains in force he'll
earn 5% or $85.40. In addition, the general agent he works
for (he may very well be the general agent himself) will earn
half the agent's commission the first year (32.5% or
$555.10), and 7% of the premium each year thereafter
($119.56). Between the two of them they will earn 97.5% of
the first year premium, or $1,665.30, and 12% each year
thereafter, or $205.00. Pretty profitable, right? And what if
the agent had sold you an annual renewable term policy for
$100,000? The premium would have been $290 and his
commission only 40%, or $116.00, and the second year 10%,
or $29.00. The general agent again would get an amount
equal to half the agent's commission, or $58.00, and 7% the
second year. Do you think that this commission structure
would have any bearing on what type of insurance that agent
is going to present? In one case, he and his general agent
make a commission of $1,665 with renewals of $205 per year
thereafter, and in the other case, they make $283 with
renewals of $49.30. They make six times the profit selling
one over the other. Is it any wonder that most of the
insurance in force is cash value insurance?

Are the agents dishonest? Not at all. Many agents do sell
term. Many of those who push cash-value insurance simply
don't know the facts themselves. They have been literally
brainwashed by the insurance companies to believe that cash
value is the greatest thing since the wheel. I constantly meet
agents who have enormous amounts of cash-value insurance
on their own lives. The idiocy of it boggles the mind. When
confronted with the truth they put on blinders and turn up
the background noise, for the truth is an absolute threat to
their entire careers and their self-esteem. They must either
admit you're right and stop selling cash-value insurance (thus

cutting their income to one sixth of what it formerly was), or knowingly con their clients. Instead of doing either, they just refuse to listen.

Mutual vs Stock Companies

There are two types of companies or policies that can be purchased in life insurance. One that pays dividends or one that doesn't. One is called *participating* and the other *nonparticipating,* or par and nonpar for short. A mutual company sells participating contracts. Nonparticipating contracts are sold by stock companies. Stock companies are owned by stockholders who share in the profits of the company, while the mutual companies are *supposedly* owned by the policyholders, in a kind of cooperative.

The advertising of the mutual companies would lead you to believe that your costs will be far less due to the fact that the mutual company will let you participate in the profits of the company through dividends. They do pay dividends; however, these are not part of the profits of the company, as they would lead you to believe. They simply charge a higher premium for the same type of policy than does the average stock company and later on refund you the overcharge in the form of a dividend. Since they hold this overcharge for some years before returning it, you lose the use of this money. The company, because it ostensibly is not seeking to profit from your business, is run like any nonprofit organization. Extremely high overhead, high reserves, and low efficiency eat up any savings that you might have realized.

If there is any doubt that a dividend is not really part of the profits of the company, check with the IRS. They state that dividends on insurance policies are not taxable inasmuch as they constitute a *refund of overpayment of premium.* In general, buy nonparticipating, nondividend-paying insurance. It'll save you money in the short run, and the long run.

How to Choose a Company

The way to buy life insurance is to buy the cheapest you can find that meets your needs. In most states insurance laws are strict enough to prevent insurance companies from selling insurance if they are not financially able to meet claims, *Equity Funding* notwithstanding. The odds against your buying from a company that might go defunct are minimal. Assuming you're only buying term, they'd have to go under at the same time you die, which would compound the odds in your favor. You should be buying by net cost alone, and the only way I can suggest that you approach this problem is as follows:

1. Determine the amount of insurance you need before contacting any agents.
2. Determine the length of time during which you'll need to carry the insurance.
3. From the above, determine which you think might be the best form of insurance to buy; that is, level term, declining term, or minimum deposit.
4. Call several independent insurance agents and tell them what you're looking for. Make it *clear* to them that you're knowledgeable and you're shopping the market to find the lowest cost policies.
5. Compare the rates that are submitted to you.

If agents know you're shopping and they fear being underbid, they'll go to their rate books and try to find a term rate that will beat out the competition. Don't hesitate to tell them the rate that the competition has quoted. That will force them to find a cheaper company. The first companies they select will be the companies that offer the highest commissions. They'll only look at the other companies if they're sure that they are going to lose the business. After all, a small commission is better than none.

Riders

Insurance agents will recommend a variety of riders that can be added at extra premium to a life insurance policy. The most common are accidental death benefit, waiver of premium, and insurability options. There is usually no reason to buy an accidental death benefit. If you need insurance you should buy enough to cover your need no matter what the cause of death. Any extra premium that would be paid for accidental death would create surplus coverage in excess of your true needs. Don't ever buy insurance you don't need; it's a very bad gamble. If you want to gamble, you'd be farther ahead to play the extra premium at the crap table in Las Vegas.

Waiver of premium is actually disability income insurance. When you buy it you are buying enough income in the case of disability to pay your life insurance premiums. Generally I recommend that this rider be added, except in the case of minimum deposit or cash value insurance. In that case the person would be buying disability income insurance on the cash value portion of the policy, too. It would be better to use those premium dollars to buy regular disability insurance, because the provisions of the waiver of premium clause in a life insurance policy are generally not as good as the provisions of a disability contract from one of the better disability companies. That subject will be covered in detail later in this chapter.

As far as the future insurability option is concerned, if you are certain you will be needing more insurance in the future, but don't want to take it out now, then it may be a reasonable thing for you to buy.

Just remember that the riders added on to a policy are some of the most profitable things an insurance company can sell, so buy them only if you're certain you need them.

Business Insurance

So far I've been discussing life insurance from the standpoint of an individual purchasing a policy for himself. A great deal of the life insurance sold today is sold to businesses or individuals through businesses. The life insurance industry uses business as an inroad to sell cash-value life insurance in quantities individuals would never buy. Business life insurance falls into three major categories: pension plan insurance, group term, and buy-sell insurance. Pension insurance is discussed in Chapter Five.

Group Insurance: Under current IRS regulations any corporation is allowed to purchase up to $50,000 worth of group-term life insurance on an employee and deduct the premium as a business expense without the premium being charged to the employee as taxable income. This is currently the only way that the cost of life insurance can directly become a deductible expense. In many circumstances this can result in a much lower net cost than any other method of purchasing insurance, and is most effective in a situation where there are only one or two full-time employees; for example, a professional corporation where there is only a doctor, or a doctor and a nurse.

One of the confusing elements of group term insurance deals with how much insurance is required to be carried on the other employees of a corporation in relation to what is carried by the top men. This ratio is determined by the laws of the state in which the insurance company is domiciled, rather than the laws of the state in which the policy is sold, with the result that different companies will have different requirements for employee participation in the plan. Many companies purposely register their group policies in states favorable to this problem. In Delaware, for example, the rules stipulate that for corporations with under ten employees, all full-time employees must be covered and the ratio of coverage can be either a uniform percentage of salary or a fixed amount of insurance for each salary bracket. In the latter case the employees are grouped arbitrarily into classes such as officers, supervisors, and all other employees. No bracket can exceed 2½ times the next lower bracket, and the lowest bracket must be at least 10% of the highest bracket. Since there is no requirement that there be any employees in any of the brackets, an employer could and would probably wind up insuring his full time employees for 10% of what he insured himself for. The doctor who took $50,000 worth of insurance would insure his employee for $5,000 under this method. The whole procedure is simple, and the time required to make the calculations minimal in relation to the potential premium savings available.

Life insurance companies, ever trying to find ways to sell cash value insurance, have come up with what is called *group ordinary*, a method of selling cash value insurance in place of group term. They simply substitute an ordinary life policy for the group term, and the corporation pays for and deducts the premium for the term portion of the policy while the employee pays the cash value portion. Any way it's examined it's nothing more than a regular cash value insurance policy, and the comparison should be made as to whether it is cheaper to buy the group term or *minimum deposit* the group ordinary. It all depends on the cost of the particular policy and the tax bracket of the employee.

Buy-Sell Insurance: In *professional* corporations (corporations of licensed professionals such as doctors, dentists and attorneys) the law requires that provisions be made to retire the stock of any shareholder who dies, becomes disabled, or leaves the corporation. Additionally, in corporations of two or more producing shareholders, the corporation will normally suffer some financial strain from the loss of one producing shareholder due to the continuing overhead burden.

In cases of death or disability, the corporation has the option of covering its financial risk through either insurance, or by having the remaining shareholders pay their pro-rata share of the losses personally. In order to determine when insurance should be used, and in what amounts, consideration should be given to the interests of the remaining shareholders, as well as the one who dies or is disabled.

The decedent shareholder will want his estate to realize the full value of his corporate stock including both corporate assets and receivables. Whether the value of these assets passes to his estate in an immediate lump sum payment, or in a series of payments over two or three years is normally not critical. Personal life insurance policies plus other assets would normally cover the immediate needs of his beneficiaries.

The surviving shareholders are liable for redemption of the decedents stock at its agreed upon value. By arranging to pay out the value of assets over an extended period of time, and to pay out the receivables either as collected, or over an extended period of time, there is a negligible financial burden of the remaining shareholders. The fixed assets are normally low, and the collection of receivables offsets the payment. Also, the assets become the property of the remaining shareholders, and can be resold to a new shareholder. In either case, there is no net loss.

There can be, however, a substantial overhead burden that may continue until a replacement can be found for the decedent. Assuming the decedent's share of the overhead could be reduced by 10 or 20% and that a replacement could be found and be on the job within six months, then the potential loss to the remaining shareholders could be defined as 80% of six months' overhead.

From the decedent's point of view, life insurance contracts funding the liabilities of overhead, assets, and receivables are not a good investment. He has paid his share of the premiums up until his death, but his estate does not benefit. It receives only the value of his shares of stock, which it would have gotten even without the life insurance. From the point of view of the remaining shareholders, however, the financial burden of the decedents death could be absorbed by life insurance proceeds. Insurance to fund the death risk in a corporate stock redemption plan is protection for the surviving shareholders, and is of no value to the decedent.

Since the only risk of loss is in the overhead burden, this is the only risk that calls for insurance.

SUMMARY

If you haven't yet reached financial independence, and others are dependent on you for support, you probably need life insurance. Recognize that life insurance companies are your friendly adversaries. They and their agents can't be trusted to calculate your true needs, tell you who in your family should be insured, or recommend the correct type of insurance. You must be your own informed counsel on insurance.

After reading this chapter, you should have a good understanding of the types of products available to you. Buy only term or minimum deposit, buy from a nonpar company, and skip the fancy riders. Be careful not to over-insure when you calculate your needs, and review your coverage every two years. The money you save is yours to keep.

DISABILITY INSURANCE

Throughout the discussion on insurance I have emphasized that you only insure a potential economic loss that would seriously affect your standard of living or your program for accumulating wealth. The most significant loss that any producing person can suffer would be the loss of the ability to earn. Yet this is one loss that is seldom properly covered by insurance. Only in the last few years have disability income insurance policies been widely sold, and their sale is still limited primarily to the highly-paid professional market.

How many people who own a $50,000 home fail to cover it with fire insurance? Not very many. And rightly so, as a $50,000 loss would be a serious setback to most people. Contrast that loss with the loss a 35-year-old earning $25,000 per year would suffer if disabled. He would have lost $750,000 by age 65! A loss few could stand.

What are the chances of becoming disabled? According to

the 1964 Commissioners Disability Table, 50.3% of all men now aged 35 will suffer a disability lasting at least 90 days prior to age 65. One in ten will suffer permanent disability. The chances of suffering a disabling sickness or injury are substantially greater than the chances of dying during any time period.

If you don't carry disability income insurance, carefully review this chapter to see if you should. If you have it, review your coverage after reading this chapter to see if you have the right kind, the right amount, and the lowest premium. It's probably the most important insurance you carry.

HOW MUCH SHOULD YOU CARRY?

The amount of insurance you carry is not related to your income, but to your monthly living expenses. The budget sheet on page 81 is your first tool in determining the size of your need. Column three lists your expenses as they would be in the event of disability. From this figure you could subtract the amount of any coverage you might have under Workmen's Compensation, State Disability Income Insurance, salary continuation plans from your employer, or Social Security. If you don't already know the amounts of benefits you would receive from these sources, contact your local agency office and inquire.

The other two sources, outside charity, that you'd have available to meet your expenses in the event of disability would be your accumulated assets and individual disability income insurance. By adding up your total assets and subtracting your total liabilities you'll arrive at your net worth. Dividing this figure by the annual income needed to live, will give you the number of years you'll be able to survive without income. Unless that number of years substantially exceeds your life expectancy, you'd be wise to conserve those assets for later, covering your immediate needs with insurance and keeping the nest-egg for later years when the insurance runs out or becomes worthless due to inflation.

Policy Variables

There are three variables to any disability income policy. First is the amount of the benefit during periods of disability, second is the length of time for which the benefit will be paid, and third is the waiting period after disability starts and before the benefits begin. Disabilities are categorized as either accident caused or sickness caused, and waiting periods and benefit periods can be different for the two. Your premium will depend on the structure of the benefits you choose.

DISABILITY VS. INFLATION

By mid-1974 prices were rising at 12% a year. If your current living expenses are $2,000 per month and prices continue to rise at that rate, in ten years your expenses will be $6,300 per month, in twenty years $19,000 per month, and in thirty years a staggering $60,000 per month!!

Don't panic. If you continue to work, your income should rise proportionately. However, a problem will arise if you become disabled. If you're relying on disability insurance to meet your needs, you may find that what would pay all your expenses comfortably today, won't pay for your groceries ten years from now. Even policies that offer cost-of-living escalators limit the increase to 3% to 5% a year and charge an extra premium for that benefit. If the present rate of inflation continues or increases, 3% to 5% won't help much.

How can you cope with the financial effects of a long term disability in an inflating economy? With great difficulty. Figure 18 shows roughly what one dollar of premium will buy in annual disability benefits (30 day wait) from a typical company for three standard benefit periods, and what the purchasing power of the total benefit would be at two levels of inflation.

The important conclusions that should be reached from looking at these figures are: 1. On long term coverage, the purchasing power of total benefits could be cut down to one-fourth or one-fifth by inflation. 2. You wind up with more total purchasing power by buying an *age 65 benefit* than by spending the same premium dollar to buy a *lifetime benefit*.

AGE	BENEFIT PERIOD	ANNUAL BENEFIT	TOTAL BENEFIT	Purchasing Power of Total Benefits In Todays Dollars	
				8% Inflation	12% Inflation
30	5 Years	$52	$ 260	$208	$187
	35 Years (age 65)	$35	$1,225	$408	$286
	45 Years (life)	$31	$1,395	$375	$255
40	5 Years	$35	$ 175	$139	$126
	25 Years (age 65)	$25	$ 625	$266	$196
	35 Years (life)	$21	$ 735	$250	$172

WHAT $1 OF PREMIUM WILL BUY

Figure 18

There is no way you can be sure that the benefit you buy, no matter how large, will not be outdistanced by inflation. One way to partially secure yourself against this risk is by not buying any long-term benefits, but rather by buying very large short-term benefits. Suppose you're 40 now, your living expenses are $2,000 per month and you want to have enough money to meet them until age 65, but you don't know how high prices will go. Since $2,000 times 12 months times 25 years equals $600,000 you'll need a $600,000 benefit, but in today's dollars. You might solve this by buying $10,000 per month of coverage for a five year benefit period. The total amount you'd collect would be $10,000 times 60 months or $600,000. The purchasing power of the $600,000 would be somewhat eroded even in the short period of five years, but it would be much better than collecting the same amount over 25 years. Since you would be collecting high benefits even for short term disabilities, and there are many more short term disabilities than long term, the premium will be much higher in buying your total benefit in the first five years of disability.

In summary, when you determine how much coverage you want, don't rely on the disability salesman. Figure out your budget, tally your assets and liabilities, and compensate for inflation. When the salesman says you can help offset inflation by purchasing future insurability options (the right to buy more insurance in the future), remember this isn't going to help solve the problem unless the option gives you the right to buy the additional insurance even when you are disabled and collecting benefits. Don't buy benefits more than fifteen years in the future if you can help it. Remember, paying extra for a lifetime benefit as opposed to an age 65 benefit is a waste of money if that income will be received 30 years in the future, when dollars will have depreciated. You'd be better off to save the difference and invest it.

TYPES OF POLICIES

There are two types of policies available. First is a noncancellable, guaranteed renewable policy issued to an individual. It is, as the name suggests, not cancellable by the company as long as premiums are paid on time, and guaranteed to be renewable to some future age such as age 65 or for life. The second type of policy is a group policy which covers members of a group or association (usually on a voluntary basis). Typically, group policies are renewable to group members at the option of the insurance company, and rates are subject to change by the company.

Disability companies believe that if they insure an individual for too great a benefit he may decide that it is more profitable to become disabled than to continue working. Consequently those companies that offer individual policies will only issue between 40% and 60% of a person's regular earned income. The higher a person's income the lower the percentage the insurance company will cover, and in addition they usually set an absolute upper limit of around $3,500 a month regardless of the income of the insured. These limits are both issue and participation limits, so the insurance an applicant already has in force is considered when determining the upper maximum. If your income qualifies you for $3,000 a month of coverage, and you already carry $1,500, an individual noncan carrier will only issue another $1,500. Group carriers don't operate according to the same rules. If you belong to an association that is covered by a group carrier and apply for group coverage, they normally won't inquire about your current coverage. They'll issue according to their maximum limits regardless of how much other insurance you're carrying. Thus, if you want to insure for more than the maximum limit that a noncan carrier will issue, first buy his maximum and after it is issued and in force, apply to your group carrier for the maximum they will issue. Once the policy is in force with the noncan carrier it can't be cancelled.

Another method of buying a larger amount of coverage is through a buy-sell policy. If you are in business with partners, some companies have come out with policies that will buy out a disabled partner's share of the business by paying disability benefits up to the amount of the partner's interest in the business. Usually these policies have a one-year waiting period, and benefit periods of between two and five years. They can be issued in excess of any individual policies carried by the participants, and frequently carry a reduced premium over the cost of a regular noncan policy with the same benefits.

DUAL BENEFIT PERIODS

Should accident and sickness-caused disabilities have different benefit periods? I can't imagine why. It's strange to find individuals with policies that have lifetime accident benefits, but only two to five year sickness benefits. If you're totally disabled, why would the way in which it happened have any effect on the length of time that you'll need to have income? Long term accident benefits are usually sold on the basis that they're so cheap, why not have them? Statistically anyone over age 35 is far more likely to suffer a long term disability from sickness than from accident. Accidents usually result in quick recuperation or death, and that's why those benefits are cheaper.

WAITING PERIODS

How long should your waiting period be? How long can you go without income before you begin to suffer serious financial problems that affect your standard of living or your wealth accumulation goals? Since the key to savings is to be your own insurance company whenever possible, you should have as long a waiting period as possible before the benefits start, thus reducing your premium. The insurance companies lower the premium as the waiting period lengthens, but unfortunately they load the basic policy so that you don't save as much in premium as the reduced risk would seem to warrant. For a forty-year-old male professional a $1,000 per month benefit (to age 65) with a ninety-day waiting period would cost about $388 per year. The same benefit with a thirty day wait would cost $492 per year. Thus for an extra $104 per year you would be paid an extra two months benefit in the event of a prolonged disability. This would mean if you were disabled for 90 days you would receive $2,000 that you wouldn't have otherwise received and the total cost was $104. If you had a ninety day disability only once in the first 19 years of the policy you would collect enough to pay the extra premium (discounted for 12% inflation it would be 11 years). You must realize that the insurance company has already calculated the odds against that disability occurring, and the odds are against you collecting on the bet. So even if it seems cheap to buy that extra coverage, don't buy it unless it's needed.

SELECTING THE POLICY

Once you have decided how much you need, how long a benefit period you need, and how long a waiting period you can handle, select the least expensive policy that provides the best contract. Unlike life insurance, the wording of disability income insurance contracts is not as fixed by law. Contracts vary and every clause must be carefully reviewed and compared against other available contracts before a selection can be made. The only way to do it is to read the contracts thoroughly yourself. Don't rely on an agent who works for one of the companies. Although there may be as many as fifty contractual points that must be compared, here are the more important ones.

Definition of Disability: When is the insured considered totally disabled? First, is it when he can't perform his regular occupation or when he can't perform *any* type of work for pay? Second, does this definition change after a short period of time? For example, one contract says that the insured is "considered totally disabled when he is unable to perform the duties of any gainful occupation for which he is reasonably fitted having due regard for his age, education, and experience." While another says the insured is totally disabled "when completely unable to engage in his regular occupation: however, after Monthly Indemnity has been payable to the insured's 55th birthday or for sixty months, whichever is longer, the insured is totally disabled when unable to engage in *any* gainful occupation for which he is reasonably fitted by education, training, or experience, giving due consideration to his economic status at the beginning of disability."

The first contract will only pay benefits if the insured is so completely disabled that he can't do anything for a living. A physician, insured under this type of contract, could lose an arm and an eye, but still be able to function as a clerk in a grocery store so he wouldn't be able to collect payments. Under the second example a surgeon would be paid if unable to act as a surgeon even though he might be able to perform as a general practitioner.

Most contracts redefine disability at some point in time, If a person is being paid benefits under a lifetime benefit provision and reaches age 55 (or collects for 60 months) this contract would require that his ability to earn be reassessed, and, for example, if a surgeon were able to become a teacher or a general practitioner, then at that point he would no longer be considered totally disabled. Provided, of course, that the income from his new occupation was reasonably commensurate with his prior income.

Disability income insurance contracts have changed considerably in the last few years; as competition increases and the product becomes more widely used it's likely that better and better contracts will be offered. Five years ago sickness benefits to age 65 were the longest offered and a person could only be insured in his specialty or occupation for a maximum of five years before the definition of total disability changed to force him into any occupation. Today the better companies all offer lifetime sickness benefits (at least for disabilities occurring prior to age 50) and total disability is considered by most companies to mean inability to perform your regular occupation until age 65 or for at least ten years.

The defintion of total disability is probably the most important part of a disability contract. Read it carefully and compare it with the other leading policies on the market. Remember, every word has a meaning.

Loss From Sickness: The loss from sickness clause should provide protection from sickness *which first manifests itself* during the term of the policy, not sickness which is *contracted or occurs* during the term of the policy. Otherwise you may find yourself disabled from some latent disease such as tuberculosis, cancer, or heart disease that began before you took out the policy, yet be unable to collect benefits.

Loss From Accident: The disability shouldn't have to occur within a specific number of days from the date of the accident in order to qualify as an accident claim. Since sickness benefits are generally treated less liberally than accident benefits, it is usually to the insurance company's advantage to classify claims as sickness claims.

Incontestability Clause: The incontestability clause in a disability contract prevents the company from denying payment of a claim based on prior existence of a physical condition. The incontestable clause of the Series 1000 policy of Massachusetts Casualty is an example of a better clause from the insured's standpoint:

> "After this Policy has been in force for a period of two years during the lifetime of the Insured, it shall become incontestable as to the statements contained in the copy of the application. No claim for loss incurred or disability (as defined in the Policy) commencing after two years from the date of issue of this Policy shall be reduced or denied on the ground that a disease or physical condition not excluded from coverage by name or specific description effective on the date of loss had existed prior to the effective date of coverage of this policy."

A weaker policy would except fraudulent misstatements on the application from incontestability. Thus, under the weaker contract an applicant who knew he had a condition but failed to mention it on the application might be denied payment even though the two year incontestability period had passed.

Waiver of Premium: Better contracts will waive the premium during periods of disability. These clauses vary from contract to contract. Here is Paul Revere's series 811 waiver of premium clause:

> "After total disability has continued for a period of 90 consecutive days, the Company will waive the

> payment of any premium which thereafter becomes
> due while the insured remains continuously totally
> disabled, and the Company will refund any premium
> paid under a disability policy which became due after
> such disability commenced."

This differs slightly from Massachusetts Casualty in that they will refund the amount of any wiaved premiums which were paid prior to the period of disability. Thus, if you had paid an annual premium, then became disabled and the ninety day waiting period expired, the first contract would not have refunded the premium applying to the ninety days of disability, while on the other hand they would pay an entire annual premium for you had that premium fallen due while the disability was in effect. Certain policies have no waiver of premium at all, others have various waiting periods, some don't refund premium, etc.

One clause to watch out for is one in which the company only waives the premium during periods of *compensable* disability. This would mean that if your benefit period was two years, yet you remained disabled past the benefit period, the waiver of premium would cease and even though you were still disabled you would have to start paying premiums again if you wanted to maintain the policy in force. Since it would be questionable as to whether you would be insurable again in such a situation, you'd probably want to keep the policy in force.

Presumptive Disability: Presumptive disability means that although the insured returns to work, he is still presumed to be disabled by the insurance company and would continue to receive benefits for the entire benefit period. In most contracts loss of sight, hearing, speech, or the use of two members (one hand and one foot, or two hands, etc.) qualifies the insured to receive benefits under the presumptive clause. Inferior contracts recognize only severance of the two members as presumptive disability.

Air Travel: Many older policies place restrictions on

private flying or charter flying. All of the better policies would pay benefits for disabilities caused by any type of flying.

Self-Inflicted Injuries and Narcotics: Many policies exclude coverage for disabilities incurred through intentionally self-inflicted injuries or the use of narcotics except for those narcotics prescribed by a physician other than the insured. These are seemingly innocuous clauses as most policyholders don't figure they're going to intentionally injure themselves, nor do most regularly use narcotics. What about an accident that *might be construed* to be intentional? You accidentally shoot yourself in the foot while hunting. If the insurance company decides to call it an intentionally self-inflicted injury, you might have to defend yourself in court. And narcotics? Suppose you're a physician with cold and you prescribe a mild narcotic like codein for yourself. You have an auto accident that disables you and the fact comes out that you had taken the codine. Since the clause said "... prescribed by a physician other than oneself..." you're out of luck. Better policies do not exclude intentionally self-inflicted injuries and narcotic related disabilities from coverage. In fact in the better policies the only exclusions are war or acts of war.

Transplant Surgery: With the advent of popular transplant operations some companies have added a transplant donor benefit to their policies. Normally the decision to transplant an organ from your body to the body of another is a purely voluntary act. It cannot be considered a sickness nor an accident, therefore would not be covered under a normal disability policy should it cause disability. The policies, such as Massachusetts Casualty, that do cover this type of disability normally cover a transplant donor if a disability begins 12 months after the policy is in force, and restrict the benefit period to 12 months.

Return of Premium: Many of the disability companies have boarded the cash value bandwagon by offering a disability policy for which the premiums will be refunded if a person doesn't become disabled for the first ten years of the policy. Naturally the premium is significantly higher for this type of coverage. This represents a bonanza for the insurance company and a loss for the policy holder. Companies that offer this feature offer it as a rider. In selling this feature the salesman will normally compare the rate of the company's regular policy and then add on the cost of the rider. Since the regular policy is a higher priced policy, it makes the cost of the return of premium feature seem relatively small. As a matter of fact, the salesman will be able to show you that the extra premium you'll be paying will compound itself at 12% or 13% per year for the ten year period, and if you don't get disabled you'll collect a healthy profit. He fails to mention that by going to another company you could purchase the base policy without the rider for significantly less than his company is offering it, thus lowering the hypothetical rate of return. Additionally, if you get disabled during the ten year period the company will deduct the amount of any benefit payments made to you from the refund.

No one likes to see insurance money go down the drain, and the idea of getting it back if you stay healthy is attractive. Under one company's rider if an insured has no claims during a ten year period the company will refund 80% of the total premiums paid during the period. If you have a disability claim that totals less than 20% of the ten year's premiums, the company deducts the amount paid in claims from the refund at the end of the period. If your claims during the period total more than 20% of the ten year's premiums, you get no refund, but a new ten year period commences. In case number one, let's assume that the premium is $1,000 per year for $2,000 per month of coverage with a 30 day waiting period, and you have a disability that lasts 90 days. If you put in a claim, you will receive $4,000 in benefits, but you will receive no refund of premium for the period. The premium you paid for that benefit was twice as high as you should have paid. Naturally, even if you have a disability you won't file a claim because by collecting that $4,000 you would forfeit the $8,000 refund of premium. In fact, if you were anywhere near the end of your ten year period you'd be foolish to put in any claim unless it was for at least the $8,000 potential refund.

The insurance company has effectively caused you to insure yourself. Another way to look at it is that they've sold you a policy with a 30-day wait, but because of the penalty to you, you really have a policy with a five-month waiting period.

Even if you don't get disabled and get a refund of 80% of your premium, what is the net result? The company has held the money for the ten year period. In the meantime if inflation continues at 12% per year, the 80% refund will have a value of $4,500.

In short, return of premium is something to shy away from. It's bad news.

Step-Rate Policies

In order to compete in the young professional market, one of the most lucrative markets in the disability field, companies have come out with step-rate policies which offer low premiums for the first five years, with the premiums then stepping up to regular rates. A young professional age 35 or under now has the option of buying a regular policy at a constant premium for the life of the policy, or the step rate. As an example Springfield Life offers its Select Step Rate Policy. A male professional, age 30, could buy a $1,000 per month benefit with a 30-day wait and age-65 benefit period for an initial premium of $231 per year, stepping up to $424 after five years. Or he could buy their regular policy for a straight $367 per year. Inasmuch as disability premiums are falling every year due to competition and higher medical technology, it would be advisable to take the lower premium if available. By the time the rate steps up, you may be able to transfer to an even cheaper policy.

Salesmen, working on commission as they do, frequently forget to mention the step-rate plans as the commission is substantially lower. If you're under 35, be sure you inqure.

Comparing Price

Premiums for essentially equally structured contracts vary immensely from company to company, so once you've decided on what you want, don't buy from the first company that comes along. The companies that specialize in the disability income field generally offer the best contracts at the lowest prices, but even among the specialists there is a great price difference depending on the benefits you want and your age. It's been my experience that the bigger life insurance companies tend to have the highest premiums in the disability income insurance field. Four companies that currently offer excellent contracts at low rates are Paul Revere, Springfield, Massachusetts Casualty (not to be confused with Massachusetts Mutual or Massachusetts Indemnity) and Provident Life & Accident Insurance Company.

Disability income insurance is one of the most important types of insurance you can carry. Its purchase should be approached in the same way you approach the purchase of life insurance. Determine the amount you need, how long a benefit you need, and how long you can wait before the benefit starts. Then compare the contracts and prices of a variety of companies. Don't *underinsure,* and, as in life insurance, review your coverage at least every two years.

CASUALTY INSURANCE

Most good gamblers know that one of the worst bets on the crap table at Las Vegas is 'hard-way' eight. On the average it will come up once in thirty-six rolls, and when it does the house pays thirty-to-one. They wind up with a 14% edge on every roll. Compared with casualty insurance, however, those are great odds. Instead of a 14% edge on every bet, the average casualty buyer is facing a guaranteed loss of over half of all premiums paid. Surely, it's one of the worst bets going.

Buying casualty insurance is a wager; you're betting against the insurance company that you'll suffer an accidental loss, they're betting you won't. They have statistics and the laws of probability on their side. In this section we'll look at some of the ways in which you can cut your losses.

INFLATION VS THE CASUALTY INSURERS

Before we decide that the insurance industry is ripping us off by offering odds that would make Jimmy-the-Greek blanche, we should note that U.S. casualty insurers suffered a whopping $2.6 billion in underwriting losses in 1974. Even after substantial rate increases they wound up 1975 an even more staggering $4.2 billion in the red. In a scramble to recover, they're raising rates as fast as state insurance commissioners will allow, dropping whole lines of insurance, and generally streamlining operations.

Their problem, of course, is inflation. First, it causes the prices of repairs and replacements to skyrocket. For example, State Farm's crash parts price index showed that prices of parts most frequently replaced after collisions were raised 47% in 1974-75. The companies fix rates and collect premiums in advance, and then find themselves faced with increased prices when the claims come in. To increase rates they must get approval from legislators who are facing a public already irate at big business and high prices. Overhead—and premiums—go up as companies spend time and money fighting the bureaucracy.

Furthermore, inflation causes the business cycle with its concomitant unemployment. Along with hard times comes a flood of increased claims as people feign illness, burn their own buildings, and generally seek to ameliorate their financial distress at the insurance companies' expense.

You'll still be getting bad odds, though, even when they're losing money, because your premium dollar goes into many things besides profits. First, it pays commissions—about 20%

to the broker up front. Then comes the companies' operating expenses, salaries to adjusters, attorneys' fees (yours and theirs), and taxes. What's left after paying claims to you is added to income from the investment of reserves, and that becomes the companies' profit.

The point that I'm making is that buying casualty insurance is a very poor bet. It should be done only when necessary, and that's the next problem we'll explore.

HOW TO FIGURE YOUR NEED

The last place you go to find advice on how much insurance to carry is to your insurance agent. First, he's on commission, which usually fogs his judgment, and second his time is limited. Since he makes only 15% to 20% on each policy, the average homeowners' policy will net him about $30. To make a good living he has to see a lot of people, which limits the time he can spend analyzing your case.

You should make your own determination of how much and what kind of insurance you need before you see an agent. Do this by studying your own assets in light of the risks that might affect them. *Any potential loss that would result in a substantial alteration of your standard of living, now or in the future, is a candidate for insurance.* If the loss of your house would cripple you financially, then it should be covered by insurance. If the loss of your automobile would do it, then it, too, should be covered.

However, *if your net worth is such that you could afford to replace an asset out of your capital or earnings without financial hardship, never insure it.* The odds are against you; you'll have an easier time beating the croupier in Las Vegas. By refusing to carry insurance on any property, you are effectively agreeing to act as your own insurance company, and all the commissions, expenses, lawyers fees and profits go right into your own pocket. A wise investment, indeed.

As an added bonus when you insure yourself, Uncle Sam will pick up half the losses you suffer in excess of $100 by allowing you to deduct them from your income. One more reason not to insure if you don't have to.

The two most common forms of casualty insurance carried by individuals are automobile and homeowners' policies. Let's study them in detail.

AUTOMOBILE INSURANCE

Bodily Injury

This coverage protects you against legal liability to others you might inadvertently injure or kill. Most policies offer limits starting at $15,000/$30,000 ($15,000 per person, $30,000 per accident), but can be increased for additional premium. Since six-figure judgements are not uncommon in liability cases, low limits are unacceptable. Either carry the highest limits available in the policy, or buy $100,000/$300,000 and add an umbrella liability policy on top of that. Ignore advice that tells you to insure for the amount of your net worth. The judgement could exceed any insurance and get your assets as well unless your limits are high enough. In liability coverage your net worth has little bearing on the amount of insurance you should carry.

Property Damage

This will pay for replacing or repairing the property of others that you may damage. While most policies set limits at a standard percentage of the liability limits of the policy, you can raise the limits if you wish. At today's prices it's not too hard to imagine a situation in which you could cause $25,000 in damage (run a motor home off the road, for example), so $50,000 might be a sensible limit. If you couldn't stand that kind of loss without undue hardship, buy the insurance. Buying $5,000 in coverage in this area makes no sense. You either need higher limits or no coverage at all. You might save premium dollars by asking for a high deductible on this coverage.

Medical

This pays medical bills for you, your family members, your passengers, and anyone you hit up to the policy limits and regardless of fault. Most agents routinely include $2,000 or $5,000 per person for this risk. If you're legally liable for the accident, your liability coverage will meet these costs for anyone you hit. Your own and your families' expenses would probably be met from your personal medical insurance. However, in some states a passenger in your car has no legal recourse against you if injured unless he can prove you were intoxicated or guilty of willful misconduct. Because of these "guest" laws, passengers have little recourse against the driver even when he's at fault, and consequently aren't covered by the liability provisions of the policy.

Conclusion: buy this coverage if you feel a moral obligation to passengers and you don't feel that you could cover the costs provided by the policy coverage out of your own pocket.

Uninsured Motorists

This protects you if you're the victim of a hit-and-run accident or are injured by an uninsured motorist. It will pay medical bills and death benefits for you, members of your immediate family, and guests riding in your auto, but doesn't cover property damage. Since the coverage is limited to medical and death benefits, and the limits are low, you may be covered by your medical policy or the medical provisions of your auto policy (above). You may also decide that you could handle this expense out of your own wealth or income. In any of these cases, this insurance would be a bad buy. Although the coverage is a mandatory part of policies in most states, it can usually be excluded by waiver.

Collision

This will pay for replacement or repair of your car when the damage is caused by collision or upset, regardless of fault.

This coverage is a waste of money unless you're in such a financial condition that the loss of your auto would significantly affect your financial well-being. If you have to carry it, buy the highest deductible available.

Comprehensive

This covers most damage or loss to your own auto other than collision or upset. It includes fire, theft, windstorm (pitted and broken windows are the most common claim), vandalism, falling objects, etc. It makes as little sense as collision insurance, and will simply result in the long run in doubling the cost of repairing your car. Buy it only if it's an absolute financial necessity.

The above are the major coverages standard to most auto policies. In determining your premium cost for these items, the insurance company will take into consideration your age, type of car, number and ages of other drivers in the family, distance the car will probably be driven, and your locality. In addition, and most important, the company will look at your driving record. Since there are so many variables, and since companies differ so much in their attitude toward each variable, blanket cost comparisons don't mean much. You must first decide what coverage is right *for you* and then aggressively shop price. The company that may be lowest for an adult male driver, age 40, with a perfect record, may be the highest for a young female with a poor record, and vice versa. I'll have some more comments on selecting a company after we look at homeowner's insurance.

HOMEOWNER'S INSURANCE

Homeowner's policies fall into six categories: forms 1, 2, 3, and 5 cover owners of single houses, form 4 is for renters, and form 6 is for condominium owners. Form 1 is a basic policy covering fire, lightning, windstorm, hail, explosion, riot, etc., as well as liability to others whose persons or property has been injured. Form 2 broadens and extends these coverages, adding such things as damage from freezing, falling objects, building collapse and water leakage. Form 3 adds paint spills, etc., while form 5 is a comprehensive all-risk policy that covers both dwelling and contents against just about everything that isn't specifically excluded in the policy. Benefits under the standard policies are arranged as follows:

Dwelling

You select the amount of insurance to cover losses to the house, but it cannot exceed the replacement cost (excluding land and foundation). If you insure for an amount less than 80% of the replacement value (calculated at the time of the claim), the insurance company considers itself to be a co-insurer, with you as its partner. In the event of a partial loss to structure or contents they will not pay the full loss, but will pay only their percentage. If you carry $25,000 of insurance and the dwelling replacement cost is determined to be $50,000, the company would pay only 50% of any loss, up to the maximum of $25,000. This can cause a dispute at the time of claim, since the insurance company will want to fix the replacement cost of the dwelling at as high a figure as possible in order to reduce the percentage of the loss they must pay. For this reason most agents will encourage you to carry 90% or 100% coverage. Since the replacement cost is calculated at the time of the claim, you may find that you insured originally for 100% of the value, but subsequent inflation has increased the replacement cost. If it goes below 80%, you lose.

How much insurance you carry should depend again on your financial situation. If you can afford to rebuild out of your own wealth without undue strain, then you don't need this insurance. If not, you may need some or full coverage. Remember, if you buy a high deductible, you save premium dollars.

Outbuildings and Private Structures

These will be covered for 10% of the coverage on the dwelling and are subject to the same co-insurance provisions cited above.

Personal Property On Premises

It's covered for 50% of the dwelling coverage, but excludes coverage on things that are not considered normal and necessary belongings. The exclusions would include unusually valuable items such as stamp and coin collections, firearm collections, gold and silver, jewelry, furs, etc. Most of these items are covered to $500 and floaters are required if additional coverage is needed. A frequent problem after a fire is remembering and substantiating the value of lost articles. A wise precaution whether you insure or not is to make a written inventory and valuation of all belongings in the home, backed up with photographs of the interior rooms of the house. These should not be kept on the premises, for obvious reasons. They'll be extremely useful in making an insurance claim or in substantiating a tax loss.

Personal Liability

This provides insurance against liability for injury to others both on and off the premises. With a few exceptions such as auto accidents, it will protect you from lawsuits up to $25,000, and this amount can be increased at a nominal cost. This coverage is critical in the same way that auto liability coverage is. Either raise the internal limits up to six-figures, or add on an umbrella liability policy. This is no place to scrimp on premiums.

Medical

This is similar to the medical coverage provided under the auto policy, and covers nonresidents of your home for up to $500 in medical bills, regardless of fault. Since the limits (and risks) are so low, this is a bad buy for most homeowners.

Other

Standard policies also provide 10% of the personal property coverage for property lost or damaged away from the premises, as well as additional living expenses incurred when your home is unliveable after damage from an insured peril. Since these amounts are normally minimal, most people whose financial houses are in good order are wasting money on this portion of the premium. This is also true of most of the additional-premium endorsements to the standard policy, such as theft-from-auto, outboard motor and boats, credit card and forgery endorsements. They swell your premium but not your wealth.

Two endorsements, however, might be prudent. Both earthquake and flood damage are excluded from standard policies but are available separately; earthquake from private insurance companies and flood from the federal government. Most agents recommend against earthquake insurance, even in high-risk areas like California. The argument is that the premium is too high and the risk too small. When the premium is high for insurance it normally means that the risk is high, as well. Those of us in earthquake zones would be well advised to consider paying the high premium (it runs around $2 per $1000) if we couldn't stand the loss. Flood insurance is similar, but in this case it must be purchased through the government since private insurers are unwilling to stand the risk at any price. Your agent can help you get it.

ON SELECTING A COMPANY

There are four basic criteria to be used in selecting an insurance company.

Financial Stability

The company must be able to meet its obligations to policyholders without compromise. While state insurance commissions attempt to restrict the field to financially stable companies, the system is not foolproof as is evidenced by the fact that dozens of companies have gone under in the past two years. *Best's Insurance Reports—Property & Liability*[34] is a standard industry reference book that rates companies by their financial strength. Check out your company before you buy a policy.

Service

Most experts suggest staying with companies that have a good reputation for efficiency and prompt payment of claims. I'm at a loss as to how to obtain this information. Relying on hearsay of agents or friends seems rather unscientific, so although you might take anything you hear into account, this shouldn't be the determinant.

Cost

Premiums for identical coverage can very 100% or more in casualty insurance. For this reason it can be very profitable to spend a few hours on the phone obtaining competitive quotes for the coverage you need. Start first with the biggest companies and work your way down. Allstate, State Farm, Aetna, Nationwide, and Travellers are a few of the largest in both auto and homeowners. Both Allstate and State Farm employ their own agents and do not sell through independent insurance brokers. For companies like Aetna that use brokers, one call can get you several quotes.

It's of little use for me to quote comparison prices of different policies here, since rates change constantly, and the specific coverages needed along with the individual's personal situation can cause any blanket rate comparisons to be misleading. What may be the cheapest company for one situation may turn out to be the most expensive in another. In relation to automobile policies, don't overlook your local automobile clubs like AAA. For certain risks they frequently offer the lowest cost.

SOME THOUGHTS ON AGENTS

There is no doubt that a knowledgeable and efficient broker can be helpful in getting the right coverage and good claim service. The danger in relying completely on your broker is that he probably restricts the bulk of his business to two or three companies in each line of insurance (in order to give enough volume to those companies to get favorable commission rates and claims service), and therefore is not likely to shop price for you beyond those companies. Furthermore, brokers stay away from companies that pay low commissions, even though those companies often offer the lowest rates. The independent broker thus becomes only slightly less narrow in his viewpoint than the agent who works directly for an insurance company like State Farm. To get the job done correctly you must do it yourself in shopping for insurance.

Remember, when asking your agent for advice about coverage, don't let him sell you on picking up lots of little extras on the policy, just because they're "so cheap". Those extras add up to massive losses of premium dollars over the years and years you'll be carrying insurance, and would be much better spent on increasing your wealth or improving your coverage in high risk areas.

CONCLUSION

Auto and homeowners insurance are only two of the many types of casualty insurance you may need. If you're in business you'll be considering such things as fire, marine, transportation, directors and officers liability, and so on. Although there is not room in this brief presentation to discuss each of these in depth, the basic rules of insurance buying still apply. Don't be a sucker and play the 'hard-way' eight. Buy only coverage for risks that would cause severe financial strain, and avoid frills. Finally, get on the phone and shop.

CHAPTER FIVE

The Income Tax

LEGAL FOUNDATIONS

Our founding fathers were painfully aware of the power that could be wielded by any despot who had the authority to tax. (Thomas Paine himself, prime intellectual force behind the revolution, had been a tax collector in England prior to coming to the colonies.) However, even though our revolution was partially seeded by a resistance to the taxing policies of King George, there was never any real opposition to the concept of taxation. Rather, it was taxation without representation that was at issue. In order to protect the people against the abuse of the tax system, the Constitution provided that any direct taxes (taxes directly on individuals, as opposed to indirect taxes like excise taxes on products) had to be apportioned among the various states on a per capita basis, just as representatives to Congress were, whereas indirect taxes could be levied at the will of Congress. Falling on rich and poor equally, direct taxes would always be unpopular and difficult to collect.

The concept of a progressive income tax was highly popular, even if unconstitutional. Poorer folks always felt that the rich should pay more of the tab for government expenditures. Whenever need for more money arose there was a clamor for a progressive income tax.

In 1894 Congress passed such a law, levying 2% taxes on all incomes over $4,000. The tax was challenged however, and the Supreme Court invalidated it, calling this a direct tax, and therefore not properly apportioned. Undaunted, the proponents of the tax went after a Constitutional amendment, and in 1913 the 16th Amendment brought in the income tax with a vengeance.

It could be viewed as poetic justice that those who were jealous of the wealth of the successful few should wind up being the principal victims of the tax they brought into existence.

THE TAX PROTEST MOVEMENT

Ever since the inception of the income tax, there have been those who have resisted paying. In the last few years the tax protest movement has grown into somewhat of a *cause celebre* with a number of protesters even writing books about it.

It's Spent On The Wrong Things

The reasons protesters give for refusing to pay their taxes are varied. Many simply don't like the purposes to which the taxes are put. Carl Hess, Barry Goldwater's chief speechwriter for his 1964 presidential campaign and ghost writer for both Ford and Nixon, became a tax resister after being audited for returns filed while working in politics. He says in his recent book *Dear America:*[3][5]

> "The auditing of the losers in a political campaign has by now become simple routine for the victors. Although aware that the decision to stop paying taxes grew out of general anger, I did think that there were particular and publicly responsible reasons for doing it ... I had concluded, in all conscience, that the tax money was used for a warfare system that killed to preserve the power of the privileged few and a welfare system that regimented the poor for the same purpose, all within a federal system that had absolutely taken over and overpowered every right of

> individual or community-based freedom that had
> been envisioned in the settlement of the country. . ."

What happens to someone who doesn't pay his taxes? Hess is now unable to own anything, or even receive a salary.

> "The IRS has systematically slapped a 100% lien on
> every piece of my life they could locate. Once, when
> I asked the IRS how I might handle a situation in
> which they took 100% of everything I earned while
> the corner grocer still demanded a smidgen for
> rutabagas, the IRS robot facing me at the moment
> replied, with simple clarity: 'That's not our
> problem.' "

Hess has turned to the barter system to survive, trading his work for whatever he might get in provisions.

Another protester who feels strongly about the uses to which tax monies are put is Marvin Cooley, author of *The Big Bluff*, who has this to say:

> "Virtually all of our income tax money is being
> spent not only illegally but to the detriment of our
> country. Our taxing system has been subverted and
> changed into an instrument of plunder and a source
> of financing for the enemies of America.
> "Tax monies used for welfare, grants, subsidies,
> and other special favors are completely contrary to
> the intent and structure of the Constitution. It is
> theft in the guise of law. The Fourteenth Amendment
> to the Constitution, Section 4, specifically states:
> 'But neither the United States nor any State shall
> assume or pay any debt or obligation incurred in aid
> of insurrection or rebellion against the United
> States. . .'
> "In direct and treasonous violation, billions of our
> tax dollars are financing Marxist governments abroad
> and Marxist revolutionaries at home. Both have
> avowed our destruction."

IRS Violates The Law

All tax protestors are particularly critical of the IRS, as most of them have felt its wrath. Henry J. Hohenstein, in his recent book, *The IRS Conspiracy*, claims that:

"... the IRS is a secret organization operating with
secret methods and sometimes illegally and under
secret orders with the dual objectives of (a) terror-
izing the individual taxpayer into doing or paying
anything the IRS demands while avoiding combat in
any case that might be won by the taxpayer or might
get publicity that could be adverse; and (b) protecting
its own personnel and policies from public gaze while
attempting to give the impression of openness and
reasonableness ... the IRS can and will seize your
property without notice and without a court order
and without due process of law ... The IRS can and
will deny you equal protection of law, in that the
taxes you pay may be much higher than those paid
by someone in identical circumstances ... If you take
a case to tax court you will discover that you are
guilty until proven innocent—that you must prove
your case; it is not incumbent upon the IRS to prove
the case against you."[36]

The IRS consistently uses illegal means to gain its ends,
according to many protestors. Hohenstein says that

"Senate hearings a few years ago disclosed that the
IRS had defied court orders, illegally picked locks,
stolen records, illegally tapped telephones, opened
and read personal mail, threatened reputable citizens,
hidden microphones to spy on the privileged con-
versations between taxpayers and their lawyers, and
maintained a staff of specialists in illegal snooping
activities. 'I violate the law at all times,' said (IRS)
special agent Thomas Mennitt. 'It's part of my
duties.' "

Marvin Cooley wholeheartedly agrees with Hohenstein on
this point. He, too, points out that the IRS has a history of

"illegally picking locks, cracking safes, stealing
records, tapping telephones, harrassing, bullying,
threatening, and imposing arbitrary and unjustifiable
assessments on innocent and virtually helpless
citizens. IRS agents arbitrarily seize bank accounts,
safety deposit box contents, wages, automobiles,
homes, and anything else they can get their hands on.
All this is done without leave of any court, without

due process of law, without court order, and without trial. Sovereign immunity provides a shelter for IRS agents to commit criminal acts such as assault, libel, false imprisonment, false arrest, fraud, deceit, and interference with contract rights."

To Carl Hess IRS employees are

"the most abjectly humorless, dehumanized, order-taking, weak-charactered, easily vicious, almost casually amoral people I have ever met."[37]

The Income Tax Is Illegal

Cooley really believes that the tax is illegal. Although an amendment to the Constitution brought the tax into existence, that amendment did not alter or abolish earlier protections built into the Bill of Rights.

Amendment IV. "...The right to the people to be secure in their persons, houses, papers, and effects, against unreasonable searches and seizures shall not be violated..."

Amendment V. "No person shall be ... deprived of life, liberty, or property, without due process of law ... nor shall be compelled to be a witness against himself..."

Amendment XIII. "Neither slavery nor involuntary servitude shall exist within the United States..."

These guarantees of individual liberty that we think of as inviolable are not so inviolable after all when it comes to the IRS, the protestors claim.

1. Taxpayers are forced to keep records for the benefit of the IRS. (Violation of Amendment XIII).
2. Taxpayers are forced to disclose details of all financial dealings. (Violation of Amendment V).
3. Taxpayers may have their property seized and sold to satisfy delinquent taxes. (Violation of Amendment V).
4. Taxpayers' property may be searched and seized without due process. (Violation of Amendment IV).

The IRS Code, itself, claims to rely on "voluntary compliance" on the part of taxpayers, but since few would give voluntarily, the IRS has usurped the powers denied it by the Constitution.

These then are a few of the reasons protestors cite when they refuse to pay their income taxes. There are more, of course. Some of the more conservative even state that the income tax is part of a massive conspiracy on the part of the communists to destroy the American capitalistic system. They point out that a heavy progressive or graduated income tax was one of the ten points of the party platform in Karl Marx's *Communist Manifesto*.

THE LOGICAL PROTEST

What should one's reasons for resisting the theft of his provisions most properly be? Would it be that he didn't approve of the uses to which the money was put? Tax protestors use this as a major rallying point. Yet, unless a country has elected officials that are both ethical and of infallible judgment, government will always be spending money in ways that are wasteful and contrary to the wishes of at least part of the taxpayers. There never could be a situation in which all the taxpayers would agree on the uses to which the tax money was put, and it therefore follows that this type of protest would mean a great portion of the population would not pay their taxes, regardless of how honest the government was. It seems an impractical protest.

What about protesting that the theft is illegal (that is, that the citizens didn't approve); Those who protest the income tax on Constitutional grounds should question themselves as to whether they would agree to pay the tax if the Constitution were amended to provide for its easy collection. Just because an idea was promulgated two hundred or two thousand years ago does not mean that it is right, per se. This is one of the major flaws in the concept of law. Decisions are too often based on precedence rather than reason. Our founding fathers may have been brilliant, but that does not mean they were infallible. I believe this is proven by the fact that they set up a system of taxation to start with. To follow a line of reasoning that predicates everything on its constitutionality would mean that whatever country you lived in, and regardless of how irrational or unfair its laws might be, you should always abide by them. It seems weak reasoning to me for someone to protest the slaughter of the Jews in Germany based on the violation of statutes of the day. It would seem far more lucid to object on pragmatic or moral grounds.

A valid argument against taxation should not be based on the legal precedents of the community, whatever they might be nor on the use to which the plundered taxes are put, but rather on the practical reality that the theft causes the entire society to have a lower standard of living.

As far as the IRS is concerned, there is little doubt that it is an organization to beware of. Since it has been amply demonstrated that it is not interested in observing your property rights or your constitutional rights, you should make a practical decision as to whether or not you should do battle with it. Some protestors take the position that it is their duty to oppose the tyrannical practices of this organization. I'm not sure how effective martyrs have been historically, but I think that most who have spit in the faces of tyrants down through the ages have wound up in prisons or mass graves and had little positive effect on the advancement of mankind. It would seem to me that the lone fighter of the system is involved in a futile sacrifice. To resist the IRS is to subject oneself to the possibility of being jailed or put out of business, even though you may be innocent of any crime, and completely within your constitutional rights. Saying 'no, I won't pay my taxes because you're bad guys' can be compared to standing in a hungry tiger's cage with a piece of meat saying 'no, you can't have it 'cause you're not being a good kitty'. He'll likely have the meat and you, too.

It's rather sad that the great majority of tax protestors base their resistance on unfair collection mechanisms, legal precedents, and disapproval of the use of the tax monies. It's time that the tax system was brought to trial for its real flaw: that is economically unsound because it is based on theft. When that is widely understood, and the viable alternative intelligently demonstrated to the society, then and only then will a constructive change come about.

IN SEARCH OF SHELTER

If you've made the decision to pay taxes without overt protest, but you're wondering if there's some legal and acceptable way in which to reduce those taxes to a minimum, this section might be of some help. I'll attempt to break tax sheltering devices down into manageable categories, and outline a strategy for selecting those that will apply to your particular tax problem.

There are several kinds of income according to the IRS, and these types of income are subject to different tax treatments. First, is the income from wages, salaries, and unincorporated businesses. This is classed as "earned income." Next comes income from interest and dividends. While not "earned income" this is still "ordinary income". Third, comes income from the sale of appreciated assets. This is normally called "capital gains" income, and is "unearned" income. Since the tax rate on capital gains is less than the rate on ordinary income, it is usually beneficial to try and have income classed as capital gains, or to shift ordinary income into capital gains income if possible.

Contrary to popular belief, it is very difficult to avoid taxes on income. About the only income that completely avoids taxation is the income from municipal bonds. Most "tax shelters" serve to *postpone* the taxation of income, and occasionally serve to *convert* the income from ordinary to capital.

It should also be made clear that there is no "shelter" that is permanent. As government expenditures increase, there is more pressure to increase taxes, and consequently to do away with shelters. Every year we find Congress considering new tax legislation that will close the "loopholes". Any tax-sheltered investment must be considered in light of potential changes in the tax law. The first shelter possibilities I'll discuss will be those devices that might lower your taxes on earned income; that income from your salary, or business.

It's interesting that very few people ever bother to make detailed tax estimates for future years. Failing to do this simple task can be extremely costly. First, the taxpayer is unable to keep his taxable income relatively level, thus minimizing taxes. Second, he is unable to know whether tax shelters would really be beneficial to him in the long run, since he fails to calculate the effect of the sale of sheltered investments. Third, he is unable to properly plan his cash flow for the year, and frequently winds up on April 15 with a tax bill for which he has no liquid funds.

The Tax Estimator, Figure 19, is a rough worksheet meant to help you forecast your tax liability for the next three years. This estimator does not take into account certain more complicated problems including income averaging, pension and annuity income, minimum preference items, and tax credit items. If you anticipate income or expense items that are not listed, adjust accordingly. In order to minimize your taxes, it's helpful to know what your anticipated taxable income will be in advance. If you can foresee a year coming in which your taxable income will be either lower or higher, you can use some of the tax devices discussed in this article to shift income into or away from the year in question, and thus wind up with a more level annual income. Since the income tax is progressive, you'll wind up paying less income tax if your income is level every year than if it shifts up and down.

QUALIFIED RETIREMENT PLANS

Tax laws provide that a certain portion of anyone's earned income from job, profession, or business can be placed into a trust fund, and left there until retirement. The first tax advantage to doing so is that the amount diverted is not taxed to the individual in the year earned, but rather in the year the money comes out of the trust at retirement. The second advantage is that interest, dividends, or capital gains earned on the monies in the trust are not taxed when earned. They form part of the corpus of the trust and are subject to the same tax treatment on withdrawal as is the original contribution. The third tax advantage is that the withdrawal of funds at retirement may be subject to advantageous tax treatment. If withdrawn in a lump sum there can be averaging provisions that will reduce the tax, or the monies may be left in trust and a portion of them taken annually, thus reducing the tax.

There are three qualified retirement plans available and which you can use depending on the type of income you have. If you're incorporated your corporation may set up a pension plan, a profit-sharing plan, or both. If you are self-employed you may contribute to a Keogh (HR 10) plan. If you have neither of the above plans, you may set up an Individual Retirement Account (IRA).

CAN YOU HAVE MORE THAN ONE RETIREMENT PROGRAM?

If you have salary income from a corporation as well as other income from self employment, your corporate salary can be covered by one or more corporate retirement programs, and your self employment income by a Keogh plan. However, the same does not hold true for the IRA. You can set up an IRA only if you have no other active, qualified retirement plans.

TAX ESTIMATOR

	Current Year	2nd Year	3rd Year
Income			
Salary, wages, commissions			
Self-employment (From Schedule C-1)			
Interest, Dividends			
Capital Gains (50%)			
Partnership Income			
State Income Tax Refunds			
Total Income			
Deductions			
Medical*			
Property Taxes			
Sales Taxes			
State & Local Income Taxes			
Auto Licenses			
Charitable Contributions			
Home Mortgage Interest			
Other Interest			
Charitable Contributions			
Casualty Losses			
Alimony & Miscellaneous			
Partnership Losses			
Employee Business Expense			
Keogh Plan Contributions			
IRA Plan Contributions			
Personal Exemptions**			
Total Deductions & Exemptions			
Taxable Income (Income Less Deductions)			
Taxes			
Federal Income Tax			
State Income Tax			
Self-Employment Tax			
Total Taxes			
Taxes Paid to Date			
Balance Due April 15			

*See Form 1040, Schedule A
**$750 multiplied by number of exemptions.

Figure 19

CORPORATE PLANS

In these plans the company makes a contribution to a trustee who takes the money and holds it or invests it at the direction of you or a committee appointed by your employer. The contribution is a deductible business expense to the employer, but since it is placed in the hands of a trustee and not released to you until normal retirement age, it is not deemed to be part of your salary until you actually receive it. If you're in a 50% tax bracket and receive $1,000 in salary you'll pay $500 in taxes and have only $500 left to invest. If the employer contributes the same $1,000 to a plan, the entire $1,000 can be invested and you'll have the earnings on the whole amount accruing to you over a period of time. The difference between the amount you'd have left if you received the income direct, paid the tax, and invested the difference, and the amount you would accumulate if you invested the pretax amount and compounded it at the full pretax compounding rate, will be a profit to you for having participated in the plan.

Under current law the amount the corporation can contribute depends on the type of plans set up. There are two qualified plans, the pension plan (which can be either a defined benefit plan or a defined contribution plan) and the profit-sharing plan.

Defined-Benefit Pension Plans

A defined-benefit pension plan is a plan designed to give an employee a fixed monthly income at some preselected retirement age. For example, the corporation decides that normal retirement age is 65, and that it will provide any employee who stays with the corporation a sufficient length of time with a retirement salary equal to 75% of his salary at the time of retirement. Thus if the employee is making $2,000 a month when he reaches age 65, the retirement fund will pay out to him $1,500 a month for the rest of his life.

In order to calculate the amount of money that must be contributed to this plan, actuarial calculations are required. The actuary takes into consideration the number of years before the employee's retirement, the salary being earned by the employee, the number of years the employee is likely to live after retirement, and the estimated rate of return the trust will be able to earn on the money deposited. From these inputs he calculates how much money whould be deposited each year for that employee.

In some cases corporations will not hire actuaries directly, but will simply purchase retirement-income insurance policies or annuities from insurance companies, in which case the insurance company is taking on the job of making these calculations.

Under current law there is no precise limit to the amount of money that can be put away for a corporate employee to fund a defined benefit pension plan. Each plan is submitted to the IRS for approval and they have the right to disqualify it if they feel that it discriminates among the employees unfairly, or if it allows for too great a retirement benefit.

Defined benefit plans can be particularly beneficial to high income professionals. A 55-year-old doctor with a net practice income of $100,000 a year could incorporate and set up such a plan that will pay him 100% of salary at age 65. He could set his salary at $50,000 a year and contribute the other $50,000 to the retirement plan. Thus, over 10 years he would accumulate $500,000 in the plan plus interest, and under the right set of actuarial assumptions this could fund his total salary on retirement. His income taxes drop substantially, of course, as now instead of being taxed on the entire $100,000 of practice income, he is only taxed on $50,000 of salary.

The first drawback to a defined-benefit plan would be the fact that a contribution must be made to the plan every year, even if the corporation does not show a profit. The only exception would be in the case a plan were terminated.

Defined-benefit plans have the further drawback that the amount of future contributions cannot be accurately estimated when the plan is initiated. Poor investment performance of the funds might require much larger contributions in the later years of the plan in order to meet the promised pensions.

Defined-Contribution Pension Plans

If a corporation doesn't want to hire actuaries to calculate its plan contributions, or is uncertain of varying future contributions, but still wants the advantages of tax deductible contributions to a retirement plan, it can set up a defined-contribution pension plan. Here the annual contribution to the plan is a fixed percentage of each covered employee's salary, up to a maximum of $25,000. The percentage of salary is limited to 25% and the same percentage of salary must apply to all employees; thus the doctor who would put away 25% of his salary must also contribute 25% of his nurse's salary to the plan for her benefit. The ultimate retirement income available to an employee will not be a fixed percentage of salary, as in the defined-benefit plan, but rather will depend on the size to which the fund has grown at retirement. Thus, if the contributions are invested wisely, the employee's retirement check would be bigger, and if they are invested foolishly, he might wind up with very little. One should realize that under the defined-benefit plan the money could be invested unwisely also, but if the fund consistently lost money, the corporation would be obligated to make larger contributions to make up for the fund's poor performance.

Profit-Sharing Plans

A profit-sharing plan is supposedly set up to let the employees of a corporation participate in the profits of the company. Ostensibly its functions are two fold: to give the employees an incentive to produce more efficiently by sharing in the profits generated, and to provide them an additional retirement benefit. For most small corporations, the plan is not used as an incentive to employees but rather as another method of reducing the taxes of the stockholder-employees. The corporation is allowed to contribute an amount equal to up to 15% of the compensation of eligible employees, and deduct the contribution as a business expense. The money is put into a trust fund and invested until the employee's retirement, at which time it is distributed to him, either in a lump sum or in installments. The employee doesn't declare it as income until it's actually received. The corporation is not obligated to make an annual contribution to a profit-sharing plan. The board of directors determines the profits at the end of each fiscal year and decides on the size of contribution. This makes the profit-sharing plan more attractive to small corporations in which the amount of available capital is uncertain from one year to the next.

A company setting up a profit-sharing plan can also contribute to a pension plan, but when two plans are in existence at one time, they are limited to a total contribution of 25% of each employee's compensation, or $25,000, whichever is less. Thus with both plans in effect and 15% being contributed to the profit sharing plan, only 10% could be contributed to the pension plan. Most professional corporations or other closely held corporations tend to prefer a combination of the two plans in that they have the option to put as much as 25% of salary away each year, but are only obligated to put away the 10% that represents the pension plan.

Vesting

The vesting period of a plan is the period during which an employee must work for a company before being entitled to withdraw his retirement plan monies upon termination. The IRS tends to favor shorter vesting periods, especially in smaller corporations in which the stockholder employees have a large share of the profit-sharing fund. Typically a professional corporation will set a vesting schedule which will vest pension plans at the rate of 10% per year and profitsharing plans at the rate of 20% per year, thus they would be totally vested over five or ten years. The owner of a small corporation might prefer to let the participants' accounts vest even more rapidly. The faster the better as far as the IRS is concerned.

Trustees

Both pension and profit-sharing plans require that the funds contributed be held by a trustee in trust for the participants. The function of the trustee is to take the funds from the corporation, record their receipt, invest them in whatever the investment committee tells it to invest them in, hold the securities purchased, and record all transactions that occur. Currently the trustee must file from 990-P and provide the information to the corporation to enable the corporation to file forms 4848, 4848-A and 4849 with its federal income tax return.

While the corporation may set up an investment committee whose function is to determine where the plan funds are to be invested, their directions to the trustee may be ignored if the trustee in his judgment believes that the recommended investment would either violate the rules of prudent investment judgment, or would disqualify the plan's deductibility in the eyes of the IRS. Typically, banks and trust companies are set up to act in the capacity of trustee for retirement plans, and the majority of the plans in the country are trusteed by such institutions. However, there is nothing that precludes any individual from acting as the trustee of a plan, and many professionals do act as their own trustee. The only problem with doing this is that an individual, untutored in the role of trustee, might inadvertently disqualify a plan by failing to adhere to the rules and regulations. On the other hand, the services of a professional trustee are expensive, and in smaller plans the costs significantly eat into the tax savings of the program.

You must look carefully at the source of the recommendations you get in this area, as in any other. Many lawyers rely heavily on the referrals they get from banks and trust companies, and to promote the idea that a person can act as his own trustee is likely to result in offending his sources. Like most other things however, you can do it yourself and cheaply.

Administration

In addition to the function performed by the trustee, there are certain other services required that fall under the heading of administration. They consist of determining the amount that should be contributed to the plan each fiscal year, how that is to be allocated among the employees, informing each employee as to his vested interest in the plan, and filling out forms 4848 and 4849 for the corporation federal tax return. These tasks can be handled by the corporate bookkeeper or farmed out to companies that specialize in the administration of this type of trust.

Funding

Pension and profit-sharing funds can be invested in a variety of ways. They can be used to purchase:
1. Savings Accounts.
2. Time Certificates.
3. Bonds, Corporate and Government.
4. Preferred Stocks.
5. Common Stocks.
6. Mutual Funds.
7. Life Insurance.
8. Limited Partnership Interests.
9. Real Estate.

That isn't to say that the trustee of your plan will automatically purchase these things on the request of the investment committee. To the contrary, most trustees will look at several factors before investing.

1. **Is it prudent?** The Prudent Man rule says that the trustee can be liable for losses if he invests the money in something that a "Prudent Man" would not have invested in, all things considered. This is a vague rule that would probably come into play if the participant in a plan decided to sue for breach of fiduciary responsibility in the event of loss of trust funds. Nevertheless, in most states trustees are bound by this rule, and in the case of any unusual investments will always try to determine the merits of the investment.

2. **Is it liquid?** Inasmuch as participants in retirement plans occasionally retire, quit, become disabled or die, there are periodic needs to dispurse portions of the funds. A trustee will want a substantial part of the monies in the plan to be in readily marketable investments such as common stocks, bonds, and savings accounts in order to meet these payments.

3. **Is the investment a problem in terms of paperwork or handling?** Trustees like to deal with simple paperwork transactions. Most will not get involved with storing things like gold coins, or investigating the merits of small offerings. The fees they charge just aren't enough to justify anything but investments that can be handled routinely.

4. **Is the investment a business to be operated directly or indirectly by the plan?** If a pension plan owns a business, the income from that business will not be

tax free, as is the income from other passive investments. It will be treated as unrelated business income and taxed to the plan. While this type of investment will not disqualify the plan, it does make the plan lose some of its attraction as a shelter.

Life Insurance

Of the things available to a pension plan as investments, what are most logical? Well, certain things can be eliminated right off. One of the most common vehicles for plan funding is life insurance. The insurance companies of the United States have developed immense divisions to do nothing but sell life insurance to pension plans. Their arguments to justify these sales follow these lines:

1. The growth is guaranteed. It's risk free.
2. The insurance portion of the whole life is taxable to the employee, but at favorable rates.
3. The death benefit is free of estate tax.
4. You're buying your insurance with pre-tax dollars.
5. The insurance company provides the actuarial services free or at a very low cost.

That list is by no means complete, as you well know if you've ever been approached by an insurance agent regarding pension plans. Let's examine it point by point.

1. The growth is guaranteed. Right, you get a guaranteed 3 to 4% return on the invested funds. Let's face it, in a conventional cash value insurance policy outside a plan the 3% return has some tax advantage in that the income isn't taxed. But inside the plan income wouldn't be taxed anyway. Why not a bank savings account, or better still, Treasury bills guaranteed by the U.S. Government that might double the yield of the life insurance contract but still give you the

safety you want? They shouldn't say the growth is guaranteed, they should say *the loss* is guaranteed because that's exactly what you'll have in our present economy if you put your funds to work at 3 or 4%.

Of course, the insurance agent will counter that the true rate of return on the insurance policy is effectively double because the contribution to the plan was tax deductible. Of course, but the true return of *any* investment made with those dollars would be doubled by the same token. When considering returns, look at your pension or profitsharing dollars as an isolated fund, not affected by the fact that it was contributed to the plan originally. In reality, it is simply part of your overall net worth; part of your investable assets. Would you buy cash value insurance if it were outside the plan?

2. The fact that the term insurance portion of the premium is taxable income to the employee at favorable rates is no advantage to buying insurance within the plan; it simply raises the cost and defines the problem by illustrating that you are really just making an investment in the cash value portion of the contract with those pension funds. By buying that term insurance portion of the contract with plan dollars you are lowering the available dollars in the plan with which you can build an investment portfolio. If those premium dollars were put to work in investments, you would have that many more investment dollars growing tax-deferred.

3. The death benefit is free of estate tax, true, but there are other ways this can be accomplished even buying your insurance outside the plan. For example, you can make someone other than the

insured the owner of the policy, thus taking the proceeds out of the estate of the decedent. Even if you considered this to be a benefit, it can be measured in dollars (the dollars required to buy the additional amount of insurance to fund the taxes), and you would probably find that the dollar benefit didn't significantly raise the true rate of return on the investment in the policy. Another point to remember: while life insurance proceeds are not taxable to the estate, neither are any other assets held in the plan.

4. You're buying your insurance with pre-tax dollars, all right, but by doing so you are *not* able to buy other investments with those pre-tax dollars. This argument simply overlooks the fact that you either buy insurance in the plan and investments outside the plan or vice-versa. You'd be far better off buying investments within the plan, since one of the major advantages of a pension plan to begin with is the fact that investment income is not taxed. Always compare the investment with what else could be done with those same dollars in the plan.

5. Granted they do provide actuarial services at a low cost, because the actual cost is built into the profits they make by being able to borrow your cash value at 3% interest and lend it out at 12%. Since most smaller corporations would be better off with a defined-contribution plan in which no actuaries are involved, this savings may not exist.

What about other disadvantages of buying insurance in a plan? How about the losses of capital involved when employees terminate in the early years of their employment? Remember, cash value builds slowly in the first couple of years of a policy, and if the employee quits, that premium paid and not credited to cash value is lost to the remaining participants. Had those premiums been invested in bonds, stocks or savings accounts, nothing would have been lost.

Plans set up with a provision for a certain percentage of the plan contribution to go into insurance initiate a cycle that is increasingly wasteful. Every time the salaries of employees go up, new policies on those employees are purchased by the plan. Over a period of time, an employee finds his insurance coverage going up and up. This would be fine if the person were underinsured, but most people aren't. In fact, most people don't bother to cancel out their personal policies when they become insured under a pension plan and wind up paying for twice as much insurance as they really need.

Don't buy insurance through a pension or profit-sharing plan except under the following circumstances:

1. You can't afford to make the maximum contribution to the plan except by cancelling your personal insurance policies and rebuying the insurance within the plan. In this case it might make sense in order to get that deduction.
2. You're uninsurable and have a chance to pick up some additional insurance without a physical.
3. You like to throw money away.

Other Investments

One of the advantages of placing money into a qualified retirement plan is that dividends, interest, and capital gains are not taxed until the money is distributed at death, disability, or retirement. Therefore, it makes sense to use this feature by making your pension fund the vehicle for those types of investments that normally yield taxable income. In any well planned pottfolio there are a variety of types of investments used. A person should have assets in all the major categories like store-of-value, loans, investments, etc. Balancing a portfolio means diversifying your assets in such a way as to hedge against all the major economic and financial risks that were outlined in Chapter Two.

Since certain of these assets yield taxable income and certain do not, it makes sense to buy income-yielding investments through your pension or profit-sharing plan while buying those that don't carry a taxable yield outside the plan. Coins and bullion, for example, earn no interest whatsoever. They are passive store-of-value assets. Carrying them in the plan while at the same time keeping a substantial savings account or high-dividend-yielding stock outside the plan is not sensible. Likewise real estate limited partnerships frequently throw off tax-free returns, as do municipal bonds. All of these would be more beneficially carried outside the plan where their tax advantages could be most fully realized, while types of securities with high yield could be used within the plan.

Secrecy is another consideration. Many investors would like to have as little of their business as possible open to scrutiny; some because they fear the possibility of state confiscation of property as economic conditions worsen; some because they want to minimize taxes to whatever extent possible; some because they just don't want their spouse or business associates to know what they're doing. A person can buy gold coins for cash, store them in a secret place here or abroad, and sell them for cash when needed. The transaction is not recorded, and if gains are made no one is the wiser. This can be done outside a pension plan, but not within the trust.

The Most Suitable

The best investments to put into the pension or profit-sharing trust are those which would take the maximum advantage of the tax free nature of the vehicle. Assets in which you expect to realize large capital gains for example. This allows you to postpone the taxes on the gain. The trust would be a good vehicle in which to play stock market strategies that required substantial short-term trading. Remember, you shouldn't go into any investment within the pension trust that you couldn't plan to use assuming you had no trust.

The first step in developing a rational wealth-accumulation strategy is to design a balanced investment portfolio that will accomplish your financial goals while protecting you against risks. After the design is complete, then decide which of the selected assets would most logically be owned by the trust.

The Payout

Under current IRS regulations a participant in a pension or profit-sharing plan gets favorable tax treatment on distribution of the trust. In situations where the employee has made no contributions to the plan, and all funds were employer contributions made after 1973, if the recipient takes the distribution as a lump sum payment in one tax year, the total distribution is taxable and the tax is figured by taking ten times the tax (using the single person's tax rate table) on 1/10 of the total taxable amount. This represents a sort of ten year averaging, and is based on the theory that a person lives for about ten years after normal (age 65) retirement.

Another alternative is to take the payments from the trust over a number of years. This usually results in an even more favorable situation for the participant. The trust is maintained in force, and the capital accumulated within it continues to earn. The payments made to an individual are all taxable income to him. Figure 20 illustrates how this might work in a hypothetical situation in which invested funds are earning 10%.

The IRS would require that a percentage of the principal of the account be paid to the participant each year in order to amortize the plan capital out over the participant's life expectancy. Even so, the benefit is substantially greater to the participant if the total amount of the accumulated capital can be left working.

The above statements regarding payouts from a qualified plan aren't meant to cover the subject in any depth; there are many complicating factors. Payout rules should be carefully reviewed when the plan is set up.

PLAN PAYOUT COMPARISON

	Lump Sum Payout	Income Payout
Accumulation In Plan	$250,000	$250,000
Lump Sum Distribution	$250,000	$ 0
Tax On Distribution	72,000	0
Capital Balance	$178,000	$250,000
Annual Income from Capital	$ 17,800	$ 25,000
Tax on Income	4,000	6,000
Net Spendable	$ 13,800	$ 19,000

Figure 20

Covering Other Employees

When a small corporation considers setting up a qualified retirement plan one of the primary considerations is the ultimate tax savings to the stockholder-employees. If any other employees must be covered under the plan, this subtracts from the tax benefits enjoyed. This loss can be partially offset by proper structuring of waiting periods and vesting schedules.

The waiting period is that period of time after a person is hired before he becomes eligible to have a contribution made on his behalf by the corporation. The law limits this period to a maximum of one year except in cases where there is 100% vesting after three years, in which case a three-year waiting period is acceptable. Waiting periods must apply equally to all employees including stockholders.

Vesting Periods

It would be to the advantage of the stockholder employees to have as long a vesting period as possible in order to recycle as much of the employer's contributions as possible back to the fund and eventually to the stockholder employees (who in most cases would tend to outlast the regular employees).

In a pension plan, amounts forfeited by terminating employees are allocated to the remaining plan participants on a pro-rata basis, but additionally reduce the corporate contribution by the amount of the forfeiture in the year it occurs. Therefore, there is no real advantage to the plan participants, but the corporation is that much richer by not having to make the contribution. In profit-sharing plans, the forfeitures accrue directly to the accounts of the other plan participants on a pro-rata basis, and this forfeiture does not affect the corporate contribution for the year. So the plan participants get the windfall of the forfeiture, and a regular yearly contribution as well.

Social Security Integration

One way in which stockholder employees can increase their share of the annual corporate plan contribution at the expense of the other employees is by integrating the plan with social security. The law recognizes the fact that the entire salary of lower paid employees is covered by social security benefits, while higher paid employees are only covered for the first $15,300 of income; thus lower paid employees might have most or all their income covered with social security while the higher paid employees would not. In order to equalize this discrepancy, it allows a pension or profit-sharing plan to allocate a portion of the corporate contribution to the portion of salaries in excess of $15,300 before the contribution is divided up among the plan participants. This is a feature that shouldn't be overlooked in the drafting of a pension or profit-sharing plan.

How To Set One Up

If you're incorporated and haven't yet installed a pension or profit-sharing plan, you should carefully investigate the idea of doing so. The first step is to find a competent corporation/tax attorney who has had significant experience in setting up professional corporations. Since these corporations are usually set up with the tax benefits of pension plans as their primary motive, an attorney that specializes in this area will be most familiar with tax laws and benefits from your point of view. He'll be able to guide you to the proper trustee, and administrator.

It would probably be wise to seek advice on what investments to buy with plan assets from outside sources as this is generally not the forte of tax attorneys. Be extremely wary if your attorney introduces you to any insurance salesmen. Inasmuch as insurance men direct a lot of business to attorneys, there is often a need to reciprocate, and attorneys will frequently push insurance-funded plans for just that reason.

If your business is not incorporated, you might find it profitable to explore incorporation simply for the tax benefits offered by qualified pension and profit-sharing plans. In order to help you make your own calculations about the net economic effect of incorporation, pages 323 and 324 in the Appendix will be useful.

A PENSION PLAN FOR THE SELF-EMPLOYED

In 1962 Congress passed the "Keogh" bill, sometimes known as the H.R. 10 bill, which made it possible for individuals who are self-employed to set up retirement plans for themselves and enjoy some of the tax benefits formerly only available to corporate employees. While not as liberal as the corporate plans, these Keogh plans are extremely lucrative from a tax standpoint.

Who Can Contribute to a Keogh Plan?

Anyone who has income from self-employment can contribute. A commission salesman, a physician, dentist, small businessman, farmer, or just about anyone who is not an employee of another person or corporation can set up a plan. In cases where a person has income from two sources, it might be possible to have a Keogh plan covering one source and not the other. For example a school teacher might be in business as a consultant as well as being employed by some school district. If the income received from consulting does not pass through the school district, then a portion of that income could be contributed to the plan. If a professional incorporates in the middle of the year, any income received by him prior to incorporation is considered income from self-employment, and a contribution to a Keogh plan could be made for that year even though he might subsequently set up a corporate retirement plan.

How Much Can Be Contributed?

Under the legislation passed by Congress and the Ford administration, a self-employed individual can contribute 15% of his net business income up to a maximum of $7,500. This contribution is considered to have been made on the last day of the plan year, providing it is made not later than the day authorized for filing the return (including extensions). The entire contribution, up to the maximum limit above, is deductible and thus could save the taxpayer up to $3,750 on his federal taxes.

In addition to the above mentioned tax-deductible contribution, a participant in a Keogh plan can make a "voluntary" contribution to the plan of up to 10% of his net self-employment income up to a maximum of $2,500. This voluntary contribution is not deductible, but once the money is in the plan, the income or capital gains earned by that money is not taxable to the participant until it is taken out of the plan. A person who is currently keeping some of his assets in unsheltered, income-producing situations could transfer them into the plan via the voluntary contribution and save the taxes on the income those assets were producing.

The above voluntary contribution is not possible for a self-employed person unless that person has one or more employees who are also covered under the plan.

Employees

If a self-employed person has employees, it may be necessary to make contributions for those employees. According to the regulations he must initially include in the plan all full-time employees with three or more years of service. His employees are considered full-time if their customary employment is more than 1000 hours a year. If the owner-employee has less than three years service himself, then the waiting period is reduced accordingly.

The contribution for the covered employees must be a percentage of their salary equal to the percentage contributed for the owner-employee. Thus if the owner has an income of $75,000 per year and contributes $7,500 for himself, since that contribution is 10% of his compensation, he must contribute 10% of the compensation of each eligible employee. The contribution made for the employee vests immediately and that employee will have the right to withdraw it upon termination.

What Becomes of the Money?

The law allows you to put away money for your retirement providing that's what you do with the money. To insure that you don't misappropriate the funds from your own retirement plan, you are required to give those funds to a trustee. Once the money is in the hands of the trustee you can tell the trustee what to do with it. You can direct that it be held in cash, placed in a savings account, used to buy bonds, stocks, treasury bills, mortgages, or life insurance. In other words, the money can be invested in much the same way you might invest it if it were not in the plan. The only difference is that you must work through the trustee.

Your selection of a trustee or custodian bank depends to a certain extent on what you intend to do with the funds once they're in the plan. Since trustees are in business for a profit you'll have to pay a fee to get them to handle your plan, and they'll get remunerated based on the amount of work involved and the risk to themselves. Certain organizations will act as trustee for your funds for little or no fee, just in order to have access to your funds. Life insurance companies, mutual funds, and some savings and loans and banks will offer to let you use their prototype plan document, and to act as trustee or custodian providing you buy their product with the money. If you want flexibility with your funds, that is, if you want to invest in several different products or want the ability to move from one investment to another, then you'll have to hire a trustee that will allow you to do this. Here the fee will be higher, naturally. Below are listed three independent trustees that charge a fee and allow some diversification of investments:

Lincoln Trust Company
P.O. Box 5831
Denver, Colorado 80217

First Trust Corporation
444 Sherman
Denver, Colorado

Certified Plans, Inc.
P.O. Box 2090
Newport Beach, California 92663

What Should Keogh Plans Invest In?

The same philosophy that guided corporate pension plan strategy applies to Keogh as well. Since all income is tax deferred within the plan, this would not be the place for tax-sheltered types of investments like municipal bonds or real estate. Since life insurance is low yielding and tax deferred, there is no sense to putting it in a Keogh plan. If you plan to keep certain of your assets in fixed income loans, this would be a good place to put them, as the income wouldn't be diminished by taxation. It would be a good place, also, to do any securities trading, as short- and long-term gains would also be sheltered.

When Can I Get My Money Out?

Anytime you want it. If you take a distribution from the plan prior to age 59½, then you'll have to pay 10% of the money in the plan as a tax penalty, plus having to add the entire amount to your taxable income in the year of the distribution. For that reason you'd probably be wise to leave the money in the plan until retirement. The penalty does not apply to your voluntary contributions, however. Since you've already paid taxes on them you can withdraw them without penalty, so long as you leave their earnings in the plan.

How Do I Set Up a Plan?

Simply write to any of the above mentioned trustees and they'll send you complete information along with enrollment forms.

OTHER TAX DEVICES

If you're self employed, once you've explored the feasibility of a Keogh or IRA, the next step is to see if there are other business expenses you can incur that can be deducted. First, you can stock supplies that you might normally not buy until next year. This will have the dual effect of lowering your taxes and simultaneously insuring that the cost of those supplies won't rise due to inflation. If you're a dentist, you should consider stocking dental gold. It's a deductible business expense and you'll have an investment in a real and solid commodity. You can also consider prepaying rent, lease payments, interest on loans, and even employee salaries.

Additionally, you can lower your taxable income by slowing down billings in December and stepping them up again in Janaury. If you're planning on buying equipment in the near future, buy it this year and take the liberal tax credit offered. If your lawyer and accountant will accept it, you can always pay those bills early as well.

YOUR PERSONAL RETURN

After you've reduced your business income by the maximum amount with the above devices, you should turn to personal, nonbusiness items to see what can be done. Here are a few suggestions.

Pay all medical bills by December 31 if your medical expenses for the year exceed 3% of your estimated adjusted gross income. If not, put them off and pay them next year.

Consider prepaying any state or local taxes that have been assessed, even though not due till next year. This includes state income taxes, property taxes, and even your automobile registration fee.

If you're planning charitable contributions for next year, you can make them this year and take the deduction on this year's return (providing it does not exceed one-half your income). Best idea is to donate appreciated assets rather than cash as you get the same deduction but avoid the capital gain tax.

Interest on loans and mortgages can sometimes be prepaid for a year and become deductible in the year paid.

You can offset ordinary income up to $1,000 with capital losses, so consider selling losers this year. Remember, it takes $2,000 of capital loss to result in a $1,000 ordinary loss.

After you've assembled all your potential deductions for your business, set up the most feasible retirement plans, and maximised your personal deductions, then and only then should you consider investing money into tax shelters.

INVESTMENT TAX SHELTERS

Investment tax shelters include such things as real estate, cattle, and oil-well drilling. These are essentially unincorporated businesses that the investor owns in whole or in part. If these businesses lose money, the investor gets to take the loss on his personal return. They are set up in hopes that the expenses comprising the losses will come back in future years as profits. In this way the investor gets the deduction for the loss this year and will realize a gain in some future year. By postponing the tax in this way, those tax dollars are theoretically at work for the investor, rather than in Uncle Sam's pocket. Most tax shelters take the form of limited partnership syndications. The selling organization will usually sell the limited partnership on the grounds that it (a) protects the investor from future liability; (b) allows him the opportunity to pool his money with others and achieve economy of scale; (c) allows him to team up with management professionals in the form of the general partner.

What they fail to tell you, even in the prospectus, is that if anything goes wrong in the business that the partnership is engaged in, the legal problems can strangle you. This is documented in any number of real estate syndications of the past few years. When the boom hit the apartment house market in 1969 and syndicators bid up the price of units and new construction expanded, tens of thousands of investors were lured into these syndications by the attractive cash flow and appreciation potentials as well as the tax benefits. What appeared to be a sure thing turned out quite differently. When the economic slump hit a couple of years later, there was a glut of space with few renters. Expenses for the operation of the projects soared with inflation while competition in the market prevented rents from being raised. Additionally, vacancy rates climbed well beyond the five percent figures that had been projected in the prospecti. Consequently, projects began losing money on a monthly basis and soon the limited partners were told that if they wanted to save their equity in these projects they would have to meet cash calls to pay the mounting expenses.

Now, if you own a house which you're renting out and your tenant moves out, you don't think too much about meeting the mortgage payment out of your pocket until you can get another tenant. If you're a limited partner who has been sold on the idea that you'll be getting regular cash payments out of your investment and suddenly you're asked for money instead, your reaction is different. You're likely to say, "let the other partners do it. I'm not throwing good money after bad." Or, you'll rely on the general partner to handle the problems because you've been led to believe that he has a substantial stake in the project as well as plenty of cash reserves. Unfortunately, the general partner was probably living on the cash flow generated by sales of partnership interests and his overhead began to eat him alive when sales fell off. And sales did fall off when investors missed their first cash flow checks. Suddenly, the syndication as well as the project is in financial trouble, and the investor is told that his apartment building is headed for foreclosure.

The limited partner was originally told that if the general partner had problems a majority of the limited partners could get together and elect a new general partner and thus take over the project. Easier said than done. First, most of the limited partners are too busy or too disillusioned to even bother coming to a meeting. The few who do are faced with the problem of putting up twice their share to bail out the project. Additionally, the mortgage lender has a clause in the mortgage that says if a new general partner is brought in, that constitutes sale of the property and the entire mortgage is due and payable or must be refinanced. Investors find that mortgage rates have skyrocketed and refinancing at the new rates makes the cash flow problems disastrous. The attorneys who are willing to represent the limited partners in the takeover then ask the few partners at the meeting for a $10,000 retainer to get the process in gear, and soon those who were willing to fight throw up their hands and call it quits.

In cases where the general partners are forced into bankruptcy the situation gets even gloomier. A court appointed referee (normally an attorney specializing in bankruptcy) takes over as controller of the general partner's business and the court supervises the assets of the general partner on behalf of the creditors. The fact that the limited partners put up all the money for the apartment buildings (and in reality own them completely) is shoved aside. They become helpless pawns as the lawyers for the creditors and general partner battle it out. The referee will get his fee from the assets of the general partner when the dust settles. The major source of assets is the real estate commissions that the general partner will realize on the sale of your apartment building (remember that clause in the partnership agreement?). Consequently, the court is going to do everything it can to prevent the limited partners from substituting their own general partner and thus stealing this source of revenue.

Limited partnerships don't always work out too well in the cattle business either. Lured by the high writeoffs and promises of fat prices from fat cattle, multitudes of high-tax-bracket investors bought partnership interests in cattle feeding operations over the past few years. The figures showed that people were eating more beef than ever, prices were rising, and cattle showed a profit in four years out of five. In addition, the figures proved that even if the cattle feeding operation lost money at the rate of 10% a year, after five years the investor would still come out with a tax profit on his investment. Many funds offered 200% initial write-off, meaning that an investor in the 50% bracket was really only investing dollars that would go to taxes anyway, so what could be the risk?

To start with, the losses can amount to far more than 10% a year, for along with the 200% writeoff come massive borrowings from banks. The investor is leveraged to the hilt. In the early seventies a drop in cattle prices due to a recession, coupled with price controls on meat, followed by a trucking strike and soaring feed prices in the wake of the Russian grain deal left most cattle investors with their small equities completely wiped out. Furthermore, the partnerships were forced into liquidation and terminated. The 200% writeoff was back to haunt them. Not only was the cash investment gone (that would have been gone to taxes anyway, of course) but now investors had to recapture their excess deduction, and thus were faced with adding half of the amount of the investment to their taxable income. The investors had originally been told that the general partner would defend any tax litigation, but where was the general partner now?

The tax consequences don't end there. When an investor originally wrote off the investment he took an ordinary loss from his ordinary earned income. That income was subject to the maximum tax of 50%. When that income comes back, it is no longer earned income, and thus no longer subject to the 50% maximum. It might get taxed at a much higher rate the second time around.

When an investor is considering buying a limited partnership interest he should first look carefully at the projected return. If it appears high, he'd better start asking himself where the risk is, because high return means high risk. It's hard for the unsophisticated investor to realize that passive investment capital is not worth much in the business world except in cases of high risk. When the syndicator is taking 10% to 20% off the front end, as well as a handsome profit along the way for managing the affairs of the partnership, an investor should wonder where the goose is that's going to lay all these golden eggs. In most cases he'll realize that he's the goose.

There are three primary tax-sheltered investments available to the average investor; cattle feeding, oil drilling and real estate.

Cattle Feeding

The basic tax shelter from cattle feeding occurs when the calf and feed are purchased in one tax year and the fattened calf is sold the next. The feed is a deductible item when purchased, and when the fattened calf is sold, the difference between the purchase price of the calf and the sale price comes back as taxable ordinary income to the investor. As a simple illustration, say that an investor buys a $150 calf and $200 worth of feed in 1975, and after feeding the calf, sells the fattened calf in 1976 for $350. He has broken even. However, he received a $200 deduction in 1975 for the feed and will realize $200 of income in 1976 for the difference between the cost of the animal and the selling price. Thus, he has shifted $200 worth of ordinary income from one taxable year to the next.

The risks to this type of deduction are many. First, a loss could be realized on the calf, and although income would be shifted, the investor would wind up with a real loss. Second, when the income comes in the second year, it may throw the investor into a higher tax bracket. It may also be taxed at a higher rate than the 50% maximum on earned income, since it may no longer be classed as earned income.

Third, the investor may subject himself to tax audit, since this type of investment is often scrutinized by the IRS. If the operation is not carefully structured, the IRS might disallow the deduction and thus throw off the individual's tax planning.

If you intend to use this type of shelter, my recommendation would be to do it through an independent feed yard, or on your own ranch, but not through a public syndication. You can buy a few head of cattle and contract with the feed yard to handle them for you. While the financing terms and the percentage writeoff may not be as favorable as in a public syndication, the risks of mismanagement are probably less.

Oil Drilling

Tax laws provide that the intangible costs of drilling an oil or gas well are deductible in the year expended. Intangible costs are the costs for labor, etc., as opposed to the costs of tangible equipment such as casings, pumps, and pipes that are installed after a well is completed. Most oil shelters provide that the money invested by the passive investor will go to the intangible costs, while the syndicator or operator will pay the tangible costs. Thus, in an oil operation the investor will normally receive a writeoff about equal to his investment.

If oil or gas is discovered, the well is completed and the income from the oil or gas will be taxed at ordinary rates, less a depletion allowance of 22% of the amount recovered. If the well is sold after completion, the return will be a capital gain to the investor. Thus, if an investor in 1975 invests $10,000 for the drilling of a well and that money goes for intangible drilling costs, he'll receive a $10,000 deduction. If oil is found, the well is sold in 1976, and he gets his $10,000 back, it will be a $10,000 capital gain. Or, if he elects to take the income from production, he'll have to add 78% of the income to his ordinary income for the year.

The risks are that oil will not be found, or will be found in such small quantities that it will not be feasible to extract it; that the operators expenses will be so high that the investor will receive little return on his money; or that the operator or syndicator will go bankrupt, leaving the investors money tied up in court or lost to attorney's fees.

The tax advantages of oil are probably the best in the tax shelter field. The risks are high on any particular investment, but if an investor is willing to invest regularly in a variety of programs, this may serve as a viable tax shelter device. It has a major advantage over cattle feeding in that the income is converted from ordinary income to capital gains, or at least into ordinary income with the benefit of the depletion allowance.

With the energy crisis upon us and considering the concentrated political power of the oil industry, it is likely that the tax incentives to oil drilling will not be soon eliminated by Congress. This makes it a somewhat more long-lasting shelter possibility than either cattle feeding or real estate.

Real Estate

The tax advantages to income real estate lie mainly in the ability to leverage the investment through mortgages with their accompanying interest and loan fee deductions, and in the deductions for depreciation that are allowed. There is little doubt that the tax incentives now granted to income real estate construction and operation will gradually be eroded away by Congress. Currently, the House Ways and Means Committee is working on legislation that would curtail certain interest and depreciation deductions on commercial real estate. There is substantial pressure from liberal congressmen to wipe out the real estate tax incentives completely.

For the investor who wants to put money into a real estate tax shelter, my advice is to avoid syndications, and buy your own properties. Even though the initial tax losses might not be as great as those that could be achieved by a large syndicator, your risks are reduced substantially as was pointed out in my earlier remarks on syndications. Each property should really be looked at as an investment, with the initial consideration being its relationship to your overall portfolio, rather than its tax benefits.

The investor who intends to get involved in shelters in any serious way would be wise to spend some time reading up on the field. There are few good works dealing with this subject. Most works have been written by the syndicators themselves and are heavily biased. One book worth reading is *Corporate and Executive Tax Sheltered Investments* by Peter C. Reid and Gustave Simons.[38] It is a series of articles written by a variety of lawyers, accountants, and syndicators with fairly

objective comments after each article by tax consultant
Gustave Simons. Although there have been some changes in
the law since it was published, it's still a worthwhile book.

INVESTMENT ANNUITIES

One of the major factors affecting the yield of an
investment is the tax due on the income. $100,000 invested
in a savings account at 7% per annum will yield $7,000 a year
before taxes. To an individual in a 50% tax bracket that
return may suddenly drop to 3.5% or $3,500 a year if the
income can't be sheltered in some way. Compounded over
twenty years the results can be significant. Sheltered, the
above account would grow to $387,000 in twenty years.
Unsheltered, it would grow to only $199,000.

One of the newer ideas born in the last few years for
sheltering investment income is the investment annuity. It
has the advantage of deferral of the tax on investment
income that qualified retirement programs have without
being restricted to the IRS qualifications required of those
plans. It also allows access to higher yields than those offered
by municipal bonds.

Annuities are not new. They are one of the oldest products
of the insurance industry. To get a quick understanding of
how they function, assume that there are three individuals,
all age 65, who each have $100,000. Since this is the last of
their assets, each is concerned that the funds will be depleted
before they have lived out their lifetimes. They approach a
fourth individual who agrees to act as an insurance company.
He calculates that the average life expectancy of each is ten
years, and that if $100,000 were invested to yield 5% over
the ten year period, it could provide an income of about
$13,000 a year during that time, with the principal being
totally depleted at the end. He decides that the probability is
that one of the three will die after five years, one at the end
of the tenth year, and one will outlive his life expectancy and
die in fifteen years. In exchange for the $300,000, he offers

to guarantee each individual an income of $12,000 a year for as long as that individual lives. If calculations are correct, he should make a reasonable profit for his risk, averaging $1,000 a year for each of the three. If they die later than expected he may make no profit or even suffer substantial losses. If they all die prematurely, however, he'll have a windfall.

This, then, is the principle behind annuities: a guaranteed income for life or some specified period of time in exchange for a non-refundable cash payment or premium.

Insurance companies are set up to make actuarial calculations of risks and to make a profit by selling coverage for those risks, therefore annuities are a natural addition to their product line.

Tax laws have been strongly influenced by insurance company pressure, and from the very beginning the income on assets held by insurance companies as reserves to fund life insurance and annuity products has been exempted from tax. The tax on this income only becomes due at the point the income is actually paid out to the policy holder. Assuming this comes to him as part of a series of annuity payments, part of his payment is return of principal and part counted as taxable income.

Normally, annuities have been sold for cash premiums with the money going into a fund and the investment of the money managed by the insurance company. Since the insurance company is at risk for a fixed payment to the annuitant, they are careful to take few risks and offer a return that is usually somewhere between the bank savings rate and the highgrade corporate bond rate. A few years ago a new concept of variable annuities was brought out in which the companies offered to invest the funds in common stocks. This offered the potential of higher returns to the annuitant but also the guarantee of higher risks. They were sold to anyone who was willing to assume those risks by accepting a payment that was variable and geared to the investment performance of the fund. In as much as the variable annuity

hit the market shortly after the stock market began to fall
apart in 1970, it met with little success.

Birth of the Investment Annuity

A company in Philadelphia called First Investment
Annuity Company of America (FIAC) saw a potential market
for a new product that offered the features of the variable
annuity. They called their product a Personal Investment
Annuity Policy (PIAP), and through it offered a customer the
right to buy an annuity while retaining management control
over the funds in the annuity.

Furthermore, under this concept the buyer can contribute
currently owned assets to the annuity, as well as cash. Where
before an owner of stocks and bonds who wanted the tax
advantages of owning an annuity had to first sell those assets,
buy the annuity, and then be content with the fixed rate of
return offered by the insurance company; he can now simply
contribute currently owned assets directly and benefit by
whatever rate of return he is able to realize through his own
or his advisors' skills.

Under an investment annuity, the insurance company that
underwrites the actuarial risk does not actually handle the
assets or offer investment direction. The assets are placed in
the hands of a custodian financial institution such as a bank
or savings and loan, and the institution takes their instructions for the investment of those assets from the policy
owner or his selected advisor. Most insurance companies
handling the product will select one or two custodian
institutions to handle their assets,while others offer the
opportunity for the buyer to select his own.

Use of outside investment advisors and custodians has led
brokerage houses, banks, and S&L's to team up with
insurance companies in the promotion and sale of the
investment annuity. Everyone stands to make money: the
brokerage house can offer its customers a new tax shelter
device yet retain investment control, while savings

institutions can offer tax-deferred savings accounts.

The annuity purchaser is required to confine his investments within the annuity to a list of approved assets. This list includes government securities, listed bonds and stocks, prime commercial paper, savings accounts, certificates of deposit, credit union shares, mutual fund shares, and cash. Real estate (other than REIT shares), commodities, and commodities futures contracts are not acceptable, nor are margined stock accounts or letter stock.

The investment annuity is subject to the same tax laws as any other annuity, so the interest and dividends of assets held in the annuity are not taxed until actually distributed to the annuitant. At his discretion this may be as late as age 85. Unlike qualified retirement plans in which capital gains are also deferred until distribution to the plan owner, capital gains earned in an annuity fund are taxable during the year earned. Rather than being taxable to the annuitant, they are taxable income to the insurance company at their rates (30% for long term and 48% for short term gains). The insurance company debits the amount of any taxes it pays on these gains to the account of the policy holder. On distribution to the annuitant at a later time these gains are taxed again as income, and thus capital gains are double taxed.

Contributions of existing assets other than cash to the annuity may subject the policy owner to some tax consequences, since this is considered to be the same as a sale of those assets for tax purposes. If you own appreciated assets and contribute them to the annuity, you'll be personally subject to the capitals gains tax. Likewise, if you own securities in which you have a loss, you'll be able to take the loss on your current return. This is one method of realizing a loss for tax purposes while at the same time retaining ownership and control of the asset.

Since an annuitant has already paid the income tax on the money or assets contributed to the account, he can withdraw up to the amount of his contribution at any time without tax liability. However, as taxes haven't yet been paid on any increase, withdrawals in excess of cost will result in reportable income.

There are two phases to an annuity contract; the accumulation phase, during which contributions are being paid into the account, and the distribution phase, during which payments are made to the annuitant from the account. During the accumulation phase and prior to the commencement of annuity payments, the policy owner may at any time withdraw all or part of the money in the fund. Once the annuity payments have begun the fund then belongs to the insurance company and the only right the annuitant has is to direct the investments within the fund and to receive the agreed upon payments.

A number of insurance companies have imitated FIAC's original product. Industry sales of some $200 million were expected in 1976. Contracts, as in the case of life insurance policies, are regulated by state law and are essentially identical except for rate structures and custodian banks. Figure 21 shows a few of the companies currently offering investment annuities along with rate comparisons. Each company must register the product with each state in which it wishes to do business so not all companies are available in all states.

Company	Front End Load	Annual Fee
First Investment Annuity Company, 1845 Walnut Street Philadelphia, Pa. 19103	Under $250,000 - 4%	2/3 of 1%
American Guaranty Life Ins. Co., 1433 S.W. 6th Ave. Portland, Ore. 97201	First $50,000 - 2% Excess - 1%	.5% .375%
The Chesapeak Life Ins. Co. P.O. Box 297 Baltimore, Md. 21203	First $50,000 - 2% Excess - 1%	.5% .375%
Phoenix Mutual Life Ins. Co. Hartford, Connecticut	None	.85%

Figure 21

Most of the companies have a minimum initial purchase contribution of $10,000 and subsequent minimum contributions of $1,000. Phoenix Mutual will accept a $5,000 initial contribution. Although Phoenix Mutual has no front end load, their first year maintenance fee is payable in advance and there is a penalty of 1.5% if the funds are withdrawn during the first year, or 1.0% if they are withdrawn from the 2nd through 5th years.

Investment Annuities and Common Sense

As the investment annuity concept spreads during the next few years, investors will find themselves innundated with advertising and promotional material ballyhooing its benefits. There is no question that this is a vehicle that can be profitable to many, but there are pitfalls as well.

First, this is a tax vehicle only, and has no other benefits. Furthermore, it is only beneficial in sheltering interest and dividends from investments. It can not shelter income from your business or profession, and it is absolutely wrong to use it when short- or long-term capital gains are involved. Capital gains, as mentioned before, get double-taxed. Not only that, but the initial tax is probably at a higher rate than an individual would normally pay.

Because the benefits are limited to interest and dividends only, investment annuities are vehicles for loan-type assets such as savings accounts, bonds, T-bills, CD's, and commercial paper. Although common stocks and mutual funds are acceptable assets, these assets are normally purchased with an eye to capital appreciation; thus the gains, as mentioned above, would be subject to double taxation. Most investors who might follow the concepts outlined in earlier chapters would normally be holding very few assets in the form of loans, so the investment annuity will be of limited use.

Second, custodial and administration fees add up. Although a 2% front-end load and a ½% annual fee seem small, when you add in the charges made by the custodial bank and any potential charges for early withdrawal, etc., the annual cost could easily amount to 1%. Assuming you have a savings account or bond in the fund that is yielding 6%, you are losing 16.7% of your total return. Since the balance of that return will be subject to tax on withdrawal, you might find that you really haven't saved anything by having your assets tied up in the annuity.

These criticisms are not meant to suggest that there aren't valid cases for the investment annuity. If you hold substantial debt securities, if you intend to maintain your position in them or similar securities over a long period, and if you're in a reasonably high tax bracket, then it may be a wise choice. It can also be helpful to individuals who have Keogh or other qualified retirement plans as a method of continuing to defer the taxes on the assets in these trusts after retirement. Done correctly, retirement-plan assets can be transferred into an investment annuity and the tax deferral continued beyond the normal distribution date.

For information on investment annuities write directly to the companies mentioned above and ask for literature and the names of representatives near you, or simply ask your local stock broker, life insurance agent, or savings and loan officer.

CONCLUSION

Proper tax planning consists of first determining your taxable income for the next few years; second, considering simple devices by which you can shift income from one year to another without risk of loss; third, determining if a qualified retirement plan is worthwhile; and finally looking into tax-sheltered investments. Although the shelter industry has worked hard to sell the average person on the idea of buying sheltered investments, this is a most dangerous area, fraught with pitfalls and traps. Few investment counselors or salesmen really understand it, nor can tax attorneys and accountants really be sure of their judgments regarding the legality of the writeoffs. For most people the prudent course is to rely on simple tax planning and retirement plans, leaving the more esoteric tax schemes to the gamblers.

CHAPTER SIX

Putting It All Together

It's time to look back over your shoulder and survey the road you've followed. By now you should have a good idea of the elements that make our economy work. Production is the basis of all that improves our standard of living, and anything that tends to interfere with production reduces our standard of living. You should be painfully aware of the reasons behind our current inflation and its personal effects on you.

You should have outlined and calculated your financial objectives, and know roughly how many years you have to accomplish them. You've read about the variety of risks facing you in your search for financial independence, and should have some idea of which ones you feel are most threatening.

You have been exposed to the three basic types of investments; store-of-value, loans, and equities. You know that you can invest in these assets, or you can speculate in them by buying for short-term profits.

Now the question you must be asking yourself is, "How do I determine which of these assets is most suited to my portfolio?" How do you structure the optimum investment portfolio to meet your goals? The balance of this chapter will give you some step-by-step instructions.

Step One—Invest in Yourself

Before you place money with others for growth, make certain you have fully funded your own business. That is your soundest investment. You have control, vested interest, and maximum profit.

Step Two—Set Up Qualified Retirement Plans

Before you decide on which investment assets you should own, establish any qualified retirement programs and other tax-deferred trusts that can conserve tax dollars for your own use. Then, when you balance your portfolio you can decide which assets should be placed in the trusts and which carried outside. These programs, as outlined in Chapter Five, will be Keogh plans and pension or profit sharing plans.

Step Three—Tally Your Investable Assets and Surplus

From your financial statement you should be able to calculate the total investable assets that you have available. Identify the type of investment in each case; i.e., store-of-value, loan, or equity; and determine whether each asset is held as an investment or speculation. From your monthly Income & Expense sheet you should be able to determine how much investable surplus will be added to your net worth each year.

Step Four—Decide on the Ideal Portfolio Balance

Now decide what percentage of your total assets should be invested in each category of assets. This depends on your own assessment of the future of our economy, and the rate of return you need to reach your goals.

Following is an example of a percentage allocation of assets.

Store of Value 60%
Loans 5%
Equities
    Liquid 20%
    Nonliquid 15%

Total   100%

The amount of these assets that are speculatively invested will depend on the size of your holdings in relation to your ultimate need for capital. You shouldn't speculate with money that will be essential to meeting your goals on schedule. By the same token, if you have already accumulated enough wealth to last you for the rest of your life, then there would be no sense in speculating at all.

As economic conditions change, you might alter the portfolio balance. In a stable economy (one not suffering from inflation) a conservative stance would be to invest two-thirds of your assets in equities and one third in loans. If our economy slides into true hyper-inflation, you would want no loans at all, and probably no equities, with the possible exception of your own business.

Step Five—Balance Your Portfolio

Look at the present structure of your assets and think about how you can bring it into line with the balance that you think is correct. It will mean liquidating certain assets and buying others. You can also bring the portfolio into line by adding your annual surplus to the category that is underfunded.

Figure 22 is a hypothetical case which shows how you might categorize your assets as they are now, and as you think they should be in light of our discussions in this book.

ASSET ALLOCATION

Asset	Current Allocation	Proposed Allocation
Store of Value		
Cash, Checking Accounts	$ 1,500	$ -0-
Raw Land	7,000	7,000
Precious Metals	-0-	30,000
Diamonds	-0-	5,000
Commodities Futures	-0-	4,800
Furs, Jewelry	2,500	2,500
Total Store of Value	$ 11,000	$ 49,300
Loans		
Savings & Loan	$ 12,000	$ 2,000
Life Ins. Cash Value	7,600	-0-
U.S. Government Bonds	3,000	-0-
Second Trust Deed	4,700	-0-
Total Loans	$ 27,300	$ 2,000
Equities		
Dental Practice	$ 50,000	$ 50,000
Common Stocks	13,000	-0-
Mining Stocks	-0-	10,000
Apartment House Syndication	10,000	-0-
Home (Equity only)	20,000	20,000
Total Equities	$ 93,000	$ 80,000
TOTAL	$131,300	$131,300

Figure 22

Step Six—Pay Off Loans

In today's economy one of the individual's greatest risks is that sudden changes in economic conditions can create liquidity crises. Even though by borrowing money today you can benefit from inflation by paying off the loans with inflated currency, you can also be wiped out if unable to meet the payments. The most conservative position is to eliminate debt. Pay off mortgages, auto loans, and investment margin accounts. Although the rate of return on your investments may seem to drop when this is done, so will the risk of total loss of the equity.

Step Seven—Determine Investment Strategy in Advance

The most important piece of advice that can be given is that you should never invest on the spur of the moment without having first determined that the investment is consistent with your overall plan. You should determine at the beginning of each year just how much surplus you'll have available that year to invest, and in what categories the monies should be invested to properly meet your long-range goals. By making careful income and expense estimates for the coming year, you should know what your total income tax liability will be, and you should be able to take full advantage of any available tax shelters by allocating a portion of your after-tax surplus to the purchase of tax-favored investments. I'm assuming, of course, that the first consideration is not the tax aspect, but rather the need for that type of investment to fill out your portfolio balance.

When approached by a silver-tongued salesman, first categorize the type of investment. Is what he's offering you a store-of-value, loan, or equity? Is he offering it on an investment or speculative basis? Margin or no margin? When that's determined, does your portfolio have a need for that particular type? If not, is this one good enough to replace a similar investment in the same category that you're already holding, and if so, can you liquidate your present asset and then replace it with this one?

Most people never take this systematic approach to making investment decisions. They look at each offering as a separate decision that bears no relationship to their previous decisions.

Nothing could be more wrong or potentially dangerous. Your investments are all interrelated; your program must be carefully integrated; your decisions must be coordinated.

In summary, there is no single "perfect asset." To survive you must diversify, stay as liquid as possible, and become intimately aware of the economic conditions of the world. Above all, you must have a plan. Every investment decision must relate back to that plan, and you must review and update that plan constantly.

CHAPTER SEVEN

Conclusion

Where will the economy of the United States go in the next ten or twenty years? There are many prophets around to answer that question. Some foresee a continuation of the past with minor ups and downs. These are the establishment spokesmen who say that if we can hold on, support our president, and have confidence, all the economic battles will be won; inflation will be licked, industry will prosper, unemployment will vanish, and everyone will live happily ever after. Other prophets see runaway inflation followed by catastrophic depression. After that, rioting, starvation, and anarchy. They exhort you to prepare for the holocaust; store food, guns, and plenty of silver and gold to use for barter. All would have you believe that the spectrum of possibilities lies somewhere in between these viewpoints.

I, for one, don't believe either outcome is possible. The government, in order to survive, must pursue policies contrary to those that would solve the problems. There is *no* possibility that any actions can or will be taken by this or any administration that would stop inflation or improve the standard of living of the nation. At best the actions of governments of the world will simply redistribute the wealth; the friction they cause while doing this will lower the productive output of the people and thereby lower their standards of living.

Nevertheless, the failure of these policies, and the subsequent economic disruption will not result in anarchy and the return to a barter society. Those may have been reasonable possibilities had the same economic woes beset the world fifty or a hundred years ago when the power of central governments was relatively weak, transportation and communication slow, and man not governed by technology. Historically, debasement of a country's currency has always resulted in depression, the overthrow of the government, and anarchy, if carried to the extreme. This is no longer a possibility. What is in store for the nation if the present policies continue unchecked is simply complete government ownership of the means of production; in other words, socialism. You have watched for years the gradual erosion of individual liberty and the strengthening of the power of the state. The root cause of the economic turmoil that robs you of the ability to become financially independent lies in the ever-growing federal and state bureaucracies. As the economic troubles compound, the strength of the state grows. Never has our government been stronger, and never more able to rule completely the lives of all individuals.

As the economic scenario unfolds over the next twenty years we will see an ever-increasing disruption of the productive mechanism, a gradual erosion of the standard of living of each individual, and a total collapse of the free enterprise system. As the government continues to meddle in the marketplace (i.e., wage-price controls, etc.) the devastating effects will be blamed on the inadequacy of the capitalist system to meet the needs of modern times, and the unwillingness of selfish individuals and industries to live up to their responsibilities for the welfare of the nation. The profiteering businessman will be blamed for all the ills befalling the people, and the people themselves, driven on by the propaganda mechanism of the state, will demand that the state, itself, take over control of the sagging industries. One by one they will be nationalized, either because they go bankrupt, as did Penn Central and Lockheed, or because they refuse to be responsive to the needs of the people. We will not be destroyed by an enemy nation, we will vote ourselves into slavery.

Depression? If you define it as conditions of widespread unemployment and business failure, it will never happen. Does any communist nation suffer from unemployment? Everyone in the blissful state of socialism has a nice full-time job. Of course, the standard of living falls to subsistence levels, for it is a law of nature that man will only produce efficiently when it is profitable for him to do so. When his profit is taken away and doled out to the nonproducers, to the bureaucrats and welfare cases, to those too sick to work, too tired to work, too elite to work, and too crafty to work, then soon everyone will be crowding into the handout line, and only fools and slaves will produce anything.

Since the need of any coercive government is, first of all, for soldiers and guns to enforce the slavery, most of the work force and production will go directly to state needs, as it now does in most communist or facist countries. And if you look around you might find the United States is not too far behind these other countries in this respect. Even today one person in six is directly employed by federal, state, or local government.

So to believe that the U.S. is headed for the greatest depression in its history is, by my way of thinking, foolishness. We are headed first for an ever-increasing inflation, with rates of 20%, 25% and 30% not far off. We will see an ever-increasing manipulation of business by the government. More controls, more "consumer protection," more power to the politicians. The entire regulatory mechanism of the government will smother business in megatons of paperwork, eating up the profitability of enterprise, and swelling the workforce of the bureaucracy. As businesses fall beneath the load, they will be subsidized and nationalized. Like England, we will go from a dynamic industrial giant

with a standard of living the highest the world has ever
known, to a whining ghost of former greatness. *Atlas
Shrugged* will become a novel of prophesy.[39]

What will the economic position of the individual be? In
an economy dominated by an inflating money supply, all
forces act against the interests of the producer. The direct
effects of the inflation create chaotic investment markets and
all the economic risks discussed in Chapter Two. In addition
to the speculative fever and its inherent dangers to your
stored wealth, the state must survive. It has only two sources
of sustenance; current production or stored wealth. It will
consume both. Historically, under countries moving into the
grip of socialism, the person who has any stored wealth
becomes the target of the people themselves.

What can you do about the future? In regard to the state
of the world today, probably very little. First, educate
yourself thoroughly in economics. Then set about protecting
your wealth according to the principles discussed in this
book. Leave the government alone. It's bigger than you and
you're not going to change it. Only don't help it along by
feeding it anymore than you have to.

Produce as much as you possibly can in the next few years,
and store it away. Cut back, if possible, on your standard of
living now, and store the excess production. Pay off your
debts and mortgages, and get your assets liquid. In other
words, make yourself as strong as possible financially.

You might look at the future as would a person living in a
primitive agricultural society if he knew a seven year drought
were coming. Rather than continue to consume his production at normal levels, he would tighten his belt and store
up as much as possible for the hard years ahead. Even though
this year it might seem that times were good and there was
more than enough to enjoy his normal standard of living, he
would be careful to conserve. Furthermore, he would realize
that most people weren't bothering to store up reserves, and
these people would pose threats to his stored wealth when

the famine came. If he's to survive he'll need to protect that wealth. It would do him little good to try and protest the coming famine, or to get the complacent government to do anything about it. His most prudent course is simply to shut up and prepare for the future. And so is yours.

Good luck!

Appendix

MONTHLY BUDGET

	CURRENT	AFTER DEATH OF SPOUSE	IF DISABLED
REGULAR			
Mortgage or Rent			
Utilities			
Maid, Gardener, Pool Service, etc.			
Groceries, Milk, Liquor			
Lunches			
Entertainment, Meals, Shows, etc.			
Recreation (Skiing, Boating, etc.)			
Clothes			
Laundry, Cleaning, Shoe Repair			
Personal (Haircuts & Allowances)			
Auto Operation (Gas, Tires, Repairs)			
Tuitions, Lessons			
Donations			
Support of Others, Alimony, etc.			
Auto Loans (Or Amortization)			
Other Loans			
Other			
TOTAL REGULAR EXPENSES			
PERIODIC			
Real Estate Taxes			
Household Maintenance & Repair			
New Household Purchases			
Casualty Insurance (Auto, Home)			
Life Insurance			
Disability, Medical Insurance			
Vacations			
Gifts (Birthdays, Anniv., Xmas)			
Income Taxes, State & Federal			
Legal, Accounting			
Medical, Dental, Veterinarian			
Other			
TOTAL PERIODIC EXPENSES			
SAVINGS & INVESTMENTS			
Real Estate			
Securities			
Other			
TOTAL SAVINGS & INVESTMENTS			
TOTAL MONTHLY EXPENSES			

FEDERAL ESTATE TAX

Taxable Estate From:	To:	Tax Is:	Plus:	Of Amount Over:
$ 0	$ 5,000	$ 0	3%	$ 0
5,000	10,000	150	7%	5,000
10,000	20,000	500	11%	10,000
20,000	30,000	1,600	14%	20,000
30,000	40,000	3,000	18%	30,000
40,000	50,000	4,800	22%	40,000
50,000	60,000	7,000	25%	50,000
60,000	100,000	9,500	28%	60,000
100,000	250,000	20,700	30%	100,000
250,000	500,000	65,700	32%	250,000
500,000	750,000	145,700	35%	500,000
750,000	1,000,000	233,200	37%	750,000
1,000,000	1,250,000	325,700	39%	1,000,000
1,250,000	1,500,000	423,200	42%	1,250,000
1,500,000	2,000,000	528,200	45%	1,500,000
2,000,000	2,500,000	753,200	49%	2,000,000
2,500,000	3,000,000	998,200	53%	2,500,000
3,000,000	3,500,000	1,263,200	56%	3,000,000
3,500,000	4,000,000	1,543,200	59%	3,500,000
4,000,000	5,000,000	1,838,200	63%	4,000,000
5,000,000	6,000,000	2,468,200	67%	5,000,000
6,000,000	7,000,000	3,138,200	70%	6,000,000
7,000,000	8,000,000	3,838,200	73%	7,000,000
8,000,000	10,000,000	4,568,200	76%	8,000,000
10,000,000	Balance	6,088,200	77%	10,000,000

A credit is allowed against the federal estate tax, shown in the preceding table, for estate or inheritance taxes actually paid to state governments. Taxable Estate is net estate after community property division and after $60,000 personal exemption.

LIFE INSURANCE NEEDS ESTIMATE

Capital Requirements

    Debts $_____

    Income Taxes   _____

    Probate and Estate Tax   _____

    Final Expenses   _____

    Education Fund   _____

    Family Income Fund   _____

Total Capital Requirements $_____

Available Assets

    Cash $_____

    Marketable Securities   _____

    Real Estate   _____

    Business Interests   _____

    Other Assets   _____

Total Available Assets $_____

Total Life Insurance Needed $_____

PRELIMINARY ECONOMIC ANALYSIS
OF
PROFESSIONAL INCORPORATION

NET INCOME FROM SELF EMPLOYMENT   _____

ADDITIONAL CORPORATE COSTS   _____

    25% of Employees Compensation   _____

    Disability Income Premiums   _____

    Group Life Insurance Premiums   _____

    Buy-Sell Insurance Premiums   _____

    Medical Insurance Premiums   _____

    Corporate Taxes   _____

    Social Security   _____

    State Disability Income   _____

    Workemens' Compensation   _____

    Additional Accountant's Fees   _____

    Retirement Plan Trustee Fees   _____

    Total Additional Costs   ═══════════

TOTAL AVAILABLE BEFORE RETIRE-
MENT PLAN CONTRIBUTION   _____

RETIREMENT PLAN CONTRIBUTION
FOR OWNER (20% of Above)   _____

BASE SALARY   ═══════════

CORPORATE BENEFITS
VS.
SELF-EMPLOYMENT INCOME

INCORPORATED   **UNINCORPORATED**

INCORPORATED		UNINCORPORATED
_____	Compensation	_____
_____	Personal Exemptions, Deductions	_____
_____	Taxable Income	_____
_____	Federal Income Tax	_____
_____	State Income Tax	_____
_____	Self-Employment Tax	_____
_____	Total Taxes	_____
_____	After Tax Net (Compensation Less Taxes)	_____

Fringe Benefits

INCORPORATED		UNINCORPORATED
_____	Retirement Plan	_____
_____	Buy-Sell Life Insurance	_____
_____	Disability Insurance	_____
_____	Group Life Insurance	_____
_____	Medical Insurance	_____
_____	Total Fringe Benefits	_____
_____	After-Tax Net + Fringes	_____

References

1. Hazlitt, Henry, *Economics in One Lesson* (New York: MacFadden-Bartell Corp., 1969).

2. Browne, Harry, *How You Can Profit from the Coming Devaluation* (New Rochelle: Arlington House, 1970).

3. Hoppe, Donald J., *How To Invest In Gold Coins* (New Rochelle: Arlington House, 1970).

4. Hebling, Hans H. and Turley, James E. "A Primer on Inflation: Its Conception, Its Costs, Its Consequences", *Federal Reserve Bank of St. Louis Review* (St. Louis: Federal Reserve Bank of St. Louis, January, 1975) p. 5.

5. Sprinkel, Beryl Wayne, *Money & Markets: A Monetarist View* (Homewood, Ill.: Richard D. Irwin, Inc., 1971).

6. McCracken, Paul W., "Fighting Inflation After Phase Two", *Fortune* (Chicago: Time, Inc., June, 1972) p. 84.

7. White, Andrew Dickson, *Fiat Money Inflation In France* (Caldwell, Idaho: The Caxton Printers, Ltd., 1972) p. 38.

8. *The Economist* (London: The Economist Newspaper Ltd., June 21, 1975).

9. von Mises, Ludwig, *Human Action* (New Haven: Yale University Press, 1949).

10. Havemann, Ernest, "The Great Glut", *Life* (Chicago: Time, Inc. 1950) p. 119.

11. Curtiss, W.M. *The Tariff Idea* (Irvington-on-Hudson, New York: The Foundation For Economic Education, Inc., 1953), p. 7.

12. Armentano, D.T. *The Myths of Anti-Trust* (New Rochelle: Arlington House, 1972).

13. Rothbard, Murray N., *America's Great Depression* (Los Angeles: Nash Publishing Company, 1972).

14. Burger, Albert E. "The Monetary Economics of Gold", *Review* (St. Louis: The Federal Reserve Bank of St. Louis, January, 1974).

15. *U.S. News & World Report* (Washington, D.C.: U.S. News & World Report, Inc., October 9, 1972).

16. Swerdloff, Peter, *Money Magazine* "If It Feels Bad, It Is Bad" (Chicago: Time, Inc., November, 1973) p. 39.

17. *The Economist* (London: The Economist Newspaper Ltd., June 21, 1975).

18. *The Wall Street Journal* (New York: Dow Jones & Company, Inc., June 16, 1976).

19. *The New York Times* (New York: The New York Times, Inc., June 22, 1975).

20. Hoppe, Donald J., *How To Invest In Gold Stocks And Avoid The Pitfalls* (New Rochelle: Arlington House, 1972).

21. Burke, William and Levy, Yvonne, *Silver: End of an Era* (San Francisco: Federal Reserve Bank of San Francisco, 1972).

22. *Federal Reserve Bulletin* (Washington, D.C.: The Federal Reserve System, July, 1974).

23. Silveira, Antonio M. "Interest Rate and Rapid Inflation",*Journal Of Money, Credit And Banking* (Columbus: Ohio State University Press, August, 1973) p. 795.

24. White, Andrew Dickson, op. cit., p. 38.

25. Bresciani-Turroni, Constantino, *The Economics of Inflation* (Northhampton, England: Agustus M. Kelley, 1968) p. 158.

26. Roebuck, Melvin L. and Richardson, William Alan, *Choosing A Mutual Fund For Maximum Growth* (New York: Roebuck & Co., 1970).

27. Malkiel, Burton G., *A Random Walk Down Wall Street* (New York: W.W. Norton & Company, Inc., 1973).

28. Bresciani-Turroni, op. cit., p. 258.

29. *The Economist* (London, England: The Economist Newspaper Ltd., August 9, 1975).

30. Graham, Frank D. *Exchange, Prices, and Production in Hyper-Inflation: Germany, 1920-1923* (New York: Russell & Russel, 1967), p. 79.

31. *The Economist* (London, England: The Economist Newspaper Ltd., August 16, 1976).

32. *College Costs* (Hartford: Life Insurance Marketing and Research Association, 1974).

33. *A Guide To Life Insurance* (Mt. Vernon, N.Y.: Consumers Union of United States, Inc., 1974).

34. *Best's Insurance Reports—Property and Liability* (Oldwick, N.J.: A.M. Best Company, Inc.)

35. Hess, Carl *Dear America* (New York: William Morrow & Company, 1975), p. 92.

36. Hohenstein, Henry J. *The IRS Conspiracy* (Los Angeles: Nash Publishing, 1974).

37. Hess, op. cit., p. 90.

38. Reid, Peter C., and Simons, Gustave *Corporate and Executive Tax Sheltered Investments* (New York: Presidents Publishing House, Inc., 1972).

39. Rand, Ayn *Atlas Shrugged* (New York: Random House, 1957).